WAR BONNETS OF THREE GENERATIONS

Father, 1798-1900   Son, 1859-   Grandson, 1887-

Chief Washakie, dictator of the Shoshone indians for sixty years, taken about 1870; Chief Dick Washakie, his son; Marshall Washakie, son of Chief Dick and grandson of the old chief

WASHAKIE

Chief of the Shoshones

GRACE RAYMOND HEBARD

Introduction to the Bison Books Edition
by Richard O. Clemmer

University of Nebraska Press
Lincoln and London

Introduction to the Bison Books Edition © 1995 by the University of
Nebraska Press
Manufactured in the United States of America

♻ The paper in this book meets the minimum requirements of
American National Standard for Information Sciences—Permanence
of Paper for Printed Library Materials, ANSI Z39.48-1984.

First Bison Books printing: 1995
Most recent printing indicated by the last digit below:
10   9   8   7   6   5   4   3   2   1

Library of Congress Cataloging-in-Publication Data
Hebard, Grace Raymond, 1861–1936.
Washakie: chief of the Shoshones / Grace Raymond Hebard; introduc-
tion by Richard O. Clemmer.
p.   cm.
Originally published: Cleveland: A. H. Clark Co., 1930.
Includes bibliographical references (p.   ) and index.
ISBN 0-8032-7278-2 (pbk.: acid-free paper)
1. Washakie, ca. 1804–1900.   2. Indians of North America—Wars—
1866–1895.   3. Shoshoni Indians—Kings and rulers—Biography.
4. Union Pacific Railroad.   5. Overland journeys to the Pacific.
I. Title.
E99.S4W3732   1996
978′.004974—dc20
[B]
95-33119   CIP

Reprinted from the original 1930 edition by the Arthur H. Clark
Company. The subtitle has been added; the pagination has not been
changed and no material has been omitted in this Bison Books edition.

To my mother
MARGARET DOMINICK MARVEN HEBARD
A Pioneer in
Iowa and Wyoming

Introduction to the Bison Books Edition
Richard O. Clemmer

Washakie

Friend of emigrant, settler and soldier. Cooperator in the "transition of the West from savagery to civilization." Enemy of Blackfoot, Sioux, and Cheyenne. And "benevolent despot"—"a czar in determination though a kindly ruler." Thus does Grace Raymond Hebard describe Washakie. Fluent in French (and of course Shoshone) and conversant in English, he held the position of noncommissioned officer in the U.S. Army. Under a law authorizing Indian scouts to enlist in the Army at the same rate of pay, with rations, as cavalry soldiers, he held the rank of private until his death in 1900 at the age of (probably) 98 or, according to Hebard, 102. He was also undisputed Chief of what was first a small band, and eventually a whole tribe that became nearly synonymous with his name: the Washakie Shoshones of Wind River.

Washakie exercised diplomatic skill in balancing the political and military scales of power in the Old West of mountain men and emigrants, of tribes that were friends as well those that were foes. Dr. Hebard's study of Washakie is not an in-depth, detailed, psychologically speculative and anecdotally titillating biography. It is, rather, one of the few solid, documented, authoritative biographies that we have of a Native American leader from the era of the "Indian wars," in which most of the heroic and antiheroic figures have been turned nearly into shadow dancers in myth and anti-myth.

Grace Raymond Hebard

Grace Hebard never knew, or even met Washakie. In a departure from her previous work, she focuses on a "great man" who had influenced enough history to be regarded in her eyes as one of the makers of it. But there is a subtlety in Hebard's biography that, every now and then, counterbalances the positivistic, march-of-events voice of the narrative. This subtlety is in her perspective on the interlopers in Shoshone territory: the emigrants, the military, and those canny old, original mountain men, the trappers. Washakie and his band helped them all, and without their help, these "pioneers" might not have pioneered so well, or might never have survived at all.

Grace Hebard was professor of political economy at the University of Wyoming and, in addition to her histories of the Mountain West, she wrote textbooks and guides to civics and government for the Wyoming Public Schools, a history of women's suffrage in Wyoming, and a manuscript on the derivation of place names in Johnson County, left unfinished at her death in 1936. Thus, she was as much a local historian and applied governmentalist as she was political chronicler, and her sources reflect this orientation. She relied heavily on interviews with Dick Washakie, Chief Washakie's aging son; with other older Shoshone men; and with military men and homesteaders who had known Washakie. She also drew on published accounts of fur traders, trappers, and mountain men. Although her perspective reflects little of the Shoshone point of view, it accords a proactive position to Indians that is rare in histories of the Old Mountain West of the time. Thus she relativizes and modifies the concept of the West as having been "made" by traders, trappers, emigrants, homesteaders, and cavalry alone.

Her aim seems to have been to give a balanced account of "how things got the way they are." Because Washakie was important in that process, he captured Hebard's attention. Yet we find the same subtlety in her treatment of Washakie's military endeavors as we do in her treatment of the mountain men. In discussing the Battle of the Little Bighorn (1876) and the pursuit of the Nez Perce bands of Joseph and Looking Glass (1877) in which Washakie's son, Dick, participated, Hebard makes it clear that much of Washakie's power and influence among Shoshones resulted from the support of the U.S. military, beginning in the 1860s. Supplying scouts as well as warriors, Washakie led a contingent of over one hundred Shoshones and Utes accompanying Crook in the campaign against the Sioux, Cheyennes, and Arapahos. Hebard credits Washakie with preventing Crook from being trapped by Lakota and Cheyenne forces as Custer was.

Hebard notes, in her chapters on "the Custer tragedy," that "the making and breaking of many of the indian treaties signed by government officials were the cause of many indian wars." Hebard also notes Dick Washakie's unforgiving critique of Howard and Crook's pincer operation against the Nez Perce bands a year later, which occasioned several instances of wanton slaughter of encamped women and children as well as warriors.

Corrections

Yet Hebard's partisanship toward Washakie and her antipathy to Washakie's ostensible enemies—Lakota, Cheyenne, Arapaho, Blackfoot, and all those Shoshones and Bannocks regarded as committing "depredations" against homesteaders, emigrants, the Pony Express, and stagecoaches—led her to make some interpretations that have been corrected in recent years either by a more balanced approach or more careful research. Consider the historical and ethnographic situation of the Bannocks. Describing them as an "outlaw band," Hebard attributes to them an identity as a group on the margins of Shoshone society and as instigators of the "Bannock Wars" of 1878–79. The Bannocks were no more "outlaws" than were the homesteading interlopers into Shoshone and Bannock territory who, with such allies as Territorial Governor Caleb Lyon of Idaho, sought to confiscate the Kamas prairies and grassy valleys that yielded edible roots and seeds crucial for surviving the "starvation time" of early Spring. The Bannocks, originally from the high valleys and desert plateaus of northern Nevada, southwestern Idaho, and southeastern Oregon, have a culture identical to that of the Northern Shoshones but speak a language that is closer to northern Paiute. By the time of the "Bannock wars," Washakie's Shoshones had been secure in their reservation for ten years; in contrast, the Bannocks and the northern Shoshones—whose lifestyles ranged from mounted bison-hunting to pedestrian small mammal, root, and seed gathering—had seen their requests for a reservation denied, modified, and usurped.[1] It is no wonder they reacted strongly. The Bannocks were no more outlaws, renegades, or outcasts than any other indigenous group of the Great Basin.

Likewise, Hebard's lumping of Shoshones, Bannocks, Paiutes, Utes, Cahuilla, and Hopi into a single ethnographic category requires considerable modification. This grouping is defensible only in linguistic terms: all are speakers of northern Uto-Aztekan languages. But Hopi and Cahuilla share less than one-third of their basic vocabularies with Shoshonean-speaking groups such as the Comanches, Kawaiisus, Panamints, and Shoshones. Culturally, the sedentary Hopi are Puebloan, not Shoshonean, and the Cahuilla share more cultural traits with the neighboring Hokan-speaking Ipai-Tapai than with the Shoshones.[2]

The term *Numic* is now used to denote the Plateau-and-basin-dwelling speakers of Ute, Paiute, and Shoshones, and the peoples' own terms for themselves, such as *Nuche* (Ute); *Numa* (Paiute); and *Newe* (Shoshone), are coming into increasingly more common use among scholars. *Shoshone* refers to "grassy area" and derives from a linguistic misunderstanding on the part of *taivos*[3]—explorers and emigrants, possibly going back as far as Lewis and Clark. In efforts to rid themselves politely of uninvited guests, Numic people would urge them back onto the trail, over the next hillock, and into the adjacent valley with the admonition "Shoshoni! shoshoni!" meaning: "You'll find lots of good grass for your mounts over that-a-way." Of course, the next valley would be home to another group. The *taivos*, then, mistook the description of the place for the name of the people.[4] Much more obscure are the origins of the now-discarded term "Snake," which was applied to Shoshones as well as to a river; Hebard's efforts to distinguish "Snakes" as the "true" Shoshones and others as "lesser" Shoshones can no longer be substantiated.

Likewise unsubstantiated is Hebard's rendering of the Bear River Shoshones as responsible for "depredations" committed against emigrants, coaches, and mail carriers between 1860 and 1862. Brigham Madsen's *The Shoshoni Frontier*[5] makes it clear that there is no evidence for linking only this small band—culturally identical to Washakie's Shoshones but largely foot Indians rather than mounted ones—to the "depredations" any more than other non-Washakie Shoshones, Bannocks, or Utes. In fact, some eyewitnesses insisted that some raiders were white men disguised as Indians. The event was not a battle but rather a massacre, in which Colonel O'Connor's "California volunteers" killed close to 250 men, women, and children encamped in Bear Valley, Idaho. The toll far outstrips any single action of any Indian group against non-Indian civilians and even many massacres of Indians by U.S. troops. (Compare: Wounded

Knee [Lakota]—more than 200 but fewer than 300; Camp Grant [Apache]—150; Sand Creek [Cheyenne]—130.)

Hebard's account of the Sand Creek massacre also deserves some elaboration. In a treaty concluded in 1861, the Cheyennes gave up claim to Kansas, Nebraska, and all of Colorado north of the Arkansas River and east of the Rocky Mountains, retaining a small tract of southeastern Colorado as a reservation. In return, the United States promised $30,000 a year in payments for fifteen years and assistance with economic development, making available a blacksmith, an agricultural consultant, a grist mill, and most important, irrigation ditches and water. By 1863 none of these provisions had been fulfilled; the Cheyennes found themselves confined to a reservation they could not use; they were prevented from going out onto the plains to hunt bison. A few dozen young men began poaching stock from nearby homesteaders and raiding emigrant trains. U.S. troops at Fort Lyon were put on alert. Black Kettle's and White Antelope's bands, wishing to disassociate themselves from the raiders and poachers, sought and were granted U.S. protection; they camped near Fort Lyon under a white flag. In a pre-dawn, unprovoked, unwarranted surprise attack, troops from Fort Lyon massacred nearly a third of the Cheyenne camp.

The troops' commander, Colonel Chivington, had acted without orders and was reprimanded and disciplined.[6] Outraged, the Army command castigated Chivington's callous stupidity. Surviving spouses and children were offered reparations.[7] But the damage had been done. The only bands of declared "friendly" Cheyenne had been made into "hostiles." Black Kettle (White Antelope had been killed) fled with the remnants of the two bands, joining the renegade Cheyennes, and calling for all loyal Cheyennes to join him and fight the traitorous and murdering U.S. Army. The drama was finally played out five years later when Black Kettle and his band were destroyed in the Battle of Washita and when Custer and his troops, in turn, were defeated by the surviving Cheyennes and Lakotas under Crazy Horse and Sitting Bull.

From Military Politics to Tribal Economics

It may seem strange that, though a political economist, Grace Raymond Hebard gives us almost no perspective on the economy of the Wind River Shoshones. But "political economy" in Grace Hebard's day meant something far different than it does now. Political economy had less to do with the securing, producing, and distributing of resources, goods, and services, and rather more to do with the use of power and authority relative to resources. In the eyes of the political economist, Washakie approximated the perfect Machiavellian prince: negotiating astute political quid pro quos (large reservation for his tribe's military service against holdouts and exceptionalists to the *Pax Americana*; demonstrable assistance to the cause of Manifest Destiny in exchange for being permitted to govern his people with a minimum of white interference) and besting all potential rivals for position of chief. But what was the real impact of Washakie's policies, economically, on the Wind River Shoshone people? How are they to be interpreted economically? How were the people in Washakie's diplomatic shadow making a living?

For a look at the economy, we must turn first to Demitri Shimkin, who gathered his data through contemporary observation and retrospective interviewing in 1936 and 1937.[8] Bison, noted Shimkin, were easily the most important economic resource until the 1880s when the last remnants of the northern herd were either slaughtered or had been situated in Yellowstone National Park. Shoshones hunted bison from horseback and their three thousand or more horses made hunting easy but not necessarily efficient: horses needed fodder and had to be moved constantly, and could not always be moved to exactly where the bison were. Shimkin estimated the Shoshones took only two thousand bison a year, and even at that, he judged "the efficiency of bison economy" to be "almost incredibly low" in terms of the time and energy expended on it. "With all their slaughter," he wrote, "the Shoshone could scarcely have had more than six months a year on bison."[9]

What did they live on the other six months of a year? In June and July they sought trade rendezvous for flour, coffee, sugar, iron pots and tools, rifles and ammunition, manufactured blankets, and other packaged and industrial goods, as well as sea shells from other Indians. They hunted deer, mountain sheep, and rabbits. In August they sought roots, and in September and October they relied on antelope. In January they relied on pemmican (a kind of sausage of dried, pounded, jerked meat preserved and seasoned with berries, salt, and herbs), or starved. They hunted bison only in October and November and February through May.

It was no wonder that Washakie was magnanimously hospitable to traders and military; forts meant goods, and goods might promote dependency but also lessen hardship. Before assuming leadership of his band in the 1840s, Washakie had experienced the economic shift that occurred after 1825 when the mountain men established regular trade rendezvous and, a decade later, trading forts. Previously, packaged goods and industrial items could be obtained only by long and dangerous trips to the Mandan villages on the upper Missouri River or to the Comanches in Nebraska or Kansas.[10] Having the traders closer at hand must have lessened risks and permitted greater territorial security.

But what the Wind River Shoshones had traded away for their horse culture and bison economy was efficient use of local resources. "The wide migrations of these people lost them their intimate knowledge of the country, vital for gaining of small game," says Shimkin. "Horsemanship, tactics, and other such learning allowed no time for knowledge of even such simple devices as pitfalls for deer, or effective traps for small animals"[11] (which Shoshones in other locations, without horses, certainly had). All their horsemanship seems to have done the Wind River Shoshones little good. No more people lived in the rich country of western Wyoming than lived in the arid desert ranges of eastern Nevada.

Recent work by Dan Flores indicates that the basic problem may have been the marginal status of the Sweetwater, Powder, Yellowstone, and Wind River valleys in terms of bison migration patterns.[12] There were just not enough bison in those areas to make complete dependence on them feasible. While Shoshones were getting fewer than two bison a year per person, the Comanches, Kiowas, Cheyennes, and Arapahos on the southern plains were taking an estimated 6.5 bison per person. Even so, their predation and that of other Native bison hunters did not come close to limiting bisons' natural reproductive increase until the 1850s, when competition from horses for the same grass, the ecological replacement of tall grasses with short ones, periods of drought, non-Indian manipulation and decimation of herds, and the impact of exotic bovine diseases took their collective toll.

The Land Grab Begins

Washakie's friendly relations with the Mormons (1857–1858), his request for a reservation, his willingness to accommodate homesteaders' demands for the best lands, and his military alliance with the U.S. Army (1855–1878) must be seen, then, as logical follow-ups to his strategy of cultivating good relations with traders of packaged and manufactured goods to make up a very real deficit in resources (1825–1850) that developed just as the Wind River Shoshones were beginning their third generation of familiarity with, and dependence on, horse-mounted bison-hunting. But even Washakie's great skills in diplomacy could not stave off the impact of the government's post–1870 policy: forced acculturation of Indians, allotting and parceling out of Indian lands, and wholesale giveaways of nonallotted tracts to non-Indians.

Washakie's reservation diminished in size, first gradually, then suddenly. From its original acreage of 3,768,500,[13] the reservation's boundaries were set to encompass 1,774,400 acres by the time Washakie signed the treaty of cession at Fort Bridger in 1868. In 1872 homesteaders who claimed their lands had been wrongly included in the reservation succeeded in having 710,000 acres sliced out of it. In 1878 Washakie agreed to let the Arapahos temporarily "camp" on the reservation for a year, but, as he put it, they came for a year and simply never left. Effectively, 1,045,000 acres were lost to Shoshones' use. In 1896 Washakie signed his last cession agreement, granting 64,000 acres of meadow and hot springs to the state of Wyoming for a resort.

But the most devastating land loss occurred in 1904 under the General Allotment Act, after Washakie's death. Congress had passed the Allotment Act—often called the Dawes Act after its congressional sponsor—in 1887. It mandated division of all reservation lands into parcels ranging from 60 to 320 acres, depending on the quality of the land in question, and allotting them to individual Indians. Coupled with a policy of training and educating Indian children in boarding schools operated by the Bureau of Indian Affairs, allotment was intended as a component of a forced acculturation policy. After twenty-five years, an allotment would go onto the tax rolls and could be sold by its Indian owner like any other piece of property. Ultimately, an end to tribes as political and social entities and reservations as administrative units would be accomplished.

Given the drop in Wind River Shoshone Indian population from a probable 1,500 in 1850 to 841 by 1900 (Arapaho population only slightly higher), the allotment process at Wind River would run out of people before it ran out of land. And indeed, such was the case on nearly all allotted reservations. "Surplus" land was to be opened up to homesteading, sold off at bargain prices, or leased for grazing.

Allotment was in the wind when Washakie died in 1900; in 1904 allotting agent James McLaughlin orchestrated a vote of the adult men intended to approve the allotting of Wind River. Opposed by the Arapahos, McLaughlin was able to obtain a plurality of "yes" votes only by persistent persuasion among the Shoshones. He got 202 Shoshones to vote yes; only 70 Arapahos acquiesced. Thomas Johnson, whose dissertation recapped the history of the Enos family to the 1960s, called the approval of allotment an outright land cession tantamount to a theft, and stated that "the McLaughlin 'theft' was probably the low point of Shoshone effectiveness in dealing with the white man."[14]

Between 1906 and 1911, 719,317 acres went out of Shoshone ownership by being declared "surplus." An additional 627,000 acres went out of Arapaho ownership, leaving Shoshones and Arapahos jointly with effective use of fewer than 700,000 acres. Of that, 285,000 acres were leased to non-Indians at $.02 an acre for a total annual lease income of $6,900. Indians had slightly more, 295,000 acres, for grazing. Another 125,000 acres were given over to individual allotments. By 1920 the Indian Bureau had realized that even at absurdly low prices, most of the "surplus" land was unhomesteadable. Therefore, it began leasing out nearly all of the 1,346,317 "surplus" acres to non-Indian cattlemen at $.05 an acre. It placed the lease income in a trust account. Indians had productive use of less than a quarter of their reservation; non-Indians had 90 percent of the rest. The allotment era was certainly the nadir of existence for Wind River Indians and for most Indians; in 1900 deaths exceeded births. The death rate was 95 per 1,000; the birth rate was only 77 per thousand.[15] Shoshone population decreased from 916 in 1890 to 841 in 1900 and remained virtually stationary until 1920, when it showed a slight increase to 880.[16]

Quality of life deteriorated and probably accounted for the decrease in population. Receiving annual rations averaging $2 in value per person and yearly grazing lease income averaging $323 per family, most families relied upon a combination of raising livestock (mostly sheep and goats for sale and for home consumption), fishing, and gathering roots and berries in season. Some men farmed.[17]

Post–1926 Developments

It was in the 1920s, however—when Grace Hebard was researching and writing this book—that the Shoshones began taking action to reverse their circumstances. In 1927 they filed suit in the U.S. Court of Claims asking $37,150,279.90 plus interest for violation of the Treaty of 1868 involving the settling of the Arapahos on the reservation. Although dismissed in 1930, it was refiled by different attorneys using different arguments and in 1938 the Court issued a judgment awarding the Shoshones $6.4 million minus $2 million in offsets that the U.S. government claimed as costs for operating the reservation and other incidentals.[18]

Congressional passage of the Indian Reorganization Act in 1934 brought hope and improvement. The Act was submitted for approval or disapproval to all reservation communities and, although Wind River voted it down, many of its provisions applied anyway. The Act ended allotment, made economic development funds available, provided for return of land, established on reservations various New Deal agencies such as the Civilian Conservation Corps and the Works Projects Administration, and made the hiring of attorneys easier. The elected Shoshone and Arapaho Business Councils, which had been formed after Washakie and most of the old Arapaho chiefs had died, as well as the Joint Business Council, began exercising more control over their own affairs.

Births began to exceed deaths with a death rate of 24 per 1,000 and a birth rate of 35.5 per 1,000 in 1928. There was a promise of better times ahead. For most families, the basis of survival was still the reservation's Indian agency, but now work was provided through the WPA, Irrigation Service, and Indian Department of the CCC.[19]

Nonetheless, Wind River Indians were starting from rock bottom. Whites' leasing of Indian land restricted availability of grazing land to Indians and thus the viability of an Indian cattle industry.[20] Demitri Shimkin described the situation in 1937: "The 1150 Shoshone were all but destitute, for they had, by this time, been deprived both of the grazing land north of Big Wind River and the fertile, irrigable land given to the Arapaho on the eastern side of the reservation. They lacked the resources, moreover, to open up the high-mountain timberland and pastures."

But contrary to expectations of the forced acculturation and allotment policy, Wind River Indians were not about to disappear. In 1939 an act of Congress restored 808,500 of the alienated 1,346,317 acres to the reservation, and the 1938 judgment funds became available. The Indian Bureau still managed to exercise considerable control by placing the funds in individual Indian money accounts and allowing only $100 per person and $500 per minor to be actually used by the Indians themselves. The remaining funds—$2,350 per adult and $1,950 per minor—were held in trust.

But this control, too, was about to end. Between 1938 and 1941 the Joint Business Council shifted from a passive role to assuming political authority. By the late 1940s, the BIA had let go its paternalistic grip and could no longer prevent Shoshones from having access to their own money, and the Joint Business Council began authorizing per capita payments. The Council also pressured companies to start production from hitherto dormant oil and gas leases,[21] and the average family income jumped from $300–400 annually in 1937 to $4,900 in 1950, most of it from oil and gas leases. In 1956 oil and gas royalties were amounting to $1.3 million annually and have been increasing steadily ever since.[22] In 1957 another claims judgment of $433,013.60 was awarded for the 710,000 acres taken under the "Brunot Agreement" in 1874 and in 1965 still another for $120,000 to compensate for gold taken from the reservation by gold miners.

By 1962, the Joint Business Council had established a Tribal government with an administrative staff utilizing oil and gas revenues for its payroll. The rest was distributed to tribal members in per capita payments amounting to $780 per month. Only 7 percent of Wind River Shoshones were on welfare, although 29 percent—mostly the elderly—received surplus commodities. Those who were employed worked largely for federal agencies (55 percent) or the Tribe itself (40 percent).[23] By 1966 the per capita payments had been cut to about $50 per month and some Shoshone families were struggling.

Even increasing oil and gas royalties and return from investments of those royalties have not kept pace with the growing population.

Beginning in 1930, population climbed steadily from 1,017 to 1,150 in 1937; 1,678 in 1950; 2,085 in 1970; 2,202 in 1976; and 2,851 in 1980. But the percentage of Shoshones living on or near the reservation has decreased from 90 percent in 1960 to less than 50 percent in 1989.[24] Poverty is once again a problem, with 41.4 percent of households falling below the poverty line, and although Shoshone per capita income is higher than that of Indians in general—$6,025 as opposed to $5,430—many Shoshones do not share in the distribution of per capita payments from oil and gas royalties and investments. In the 1970s, the Shoshone and Arapaho Tribes, exercising their sovereign right to determine membership, each implemented a one-half blood-quantum requirement for tribal membership. Those individuals who are mixed-blood to the extent that they are neither one-half Shoshone nor one-half Arapaho cannot be tribal members or share in either tribe's economic resources.[25]

Religion

While Hebard had little to tell us about religion in 1930, in 1995 we can confidently say that indigenous religions are alive and well among the Wind River Shoshones. Hebard quotes at length from a report by the Episcopalian minister appointed during the era of forced acculturation in 1887, who asserted that the Shoshones were not naturally religious but they had converted to Christianity by the hundreds. In reality, just the opposite is probably closer to the truth: Shoshones are indeed religious but did not and have not converted to Christianity by the hundreds.

Today, Christianity, Peyotism, and the Sun Dance are the predominant religions. Shoshones and Comanches appear to have developed the Sun Dance independently of other tribes between about 1720 and 1820, and continued dancing it even after it was banned in 1890. Shoshones also danced the Ghost Dance, part of a religion promising redemption and a better life, which originated among Paiutes in eastern Nevada in two different forms in 1870 and again in 1887, and spread, although in yet different forms, to dozens of other tribes. Reworked, the Ghost Dance was performed as the "Sand Dance" or "Half Dance" often in conjunction with the Sun Dance and retained some adherents at Wind River until the 1970s.[26]

Shimkin reported in 1938 that, although about a third of the

Shoshones were nominal Episcopalians, this same third were also loyal Sun Dancers and adherents of the Peyote religion. "There is no conflict internally," he reported, "when the same person is a good Episcopalian, a good Peyotist, and a leader of the Sun Dance." Omer Stewart estimated that by 1944, 67 percent of the families at Wind River had at least one adherent to the Peyote religion. Even in Grace Hebard's day, Peyote was known, with estimates of the percentage of adults using Peyote varying between 2 percent and 7.5 percent.[27] Utilizing ground-level altars of natural materials, Peyotists in groups of twelve per congregation take water and the peyote cactus as raw buttons, paste, or tea, as sacraments in twelve-hour rituals beginning at sundown and lasting until sunrise, at ceremonies held weekly, usually on Saturday nights. Emphasizing song, prayer and meditation, Peyote ceremonies are not unlike very lengthy Christian ceremonies. Some Peyote ceremonies contain a considerable amount of Christian symbolism, prayer, and reference to Jesus Christ as healer.

Peyote is a relatively new religion for the Shoshones, who obtained it from the neighboring Arapahos in 1908. But the Sun Dance remains the primary Shoshone ceremony. Shoshones taught the ceremony to the Crows in 1939–1940, who had had a Sun Dance ceremony of their own but had let it lapse a century earlier. Shoshones also taught it to Utes, and today two Sun Dances a year are conducted on the Wind River Reservation. The Sun Dance not only reunites Shoshones as a community, but also provides them with a religion that speaks to individual salvation as much as it does to group cohesion and cooperation.

Political trends in Indian country are increasingly moving back toward self-determination, nation-building, and actively maintaining traditions, languages, and home communities. Congressional legislation such as the Self-Determination Act (1975) and the Native American Graves Protection and Repatriation Act (NAGPRA, 1990), which provides for reburial of Indian people exhumed over the last century and a half for "scientific purposes" and return of religious and ceremonial items housed in museums, and various new laws covering archaeological excavations have facilitated the trend for Native Americans to take increasingly greater control over their cultural destiny as well as their political affairs. The Wyoming Indian High School at Wind River, now an Indian-controlled public school, began incorporating Indian culture and Indian-perspective history through the Shoshone Native Studies Curriculum Development Project in the 1970s, and by the 1980s, Shoshones and Arapahoes were regularly consulting with federal officials and archaeologists on locating dams to avoid flooding ceremonies and sacred sites, and working with museum curators to develop locally meaningful exhibits and displays.

Grace Hebard's work, then, is an important document linking the continuity of Shoshone life in the past of Washakie's Mountain West with the present of Wind River's reservation-based Tribal community. Hebard could hardly foresee the transition that was about to take place within a few short years of the original publication of this book (1930) and of her death (1936). She could not know that Washakie, in insisting that the Shoshone homeland of the Wind River Valley be retained as a reservation, would have been making an important decision that would have important economic consequences with the discovery of oil and gas. Nor could she have foreseen that the diminution of the Shoshone land base and population was about to be dramatically reversed. In an era when many Tribal historians are attempting to recover the histories of important individuals, following a long period when the accomplishments of Native Americans were dismissed or ignored, it is to Hebard's great credit that she bucked the tide of her time and produced a record, remarkably little flawed by her own era's prejudices, that stands more than sixty years later as definitive, authoritative, and ground-breaking.

Notes

1. Richard O. Clemmer and Omer C. Stewart, "Treaties, Reservations, and Claims," in *Great Basin,* ed. Warren d'Azevedo, vol. 11, *Handbook of North American Indians,* ed. William C. Sturtevant (Washington DC: Smithsonian Institution, 1986), 525–57.

2. Joseph G. Jorgensen, "Sychronic Relations among Environment, Language, and Culture as Clues to the Numic Expansion," in *Across the West. Human Population Movement and the Expansion of the Numa,* eds. David B. Madsen and David Rhode (Salt Lake City: University of Utah Press, 1994), 84–102.

3. The word for "whites" in Numic.

4. Just as, in similar fashion, the "Bannock" people came to be called by the Numic word for a flat seed-cake.

5. Brigham Madsen, *The Shoshoni Frontier and the Bear River Massacre* (Salt Lake City: University of Utah Press, 1985).

6. Chivington's prospects, however, were not materially damaged. A Methodist minister, he later headed the congregation of Denver's first Methodist Church and became a trustee of the University of Denver.

7. They were given a little bit of money and offered 160 acres each of land on a new reservation in Kansas. But the state of Kansas objected and the little band of "friendly" Cheyenne were shipped further east to Indian Territory (now Oklahoma).

8. Demitri B. Shimkin, "Wind River Shoshone Ethnogeography." *Anthropological Records* 5(4) (Berkeley: University of California Press, 1947) 245–88; Demitri B. Shimkin, "Eastern Shoshone," In *Great Basin*, ed. Warren d'Azevedo, vol. 11, *Handbook of North American Indians*, ed. William C. Sturtevant (Washington DC: Smithsonian Institution, 1986), 308–35.

9. Shimkin, "Wind River Shoshone Ethnogeography," 267.

10. Ibid., 269.

11. Ibid., 280.

12. Dan Flores, "Bison Ecology and Bison Diplomacy: The Southern Plains from 1800 to 1850," *Journal of American History* (September 1991): 465–85.

13. Joseph G. Jorgensen, *The Sun Dance Religion* (Chicago: University of Chicago Press, 1972), 94.

14. Thomas Hovet Johnson, "The Enos Family and Wind River Shoshone Society: A Historical Analysis," (Ph.D. diss. University of Illinois, Urbana, 1975).

15. Ibid., 160.

16. Jorgensen, *Sun Dance Religion*, 108, 94, 91.

17. Ibid., 101; Shimkin, "Eastern Shoshone."

18. Clemmer and Stewart, "Treaties, Reservations, and Claims;" Jorgensen, *Sun Dance Religion*, 112.

19. Shimkin, "Eastern Shoshone."

20. Jorgensen, *Sun Dance Religion*, 108.

21. Shimkin, "Eastern Shoshone."

22. Martha C. Knack, "Indian Economies, 1950–1980," in *Great Basin*, ed. Warren d'Azevedo, vol. 11, *Handbook of North American Indians*, ed. William C. Sturtevant (Washington DC: Smithsonian Institution, 1986), 573–91.

23. Jorgensen, *Sun Dance Religion*, 120.

24. Based on Jorgensen, *Sun Dance Religion*, 91, 143, 289; Shimkin, "Eastern Shoshone"; Joy Leland, "Population," in *Great Basin*, ed. Warren d'Azevedo, vol. 11, *Handbook of North American Indians*, ed. William

C. Sturtevant (Washington DC: Smithsonian Institution, 1986) 608–19.

25. As of 1970, Johnson "The Enos Family," estimated two hundred children were of mixed Shoshone-Arapaho ancestry and speculated that they would be ineligible to be enrolled in either tribe (230, 320). Shimkin, "Eastern Shoshone," had estimated 58 percent of the Wind River Shoshone population as being of mixed blood in 1930, with the largest number in the 1–9 year age group.

26. Jorgensen, *Sun Dance Religion;* Judith Vander, *Songprints: The Musical Experience of Five Shoshone Women.* (Urbana: University of Illinois Press, 1988).

27. Omer C. Stewart, *Peyote Religion: A History* (Norman: University of Oklahoma Press, 1987), 192–95.

Contents

Illustrations

---

* Especially prepared from original sources and special surveys by the author and Oscar Messerly.

Introduction

It is indeed an honor to be asked to say a word regarding the author's effort to place before the public a sketch of the life of that splendid old chief, Washakie, whom I knew well in 1898 and 1899 when in command at Fort Washakie, then the most remote from railroad of any of our military posts.

I shall attempt no description of Washakie's fine mental and physical qualities, for that is done in the text by a pen far more skilled than my own. No difficulty is experienced in concurring in all the admirable things which are there said of him.

Washakie's steadfast loyalty to the government, despite the ill-treatment he had received at its hands in the matter of being required to accept the Arapahoes as "guests" for a period of something like a half-century, is indeed remarkable. Our indian policy, or rather the lack of a sane one, marked by broken treaties, dishonest agents, ignorant and tactless handling of the entire subject and the infliction of untold misery on our indian wards, has been such that an army man who has had to stand by with hands tied can hardly keep within bounds when writing or speaking of it. Therefore, adopting a fashion of our indian friends, I close this feature by saying, "I have spoken."

While the title of this interesting volume is *Washakie: An account of Indian resistance of the Covered Wagon and the Union Pacific Railroad Invasions of their territory*, Doctor Hebard gives us much more than called for by the title and tells us so much regarding the early history of Wyoming, the Oregon and Bozeman trails, indian treaties and the habits and general characteristics of the tribes of that section that the book constitutes a distinct and valuable contribution to Wyoming's history. For such work Doctor Hebard is unusually well qualified by reason of her long connection with the history and government of Wyoming, as well as her authorship of such works as *The Bozeman Trail, The Pathbreakers from River to Ocean, Sacajawea*, etc. Her contributions to the history of stirring times in this section of the west have a value not to be estimated in dollars and cents, and will be more and more appreciated as the years go by.

WILLIAM CAREY BROWN
Brigadier-general, U.S.A., retired.

Preface

Had Chief Washakie been an enemy of our government and its people, battling with bow and arrow, spear, tomahawk and rifle to maintain a savage supremacy over the regions now peopled with industrious workers, he would be better known. His exploits would have been eagerly seized upon by chronicler and storyteller, and his fame would have been carried to the ends of the world. Though a great warrior, as virtually every red leader must needs have been, he was an ally of the "Great Father" at Washington, a friend of· the emigrant, the settler and the soldier, a coöperator in the transition of the West from savagery to civilization. His part in this drama makes him a less spectacular figure than otherwise he might have appeared, but at the same time invests him with signal historic importance. Time has a quiet way of mending these discrepancies between worth and renown, and those who know Washakie by the record of his life and deeds need have no fear of the rank the future will accord him.

The aim of this work is to present something more than the biography of an individual. Though the outstanding personality of Washakie is usually kept in the foreground it is environed, however roughly, by moving figures and stirring scenes from the history of the time. His own people and the stubborn resistance they maintained against the many hostile tribes that encompassed them; the dauntless trapper-explorers and their per-

sistent search for beaver, that carried them, in the face
of hourly perils, to every nook and cranny of the
region; the white migrants, in their covered wagons,
who in a resistless tide poured into the land and peopled it; the red warriors and the white soldiers and the
combats they fought during the long war to determine
who should rule – all these are drawn into the picture.
The work is, in brief, an attempt to preserve an important page in the history of the development of the great
West.

When the task first suggested itself, the personal
material available seemed too meager to warrant the
preparation of a book. But to requests for information·
came such prompt and generous response from many
individuals and institutions that toward the end, the
major problem became one of elimination. For the
material that has made the book possible, acknowledg-
ment, with grateful appreciation, is tendered to a loyal
host of friends of the chieftain whose names do not
appear; to the War Department; to the Office of Indian Affairs of the Department of the Interior; to
United States Senators F. E. Warren and John B
Kendrick; to Brigadier-generals William C. Brown,
Charles King and Walter S. Schuyler; Colonels William Henry Corbusier, William A. Arthur, E. E. Hardin, Aubrey Lippincott, W. A. McCain, George H.
Morgan and Homer W. Wheeler and Captain Frederick H. Sparrenberger, of the United States Army,
most of whom personally knew Washakie and all of
whom were at different periods at Fort Brown, or as it
more appropriately was called, Fort Washakie; to the
family of William A. Carter sr.; to Mr. John E. Rees
for translations of pictographic writings; to those who

gave personal interviews on the Shoshone reservation: the Reverend John Roberts, Captain Herman G. Nickerson, Mr. F. G. Burnett, Mayor E. J. Farlow, Mr. Albert D. Lane and Mr. James K. Moore jr.; to Miss Grace Brown, sister of Brigadier-general Brown; to Mr. John C. Burnet; to the Right Reverend Nathaniel S. Thomas of the Wyoming Episcopal Diocese, which includes the Shoshone tribe; to Senator William G. Johnson; to members of the Indian Field Service, represented by Superintendents H. E. Wadsworth, Chester E. Faris and R. Paul Haas; to the Historical Department of the Church of Jesus Christ of Latter-day Saints at Salt Lake City; to Mrs. Jeannette Young Easton; to the Historical Department of the State of Wyoming; to the librarians of the University of Wyoming; to Miss Stella M. Drumm, librarian of the Missouri Historical Society; to Mr. J. Cecil Alter, Western historian; to Mrs. L. M. Wells for endless time devoted to research among the official files at Washington, D.C.; to Mr. Robert H. Hall; to Mr. H. E. Mills; to the faithful and painstaking interpreter for the Shoshone reservation, Mr. James E. Compton; to Honorary Chief Dick Washakie, who gave the author the intimate history of the House of Washakie; to Mr. Oscar Messerly, cartographer; to the many publishing houses for the use of the books cited and to the authors of those books for quotations used.

GRACE RAYMOND HEBARD

The University of Wyoming,
August, 1929.

Sixty Years an Unchallenged Chief

For nearly sixty years head chief of the Eastern Shoshones, Washakie was the foremost indian of the Trans-mississippi West. Other chieftains, by acts of pillage and massacre, became for a time more noted; but Washakie's fame lives on because he was the bringer of peace and protection to his people and not the fomenter of savage deeds which would in turn have wrought their destruction. Born before the beginning of the nineteenth century, he lived till near its close, and he died the venerated head of a people whom from primitivism he had led far forward along the path of civilization.

Washakie (the name is accented on the first syllable) was, however, primarily a warrior. A newcomer among the Eastern Shoshones, only part Shoshone in blood, and an orphan boy, with no family connections to aid him, he rose to command by his prowess and skill in battle. Out of scattered groups, in a time of general anarchy in the Shoshone nation, he created his own band, and he saw it grow to an effective fighting force. His warfare was mainly defensive. Though generally at peace, and sometimes in alliance, with the Flatheads and the Nez Perces, his people in the early days were well-nigh surrounded by more aggressive, more numerous and better equipped tribes—the Crows, the Utes, the Sioux, the Cheyennes, the Arapahoes and the four tribes of the Blackfoot confederacy — and the strategy of Shoshone chiefs was devoted more to the maintaining of what they deemed their own than of attempting to despoil others. He was not always a victor, and yet he seems rarely to have been defeated. If he could not win by onset or strategem, he knew how, by stubborn resistance, to wear down the valor of his enemies and force them to withdraw from a profitless combat. Sometimes a body of trappers made common cause with him, and triumph was easy and complete; but most of his battles, in which as a rule he had to pit Shoshone courage and horsemanship against superior numbers and better equipment, were fought without auxiliaries.

As a ruler he was untroubled by considerations of democracy. He was, in the best sense, a benevolent despot. Under him the old Shoshonean anarchy, which left the individual free to go or come as he chose, disappeared, and his followers learned obedience and discipline. Like other benevolent despots he felt that he knew what was best for his people, and he brooked little discussion and no opposition. But though a tyrant, he did not abuse his power; he was kindly and unselfish, and what he won for his people was equitably shared among them.

From our first knowledge of him he was a warm friend of the whites. He knew most of the noted characters of the old trapping days, and well-supported tradition makes him the frequent companion and close friend of both Jim Bridger and Kit Carson. In later days he was the protector and helper of the emigrants along the Oregon and Overland trails, and still later he and his warriors were comrades-in-arms with the soldiers against the Sioux, the Cheyennes and the Arapahoes. For many years he was a regularly employed scout in the army.

He was, from his earliest contact with the government, its loyal ally. In this loyalty, however, there was no touch of servility. The great Brulé chief, Spotted Tail, was sometimes accused, rightly or wrongly, of being so much the friend of the whites and the government that he failed in his duty to his own people. The accusation was never, so far as known, levelled against Washakie. Though always the stout defender of his people's rights, and though sometimes he had to meet aggression, both from individual whites and from their government, he realized that only further evil would come from meeting it with savage reprisals. Always he kept the peace, depending upon time and the ultimate good faith of the whites for redress of grievances; and the few unruly tribesmen who from time to time, for some fancied wrong, would steal away to join the Bannocks or other pillagers, would find themselves, on their return, outlaws from his band.

Though born and reared a nomad and doubtless a passionate lover of the free life of the wilds, he had the wisdom to see that the old days were doomed; that with the oncoming of the whites, game would disappear and that his people would be compelled to make their living by more settled modes of labor than the chase. He was doubtless the first among them to favor a reservation and the practise of agriculture, with schools and other facilities for learning the white man's way of life. Peacefully and without noted incident he brought his reluctant people into the new era.

Of dignified and commanding presence, often likened in face and bearing to Robert Collyer or Henry Ward Beecher and sometimes to George Washington; of kindly and generous disposition; sagacious and shrewd; truthful in word and honest in deed, he won the esteem and affection of his white associates to a degree unattained by any other indian chief, even by the good Ouray of the Utes. When he died he was accorded a military funeral; and the official announcement of his death paid tribute to his worth in the fitting epitaph: "He was a great man, for he was a brave man and a good man."

The Eastern Shoshones are a band of the tribe known generally as the Northern Shoshones, or Shoshones proper, or Snakes, a division of the great and widely distributed Shoshonean family. It is a family which includes such nearby tribes as the Utes, the Paiutes, the Paviotsos and the Pahvants and such remoter tribes as the Kawias (Cahuillas), the Gabrielenos and the Juanenos of southern California, the peaceful and industrious Moquis (Hopis) of Arizona and the once roving banditti of Texas, Oklahoma and New Mexico – the Comanches. Except for the Moquis it was, in the old days, a jarring and turbulent family, since most of its divisions from time to time fought one another with quite as much ardor as though no tie of kinship connected them.

The Northern Shoshones ranged over the greater part of western Wyoming, southwestern Montana, central and southern Idaho, northern Utah and Nevada and all but the westernmost part of Oregon. The origin of the word Shoshone, despite various theories, we do not know. Osborne Russell, who for eight years was intimately associated with these indians and who learned something of their language, wrote about 1844 that he had never been able to ascertain either the definition or the derivation of the name.[1] Nor do we know,

---

[1] Russell, Osborne, p. 144. [For details of citations, see Bibliography.]

in spite of other theories, why the Shoshones were called Snakes. It is certain that they were so known long before they came in contact with the whites. By most early writers the name is said to have been given them because of their uncanny skill in eluding pursuit by hiding themselves – an explanation that may be the true one.

We first hear of them from the reports of Lewis and Clark. When the captains, with their expedition, were at Fort Mandan, north of the present Bismarck, North Dakota, in the winter of 1804-1805, they learned of these indians from the Mandans and the Hidatsas (Minnetarees of the Missouri). They realized that a people living about the supposed headwaters of the Missouri might be of inestimable aid in enabling them to cross the continental divide and reach the Columbia. They would need horses when it became necessary to abandon their boats, and they would also need guidance to set them right on their way. All depended on whether the Shoshones would prove friendly or hostile.

To assure friendliness the captains took with them an "ambassadress," and fate could not have granted them a better one. She was herself of the tribe – one of the two, or more, Shoshone wives of the interpreter Toussaint Charbonneau. We do not know her exact age, but at the time it could hardly have been more than sixteen. Five years earlier, near the Three Forks of the Missouri, she had been made a captive by a war party of Hidatsas, who carried her to their village at the mouth of Knife river and subsequently lost her in a game of chance to Charbonneau. The interpreter married her, in the indian fashion, and on February 11, 1805, less than two months before the expedition resumed its march, she gave birth to a boy. According to the captains her name (reduced to a simple form out of the many ways in which they spelled it) was Sacajawea – a name that they, it is believed, misunderstood to mean "Bird Woman." The name as spelled in 1814 by the first editors, Captain Clark, Nicholas Biddle, and George Shannon in the Lewis and Clark *Journals* is generally given as above indicated.[2] The word as thus used is a pure Shoshone one meaning: *Sac* – canoe or boat or raft; *a*– the; *jawe* – launcher. Regardless of spelling, pronunciation or meaning of the word Sacajawea, it is important to remember that the Shoshone woman more than fulfilled all that was expected of her and that she made certain the success of the expedition.

On April 7, with her papoose strapped to her back, she set out with the party on the long journey. More than four months passed before the Shoshones were found. After the expedition passed Three Forks it was expected that they would be met somewhere on the stream that the captains named the Jefferson. But as day after day passed without discovering any trace of them, Lewis and three companions, started ahead. They ascended Horse Prairie creek, a small tributary of the Beaver Head, and crossed the continental divide into the present Lemhi county, Idaho. On their way up the divide they had seen a mounted warrior, to whom they had made signs of friendliness, but who had viewed them with suspicion and galloped away. Two days later (August 13) on the western slope, they saw three indians a mile distant, but these also fled. A mile further on they suddenly came upon an elderly woman ,a young woman and a little girl. The young woman ran, but the

[2] Lewis and Clark (1902 ed.) ; vol. 1: pp. 237, 353, 355, 407, 439, 440, 448; vol. 2: pp. 64, 273, 317, 391.

other two, hopeless of escape, merely sat still, holding down their heads as if expecting the deathblow.

Lewis went up to them, gave them some presents, made friends with them and persuaded them to call back the young woman. They proved to be Shoshones, and with the whites they at once proceeded toward the indian camp. They had gone but two miles when a troop of sixty warriors was seen approaching at furious speed. Lewis, laying down his gun and bearing an unfurled flag, went forward to meet them. The chief and two other warriors, who were riding ahead, slackened their pace and questioned the women, who showed the presents they had received and said that the strangers were pale-faces and good friends. The three warriors then leaped from their horses and with joyous exclamations of *Ah hi e* embraced the whites.

The chief gave his name as Cameahwait, and both he and his followers showed the strangers the greatest hospitality. They were, however, suspicious that Blackfeet might be in the neighborhood, as well as doubtful about what the whites were doing there, and it was only by dint of constant urging that Lewis could induce them to return with him across the divide to where Clark's men were laboriously struggling with the boats. Slowly and reluctantly they accompanied him, and early on the morning of August 17, near the present Armstead, Montana, the boat-party was descried. The indian girl-mother, walking with her husband somewhat ahead of Clark, suddenly recognizing her kinfolk in the distance, began to dance and give every manifestation of delight. As the indians approached, a young woman who had been her fellow-captive but had escaped, darted from among them and embraced her. Soon both parties, red and white, were mingling in cordial fellowship; and when a council was shortly afterward convened the girl-mother, recognizing Cameahwait, ran to him and in a flood of happy tears made herself known as his sister.

The party remained with the Shoshones for more than two weeks. In all that time Sacajawea, the ambassadress and interpreter, was the alert and loyal representative of the captains in their dealings with the indians. She, who had uncomplainingly borne all the fatigues and hardships of the journey and in the difficult times to come was to share even greater toils and more extreme privations, now found herself in the position of an indispensable helper, and most efficiently did she play her part. The caprice of the indians, which was a sore trial to the captains, she watched with alert eyes. At one time it jeoparded the transport of the luggage across the divide, and at another time, by reason of a proposed buffalo hunt, threatened the abandonment of the party before it was properly equipped with horses. These instances and others she was quick to discover and prompt to reveal. Her influence with her brother, a man of integrity and good sense, but of a vacillating and uncertain nature, seems always to have been decisive. That the expedition could go forward, instead of returning, was pre-eminently due to her faithful service. Yet a word of praise must also go to her brother; and so also to a third Shoshone – the old guide whom the whites called Toby. When, on August 31, the party resumed its journey, Toby, with four of his sons and several companions, accompanied it. A few days later all of these except Toby dropped out; but another son came up, and father and son kept on all the way to the Snake. There, alarmed about something, they stole out in the night and without waiting for their pay rode swiftly homeward.

The captains seem to have applied the name Shoshone to this band alone. Perhaps it then had no specific name. But fifty years later the Mormons named it the Lemhi band, and as such it has since been known. Biddle, in his abstract of the journals of the captains, says of these indians:

> The Shoshonees are a small tribe of the nation called Snake indians, a vague denomination which embraces at once the inhabitants of the southern parts of the Rocky mountains and of the plains on each side. The Shoshonees with whom we now are amount to about one hundred warriors, and three times that number of women and children. Within their own recollection they formerly lived on the plains, but they have been driven into the mountains by the Pawkees [the four tribes of the Blackfoot confederacy] . . . and are now obliged to visit, occasionally and by stealth, the country of their ancestors. Their lives are indeed migratory. . . As war is the chief occupation, bravery is the first virtue among the Shoshonees. None can hope to be distinguished without having given proofs of it, nor can there be any preferment, or influence among the nation, without some warlike achievement. Those important events which give reputation to a warrior, and which entitle him to a new name, are, killing a white bear, stealing individually the horses of the enemy, leading out a party who happen to be successful either in plundering horses or destroying the enemy, and lastly scalping a warrior. . .

From the middle of May to the beginning of September, continues Biddle, they resided on the waters of the Columbia [the headwaters of the Salmon], then moving to the Missouri, where they joined the Flatheads and other tribes for greater security against the Pawkees. They had only a few guns, and those few bad ones, their arms being the bow and arrow, shield, lance and pogamoggan – a stout twenty-two-inch stick

to which a leather-covered stone was attached. They
fought on horseback, and though poorly equipped and
subject to frequent attacks from their enemies, were "a
very military people." Chieftainship among them was
not invested by any ceremony nor distinguished by any
external honors, but was gradually acquired by "merit
and good wishes"; and the chief possessed only nominal
authority, for his commands had no effect on those who
chose to disobey. The captains found these people not
only friendly but, in the main, truthful and honest.[8]

The constant friendliness shown to the whites by the
Lemhis, as well as the general friendliness of most
other Shoshones, dates from this first contact. Though
early records relate occasional attacks of this people
upon the whites, the looseness with which the word
Shoshone or Snake was employed makes it difficult to
determine who the attackers were. Certain it is that
the Bannocks – a Shoshone band or sub-tribe about
which more will appear farther along – committed
many atrocities, and also certain it is that renegade
Shoshones from various bands often aided them. But
for the Shoshones other than those of this band and its
outlaw recruits the general record from the beginning
is one of amity and fair dealing, while for the Lemhis
it appears to be one of cordial friendship and an unbroken peace. Thomas James, who was a member of
the expedition of Pierre Menard and Andrew Henry
that made the first organized trapping invasion of the
Three Forks of the Missouri (early spring of 1810),
records an incident revealing the humanity of a party
of Snake warriors. It is fair to assume that they were
Lemhis, since no other Snakes were then likely to have

---

[8] *Ibid.*, I: pp. 418-424. (Original ed. 1814.)

been in that neighborhood. On the journey from the mouth of the Big Horn most of the trappers became afflicted with snow-blindness, rendering them temporarily helpless. The advanced section went into camp on the Gallatin and waited for recovery:

While in this distressed situation [he writes] enveloped by thick darkness at midday thirty Snake indians came among them, and left without committing any depredation. Brown and another, who suffered less than the others, saw and counted these indians, who might have killed them all and escaped with perfect impunity. Their preservation was wonderful.[4]

All the Shoshones met by Wilson Price Hunt's Astoria overland expedition in 1811 were friendly and some of them most generous and helpful. The first band was found on the western slope of the Big Horn mountains. After the abandonment of the horses of the party and the disastrous attempt to descend the Snake river in canoes, other Shoshones were found at various places along the route, and from them a few horses and some food were obtained. The food supply of the indians was scanty, and their willingness to share any part of it is a striking evidence of their kindness. To this spirit two men of the expedition owed their lives. On the break-up of the party into small groups, Ramsay Crooks and John Day, with three companions, travelled together for a time, but subsequently the three wandered off and were lost. Crooks and Day, while traversing the Snake river desert, became so weak that they made a fire and settled down to rest. They had some roots they intended to cook, not knowing they were poisonous, when boiled. Their fire happily went out and for a day and a half they lay in a torpor. When at last they awoke they found two Shoshone indians bending over them.

---

[4] Douglas (ed.), p. 51.

The indians had a good fire burning and a supply of water for them to drink. They fed the starved white men and showed them how to cook the roots so they would not be poisonous. They left two pounds of venison on their departure, as an offering of kindness, and this nourished the travelers back to strength.[5]

Shoshoneland was next traversed by the returning Astoria party, led by Robert Stuart, which left the Pacific on June 29, 1812. While travelling afoot (for their horses had been stolen by a party of Crows), they encountered, on the upper waters of the Green river, a Snake village of forty wigwams and one hundred and thirty souls. The Snakes were miserably poor, for they, too, had recently been robbed by the Crows, who took their horses, most of their effects and even several of their squaws. But they were friendly and helpful; and for a pistol, an ax, a knife, a tin cup, two awls and a few small trinkets, they parted with their last horse – a decrepit old nag which the Astorians found useful as a pack animal for their few belongings, thus enabling them to make better progress on their journey.[6]

From articles in their possession the Shoshones were believed to have occasional contact with the Spaniards of New Mexico. Of one such early contact we can be fairly certain. About 1818 a party of Spanish traders, probably with a military escort, reached the valley of what the American whites then called the Spanish river, or Colorado of the West, presumably in the present Wyoming. From this visit dates the name "Rio Verde," then given to the stream. It was a name which doubtless came to the American settlements by way of

[5] Irving, *Astoria*. The quoted passage is a summary by Russell and Driggs, p. 143.

[6] Irving, *op. cit.*

Santa Fé. In its anglicized form, Green river, it soon
became generally accepted, though the Crow name,
Seeds-kee-dee (Prairie Hen), for some years persisted
as an alternative. This party very likely met some Shoshones, but of its relation with them we know nothing,
since it left little trace. We may be sure that the indians
tried to persuade the visitors to sell them rifles and
ammunition, the commodities most in demand among
them, and equally sure, from the sternly maintained
Spanish policy then in force, that their attempts were
futile.

From the Oregon country came the next invasions of
Shoshoneland. In June, 1813, only a few months before
the news of the war with Great Britain persuaded the
Astorians to sell their trading post, they sent a party of
four Canadians and three Americans, headed by John
Reed, to the Snake country to find the hunters and recover the horses left behind by the expedition of 1811.
Early in the following January the scattered members
of the party were attacked by indians and all the men
were killed. With the party was Pierre Dorion, guide
of the Astoria overland expedition, who had taken with
him his Sioux wife and two children. This notable
heroine, hardly to be matched in the pages of history
for courage and fortitude, effected her escape with her
children and after a series of almost incredible adventures reached the friendly Walla Wallas. On the Columbia, soon after, she met the last party of returning
Astorians, to whom she told the story of the tragedy.

Other expeditions were to follow. The Northwest
Company, the principal fur-trading rival of the Hudson's Bay Company, had penetrated to the lower Columbia as early as the summer of 1811, and on October

16, 1813, had acquired the American trading-post of Astoria. At various times during the next five years its trappers had penetrated the frontiers of the Shoshone country, but not until the end of September, 1818, did it send a party to the interior. This party, of fifty-five men, with one hundred and ninety-five horses and three hundred beaver traps, and known as the "First Snake Expedition," started from Fort Nez Perces (the present Walla Walla) and remained out for more than a year.

From Alexander Ross, the chronicler of this and the subsequent expedition, we have our first extended account of the Northern Shoshones as a people. He divides them into three branches. First are the *Shirry-dikas*, or "dog-eaters," though since they lived by the chase the reason for the name is not evident. They are represented as the "real Shoshones," slender, clean, well-dressed and brave, who live on the plains and hunt buffalo. Next are the *War-are-ree-kas*, or "fish-eaters," not so brave nor so well equipped, the constant victims of the hostile Blackfeet and Piegans. Last are the *Ban-at-tees*, or "mountain Snakes," generally looked upon as outlaws, robbers and murderers. They were, according to Ross, the miscreants who perpetrated the massacre of John Reed's hunting party.[7]

These Ban-at-tees were the people later known as Bannocks (among other Shoshones, Pun-naks), and they have been the subject of many contradictory reports and much confused speculation. Though often referred to as a separate tribe or sub-tribe, it seems safer to regard them as an outlaw band, hardly distinguishable except in their propensity to treachery and violence, from the "real" Shoshones. From time to time

[7] Ross, vol. 1: Vandiveer, chap. xviii.

the more lawless spirits among the other bands would
join them, remaining until some disastrous engagement scattered them with heavy losses. But though the
records of trapper days and even later times chronicle
many severe chastisements administered them, they
show that these freebooters had marvelous recuperative
powers. On the word of James P. Beckwourth they were
"annihilated" by the trappers in 1826, and on the word
of Joseph L. Meek again in 1836. The latter event,
which should be dated 1837, the year given in Osborne
Russell's *Journal*, was not, however, an annihilation,
though it was a defeat sufficiently decisive to keep them
fairly peaceful for many years. But it was again necessary to chastise them during the Civil War, and Colonel
(afterward General) Patrick E. Connor did the job
with great thoroughness in the famous Bear river fight
of January 29, 1863. They had one more fling in 1878,
when finally they were forced to realize the advantages
of keeping the peace.

For the "real" Shoshones, Ross expresses great admiration, and he especially commends their courage.
In a final tribute he writes:

The Snakes, from their inland position, have seldom been visited
by the whites . . . so that they remained, until lately, in their primeval
simplicity. Meanwhile they have been surrounded on all sides by
powerful and warlike nations, which nations have, for nearly a century past, been frequented by traders and consequently, all that time,
furnished with firearms and other weapons of war, to the great
annoyance and almost ruin of the poor and defenceless Snakes, who
have had to defend their country and protect themselves with the
simple bow and arrow, against the destructive missiles of their numerous enemies.

Hence it was that the Blackfeet, the Piegans and other tribes . . .
have made the Snake country the theater of war; and hence the
Snakes, from their unarmed and defenceless state, have been stig-

matized as a dastardly race unskilled in the art of war. . . . But arm
the Snakes, and put them upon an equal footing with their adver-
saries, and I will venture to say, from what I have seen of them, that
few indians surpass them in boldness or moral courage; my only wonder is, that they have been able, under so many discouraging circumstances, to exist as a nation, and preserve their freedom and independence so long.[8]

It is not until a later time that we find mention of the
"Diggers," also a Shoshonean people, although not a
part of the "real" Shoshones. The name has been used
with little discrimination, and we can not always be
certain who are meant by it. In general it seems to refer
to the Paviotsos and Piautes, tribes living in the barren
country to the west and southwest of Great Salt lake,
though in former days ranging considerably to the
north. Since their region supported little or no game,
they were forced to eat food rejected by other tribes.
They dug not merely for roots but for grubs and ants;
they gathered and roasted grasshoppers, and they made
a delicacy of body lice. Many stories are told of their
poverty, filthiness, treachery and cowardice. It is, however, certain that they have been in some degree ma-
ligned. Though exceedingly primitive, they had a culture of their own. If not always friendly, they at least
bore the whites no inveterate hostility; and though
sometimes craven and treacherous, they showed themselves in later days, when they obtained firearms, capable of sustained bravery in open conflict.

By the middle twenties Shoshoneland was being sys-
tematically covered by bands of trappers from both the
Missouri and the Columbia. The old Northwest Company had been swallowed by the Hudson's Bay Company in 1821, and a new leader, Peter Skene Ogden,

---

[8] Ross, vol. 2: pp. 151-153.

who had acquired an interest in the former organization a year before the consolidation, appeared in the indian country. Between 1824 and 1829 he led his men up and down the streams of Idaho, southwestern Montana and northern Utah, finding himself in close competition with American trappers who had but recently entered the region. His journals yield many references to the Shoshones. Unlike Ross, he seems not to have been concerned with noting distinctions among the various bands, for all Snakes apparently looked alike to him. He writes of them at first as peaceable and friendly, but he came later to look upon them as robbers, sneaks and murderers. His indignation reached its height on January 22, 1828, when he wrote:

> How long will the Snakes be allowed to steal and murder I cannot say. . . Acting for myself, I will not hesitate to say I would willingly sacrifice a year or two to exterminate the whole Snake tribe, women and children excepted. In so doing I could fully justify myself before God and man. Those who live at a distance are of a different opinion. My reply to them is: come out and suffer and judge for yourselves if forbearance has not been carried beyond bounds ordained by Scripture, and surely this is the only guide a Christian should follow.[9]

But this entry was written on the Portneuf, in the heart of the Bannock country, and seems likely to have been prompted wholly by the depredations of this outlaw band. The just and clement Peter Skene Ogden may have been unacquainted with, or may for the moment have ignored, the better behaved Shoshones to the north and east.

From Saint Louis, in 1822, General William H. Ashley, with Major Andrew Henry as second in command, led his first trapping expedition up the Missouri. He had intended to make his winter encampment at the

---

[9] Elliott (ed.), *Ogden Journals.*

Three Forks, and from there to dispatch his trapping parties southward into the untried fields of what is now Wyoming. But he reached the upper Missouri late in the season, the Assiniboines stole all his horses, and at the mouth of the Yellowstone he halted his expedition and began the building of a stockade. Leaving Henry in charge, he returned to Saint Louis, and in the early spring of 1823 started north with a new company of recruits. In one or the other of these two parties were Jedediah S. Smith, Thomas Fitzpatrick, William L. Sublette, Étienne Provot, James Bridger, Hugh Glass and David E. Jackson – all destined to win high renown in the trapper-explorer era – and James Clyman, a century later to become known as the chronicler of one of the most important of the trapping journeys. Near the present boundary line of the two Dakotas, on June 2, this second expedition was halted and pushed back, with severe losses, by a treacherous attack of the Arikaras. Reinforcements of trappers, soldiers and Sioux came up, and on August 9, the Arikaras, after sustaining for some time a general assault, ingloriously fled. The way to the north was now clear, but the fighting and the delay had again turned Ashley's plans awry. Henry and his detachment from the Yellowstone that had come to the rescue, returned to their stockade, and a small trapping party was organized to proceed westward, whereupon Ashley, with the remainder of his following, left for home.

This westbound trapping party was a maker of history. It was composed of about twelve men, among whom were Smith and Fitzpatrick, the leaders, and Sublette and Clyman. It left the trading post, Fort Kiowa, on the Missouri, toward the end of September, journeyed to the Wind river, ascended it to the neighborhood of Fremont's Peak, descended it later to the Big Horn, and wintered with a band of Crows. From the Crows the whites learned of the rich beaver grounds across the divide, and of the mountain gap through which they could easily make their way. In February (1824) they set out to the south and after crossing over to the Sweetwater turned westward. Late in that month or early in March they traversed South pass and descended into the valley of the Green – the first American whites to thread the pass from the east, and unless Ramsay Crooks's claim for the Robert Stuart party can be sustained, the real discoverers of that famous thoroughfare. On the Green was found a small band of "diggers or Shoshone Indians," as Clyman called them, who, after having been plentifully fed by the trappers, disappeared with all the party's horses. Six weeks later the band was surprised and the horses were recovered, but the incident doubtless left for a time a rankling resentment in the trappers' minds against everything bearing the name Shoshone.[10]

Henry's party, which included Étienne Provot and James Bridger, had in the meantime left the mouth of the Yellowstone and wintered at the mouth of the Big Horn. In the spring they started south, crossed South pass, and joined the trappers who had preceded them. From the Green they spread out in all directions, Smith's party in a short time making contact with a Hudson's Bay party on the upper Snake. Provot, leading another party, crossed the northwesterly shoulder of the Uinta range to the upper reaches of the Weber river, and descended to the floor of Great Salt lake

---

[10] Camp (ed.), see *Clyman.*

valley, near the present Ogden. Here he had a battle
with Shoshones which bulks rather large in frontier
annals. Seven whites were killed before the indians
were driven off, when the trappers settled down for
the winter. There is an account of another battle, near
the site of Provo, in which a wily Shoshone chief with
his band is said to have succeeded in killing most of
Provot's men; but as the party had not then proceeded
so far south and as there is no reason to suppose that
the trappers lost more than the seven men mentioned,
Alter reasonably concludes that the two accounts refer
to the same battle and that one of them is merely a
gorgeous exaggeration.[11] Others of Ashley's men penetrated to the Bear river country, wintering in Cache
valley; and from there, in the fall of 1824 Bridger
descended the river and discovered Great Salt lake. If
any of Provot's men saw it earlier, they registered no
claim to the fact, and by common consent, on the high
authority of Robert Campbell, the honor of discovery
belongs exclusively to Bridger.[12]

Meanwhile, in Saint Louis, Ashley was organizing
his third expedition. Learning from Henry, who with
a cargo of furs had reached Saint Louis by way of the
Big Horn and the Missouri, of the rich fields of the
Shoshone country; learning also from Fitzpatrick, who
had journeyed back to the Missouri, at Fort Atkinson,
of the easy routes overland, he started out with a new
company on November 3. Following the Platte and the
South Platte for a distance, crossing the Laramie plains
and the Red desert, he reached the Green river, above
the mouth of the Sandy, near the middle of April,

[11] Chittenden; Alter, pp. 45-46, 57-58.
[12] Alter, pp. 49-50.

1825.[13] He soon established contacts with most of his men, and to all trappers and friendly indians within reach sent messages that a general rendezvous would be held at the junction of Henry's Fork and Green river near the present Utah-Wyoming boundary beginning July 1.

The summer rendezvous, of which Ashley was the innovator, was the great fair and convention of the beaver country, and as an annual event continued almost to the close of the trapping era. At this first gathering more than eight hundred persons were present, a number more than quadrupled in some of the gatherings of after years. At the rendezvous peltries were exchanged for clothing, ammunition, sugar, coffee, flour, tobacco and whiskey, and new contracts were made and fresh trapping campaigns were planned. But though it had its business phase, it had also its phase of convivial hilarity. Here for a brief period the red race and the white mingled in holiday mood. Liquor flowed freely to red and white alike. The warriors played games, or displayed their skill in horsemanship or performed their ceremonial dances; the trappers vied with one another in contests of strength or markmanship, gambled for high stakes to their frequent impoverishment, drank excessively and sometimes participated in drunken brawls; and their gaudily dressed indian wives paraded the new finery with which their doting husbands had decked them from the trader's stores. Perhaps no other time or place in the world's history has furnished so colorful and picturesque a carnival.

To these palefaces overrunning their lands the Shoshones were, in the main, hospitable. The attack on Provot's party stands out as a notable exception. Even

---

[13] Dale; Alter, *op. cit.*, p. 59; Hebard and Brininstool, vol. 1.

so, there may have been, for all we know, gross provocation; or it may be that the assailants were Bannocks. Other records show the whites and the Shoshones in frequent alliance. An instance was the battle with the Blackfeet, in July, 1826, probably near the mouth of Weber canyon, Utah. Snake warriors and three hundred of Ashley's men, under the command of Sublette, fought together against a great horde of the northern raiders, and after a six-hour engagement, in which eleven Snakes but no whites were killed, forced them to flee, leaving one hundred and seventy-three dead bodies on the field.[14] Usually, moreover, the Shoshones sided with the whites against their kinsmen, the Bannocks. Moving northward soon after, and incidentally defeating two more bands of Blackfeet, Sublette and his men camped with a party of Shoshones near the junction of Salt river and the Snake. A large village of Bannocks was near, and Sublette, knowing their disposition, warned them against any depredations. They paid, however, no heed to the warning, and shortly afterward killed a Snake and wounded two trappers, whereupon they disappeared. On Sublette's call for volunteers to punish them, two hundred and fifteen trappers responded. With young Bridger in command, they overtook the runaways on an island in Green river. Dividing his force, Bridger attacked them from both sides of the stream, continuing to fire until all of them, except six or eight squaws, were killed. According to the none too veracious Beckwourth, four hundred and eighty-eight scalps were carried back to camp. When the Shoshones were told of the fight and its results they greeted the news with exclamations of delight. "Right!

---

[14] Alter, *op. cit.*, pp. 76-77.

Pun-naks very bad indians," they said, and celebrated the victory with a scalp dance.[15]

From Captain Benjamin L. E. Bonneville, who was in the mountains from 1832 to 1835, we have occasional mention of the Snakes, though little that will serve the present purpose. The one incident related that might have for us a prime interest is his meeting in 1833 with an intelligent and brave young Shoshone chieftain. One is tempted to believe that this warrior was Washakie, who before that had come to live with the Eastern Shoshones and who may already have become a sub-chief. The particulars, however, are too vague to warrant an identification.

We have something more detailed in narration, with a more vivid picturing of indian scenes, from Father Pierre-Jean de Smet. During his missionary journeys he came in friendly contact with many tribes, and he writes of them, especially of the Shoshones, with an engaging interest. On June 30, 1840, he arrived in the Green river valley for the annual rendezvous, then in full swing. He tells of the "Shoshones, or rootdiggers, called also Snakes" (for he had not yet learned to distinguish between the two branches) who "were present in great numbers":

They inhabit the southern part of the territory of Oregon [he writes], in the vicinity of upper California. Their population of about 10,000 souls is divided into several bands, scattered here and there over the barrenest country in all the region west of the mountains. . . Occasionally a hunting party will come east of the mountains to hunt buffalo, and at the season when the fish come up from the sea they go down to the banks of Salmon river and its tributaries to lay in their winter stock. They are pretty well provided with horses. At the rendezvous they gave a parade to greet the whites that were there.

15 Bonner, pp. 134-138.

Three hundred of their warriors came up in good order and at full gallop into the midst of our camp. They were hideously painted, armed with their clubs and covered all over with feathers, pearls, wolves' tails, teeth and claws of animals, outlandish adornments, with which each one had decked himself out according to his fancy. Those who had wounds received in war, and those who had killed the enemies of their tribe, displayed their scars ostentatiously and waved the scalps they had taken on the ends of poles, after the manner of standards. After riding a few times around the camp, uttering at intervals shouts of joy, they dismounted and all came to shake hands with the whites in sign of friendship.[16]

Next followed the smoking of the pipe of peace which the chief had lighted, first offering it to the Great Spirit and then to the sun, to the earth and the four cardinal points. To the assemblage Father De Smet gave an explanation of his purpose in visiting the red man's country, telling the indians of the work of the "Black-robes" and their purpose of helping the red men save their souls. After taking counsel among themselves for half an hour one of the chiefs arose and said: "Black-gown, your words have entered our hearts; they will never go out from them. . . All our country is open to you; you need only choose to settle an establishment." On the same evening we are told, they again assembled, and "the head chief promulgated a law, that whoever in future should steal or commit any other scandal should be punished in public."

From Father De Smet we learn that the Snakes believed "the especial residence of the Great Spirit to be in the sun, in fire, and in the earth. When they make a solemn promise they take the sun, the fire and the earth to witness their undertaking. When a chief or warrior of the nation dies, his wives, children and nearest relatives cut off their hair; that is their full mourning. They

---

[16] Chittenden and Richardson, vol. 1: pp. 296-318.

even clip the manes and tails of all the dead man's horses, giving the poor animals a most sorry appearance." [17]

Few of these writers seem to have been concerned with Shoshone history. Doubtless a people with no written or pictured records, with only the most primitive notions of computing time and with traditions deformed by myth and fable, furnishes an unpromising field for historic endeavor. Close inquiry on the part of their earlier visitors might, however, have preserved for us some approximate knowledge of the course of events among them. After Alexander Ross we have little reference to their current history until we come to Osborne Russell. This remarkable man, as a youth of twenty, came to the mountains with Wyeth in 1834, and in the summer of that year took part in the building of Fort Hall. Later he was a trapper, and at the beginning of 1836 engaged with Bridger. For eight years he remained in the mountains. Much of this time he spent in close contact with the Shoshones, and he made considerable progress in learning their language. From the beginning he kept a journal, in which he recorded his wanderings, his observations and thoughts and the talk of the trappers and indians. About 1844, after he had moved to Oregon, he prepared it for publication, but for some reason it was not printed until 1914 (another edition appearing in 1921). This book, *The Journal of a Trapper*, 1834-1843, is of the highest value as a first-hand account of the daily movements of the beaver-hunters; and it is also of great value for its references to the Shoshones. Though few and brief, they are explicit and informative. It is from Russell that we have the first known mention of Washakie and also a statement

[17] *Ibid.*

of conditions in the Snake nation that heralded his rise
to power.[18]

For at least a part of this time the Shoshoes seem to
have recognized the rule of a head chief. Though
Lewis and Clark do not mention such a ruler, Alexander Ross, writing as of 1818-1820, repeatedly alludes
to the "two principal chiefs" of the nation, Pee-eye-em
and Ama-qui-em, giving precedence always to the
former as though he outranked the other. Russell, in an
entry written in October, 1834, says that the head chief
as Pah-dasher-wah-un-dah (elsewhere spelled Pahdahewakunda), or The Hiding Bear, whom the whites
call Iron Wristbands, and again mentions him in 1840.
He died, according to Russell, in 1842, and his brother,
who apparently was to succeed him, died in 1843.[19]
Doubtless the head chieftainship was no more than a
convenient fiction, supreme authority being well-nigh
impossible among a people so individualistic in temper,
so broken up into roving bands and so widely scattered.
The time was now at hand when the nation was to be
permanently divided, and over the eastern part of it a
warrior was to assume command, which until his death,
nearly sixty years later, he was firmly to hold.

---

[18] Russell, *op. cit.*, pp. 114-116.
[19] *Ibid.*, pp. 145-146.

Washakie Wins His Name

Washakie was born near the close of the eighteenth century. The Shoshones, like other nomadic indians, kept no record of vital statistics, nor did they count time by the white man's calendar. They knew, of course, the time divisions of "snows," "seasons," "moons" and "sleeps," but they remembered them only by the outstanding events in their lives, such as battles won (the defeats being always ignored), big hunts, hard winters, dry summers and terrific storms. In such a scheme of computation the unimportant years and seasons were likely to be soon forgotten. Shoshone chronology seems to have been even more primitive than that of neighboring indians. "The Shoshones do not know their own ages," writes the Reverend John Roberts, for many years their pastor at the reservation mission. "The Arapahoes do; the Flatheads do. Washakie had lived so long with the Shoshones that he lost tally of his age." [20] Though the generally accepted date of his birth is that

[20] In a letter to the author, dated at Wind river, Wyoming, March 2, 1928, the Reverend John Roberts writes as follows: "The Shoshones do not know their own ages. The Arapahoes do; the Flatheads do. Washakie had lived so long with the Shoshones that he lost tally of his age. He said that he and Jim Bridger were 'young men together.' When Washakie died the army officers at the post, Mr. J. K. Moore, perhaps Captain Herman G. Nickerson, then United States agent, got together and decided that the old chief was born in 1804. It is therefore so recorded as the year of his birth on the granite monument that marks his grave. This granite rock with the inscription was placed there by the War Department of the United States. It will stand there while the Stars and Stripes float on the breeze.

"At Washakie's death I asked John Enos – an old friend of mine, a Flathead – if he could tell me Washakie's age. He said positively, 'I sure can.'

inscribed on his monument (1804), there is testimony that he was born as early as 1798.[21]

He was born somewhere in the present Montana, perhaps in the upper (southern) part of the Bitter Root valley. His father Paseego, who is said to have been of Umatilla, Flathead and Shoshone blood, belonged to the Flathead tribe. When Lewis and Clark came to this valley in the fall of 1805 they found two closely related bands or sub-tribes of indians, whom they called the Ootlashoots and the Tushepaws, the former of whom regarded themselves as a branch of the latter. Though there has been dispute as to the identity of these indians, they have been generally regarded as Flatheads, and it may well be that Paseego was one of their number and that Washakie was born among them. As to his mother's nation, there is also dispute; but his son Dick Washakie, honorary chief of the Eastern Shoshones, is probably right in asserting that she was a Shoshone.[22] If so, it is a reasonable conjecture that she was of the nearby and friendly band of Lemhis.

To the name Washakie have been given several meanings: "Shoots Straight" [the buffalo],[23] "Shoots-on-the-Fly," "Sure Shot" and "Gambler's Gourd." It is also said that at the time of his birth the name "Shoots Straight" was given "in appreciation of the direction of the morning sunbeams on the newborn child." The generally accepted theory is, however, that the name comes from the word "wus-sik-he," meaning a rawhide

Enos spoke English well and was a very intelligent old man. 'Washakie's sister was my mother. He was my uncle. He was thirteen years older than I am.' I so entered Washakie's age in the mission's register of burials as being one hundred and two, basing this fact on Enos's age."

[21] *Ibid.*

[22] Washakie, Dick. *Statement* to the author.

[23] Hodge.

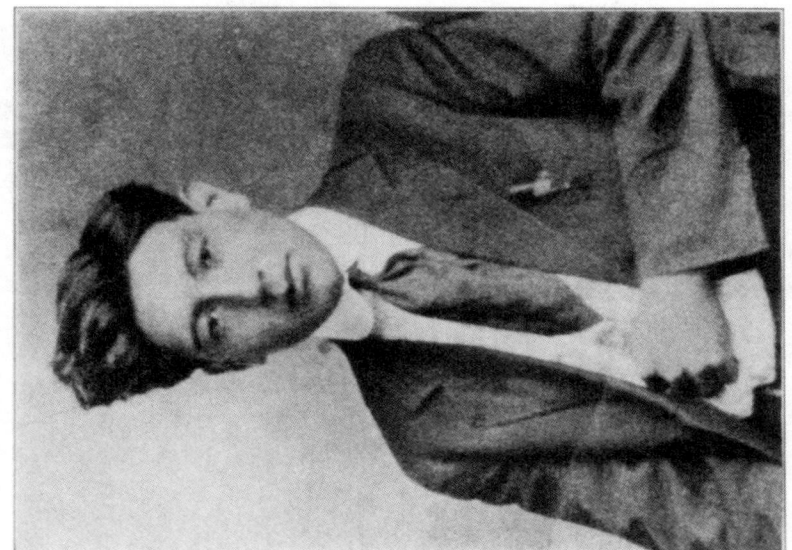

JOHN WASHAKIE

Grandson of Chief Washakie. Killed in World War in service of the United States and buried in the Wind river cemetery, Wyoming

JOHN ENOS, aetat 103

Nephew of Chief Washakie. Was Bonneville's guide in 1832 and with Fremont, in same capacity in 1842, when he climbed Fremont's Peak, Wyo.

rattle. Doctor D. B. Huntington, who had been a soldier in the Mormon battalion and who came to Utah in 1847, later serving as an interpreter for the Utes and the Shoshones, published a pamphlet in 1872, in which he says:

> Wash-a-kii is the name of their [the Shoshones'] head chief. He is a noble-looking man; is and always has been a friend to the whites. The way he obtained his name was thus: The first buffalo he ever killed he skinned the pate, took the hair off, puckered it up, and tied it around a stick with a hole in it, so that he could blow it up like a bladder. He put some stones in it, and when it became perfectly dry it would rattle, and when the Sioux came to war with them, he would ride in among them and scare their horses; so they [his people] called him Wash-a-kii, "The Rattler."

It is remembered that when he sang, as he often did, he accompanied himself with a gourd to which were attached many rattles. The name has been spelled in no less than thirty ways, and a general uniformity seems not to have been reached until early in the seventies.

What we know of his early years comes mostly from an interview between the author and his son Dick Washakie, which took place on the reservation in the summer of 1926, and in which Mr. James E. Compton, the official interpreter, participated. In prefacing the narration of incidents in his father's life the son would frequently say: "This he has often told me himself, and I feel safe in saying that I believe it to be absolutely true." When Washakie was four or five years old, the village in which he lived was attacked by a band of Blackfeet. His father, with a number of others, was killed, and the survivors scattered through the country. The mother, with her three boys and two girls, wandered about for many days, the oldest son, Com-mo-sie, perhaps twelve years of age, nobly acting the part of protector and food bringer. They reached the Salmon, and coming to a bend of the river saw on the opposite bank a large camp of indians. Though unable to judge whether they were friendly or unfriendly, the mother, in her desperate need for food and shelter, made her presence known. They proved to be Lemhis, friendly and hospitable, and they brought the refugee family safely across the river and then to their village.

Here the family lived until Washakie grew to be a young man. One of his sisters married a Lemhi, leaving descendants who are members of the band today. About twenty years after the family came to the Lemhis, the band was visited by some Flatheads, on their way to their old home, and they persuaded the mother and two of her sons and a daughter to go with them. "But Washakie, my father," says the son, "remained with the Lemhis. He never again saw his mother or the sister who accompanied her." A short time afterward a party of Bannocks, one of whom had been a close friend of Washakie's father, arrived for a visit, and when they returned Washakie accompanied them, remaining with the band for a period of from three to five years. That one who, in his later years, was noted for his close alliance with the whites, should have fraternized for even a week with these turbulent freebooters, is difficult to explain. It is unthinkable that he could have remained with them without taking part in their activities, and he could not have done this without at some time coming into collision with the whites. Perhaps this was the period in which he sowed his aboriginal wild oats, and perhaps also, as was the case with most young indian braves, he had to live through a phase of overt hostility to the whites before experience taught him wisdom. Be that as it may, he left his outlaw friends. From the region wherein Fort Hall was later built (1834), he went with a party to visit the Shoshones of what later became known as the Fort Bridger country, or Bridger valley, and among these he lived for the rest of his life. The date of his joining them cannot be fixed. It may have been as early as 1826 or as late as 1832.

Family tradition makes him the hero, about this time, of an encounter with the Blackfeet. These Ishmaelites of the mountains had penetrated to Bridger valley, committing depredations, including the theft of many horses. A Shoshone force was gathered which followed the marauders many days, finally overtaking them somewhere in the present Montana, and after a fierce fight killing and scalping nearly all of them and recovering the stolen horses. In this pursuit and battle Washakie is said to have given striking proof of the qualities that afterward brought him to the head chieftainship. Battles between the Blackfeet and the Shoshones were frequent, and though this one cannot be identified with any of those known to history, it may well have happened and have furnished the young man the opportunity of showing his new-found comrades his mettle as a warrior. Tradition gives him another signal opportunity, shortly afterward, in an engagement in which the Crows were badly worsted. Indeed, tradition makes him exceptionally active in warfare from his youth; and in his old age, long after he had settled into peaceful ways, he could say: "As a young man I delighted in war. When my tribe was at peace I would wander off sometimes alone in search of an enemy. I am ashamed to speak of these years, for I killed a great

many indians." [24] To his death he carried on his left
cheek, just below the eye, a deep double scar, the mark
of a Blackfoot arrow and noticeable enough to give
him the name Scar Face among other tribes.

War, however, did not fill up the full measure of his
days. He was known as a hunter and trapper. He is said
to have been a horse wrangler for the Hudson's Bay
Company, and may well have been so in his Lemhi
days. It was doubtless after he came to live with the
Eastern Shoshones that his familiarity with the white
trappers began. He was, wrote Captain F. W. Lander
in 1859, their "constant companion"; [25] to the Reverend
John Roberts he spoke of Bridger and himself as having been "young men together," and he is said to have
had an especial fondness for Carson, whom he may well
have known from 1833 to 1838. And since there was no
other way by which he and his tribesmen could acquire
the arms and ammunition so greatly needed for defense against the surrounding tribes, he was probably
an industrious trapper and an encourager of trapping
on the part of his followers. He must have married
young, and following the custom of his people, somewhat often, for he fathered a large family, though only
three children are now living.

The first known mention of him is in 1840, and appears in Russell's *Journal*. On Christmas day of that
year, at a camp on the Weber river, Utah, Russell took
part in a feast at which were a number of Snake warriors. The after-dinner talk was copious, and Russell
was an attentive listener. He writes:

The principal topic which was discussed was the political affairs

[24] Patten, James I., Indian agent at Fort Washakie. *Statement* reported
to the author in February, 1917.
[25] U. S. Senate Document, 42, 36 Cong., 1 sess.

of the Rocky mountains, the state of government among the different tribes, the personal characters of the most distinguished warrior-chiefs, etc. One remarked that the Snake chief, Pahdahewakunda, was becoming very unpopular and it was the opinion of the Snakes in general that Moh-woom-hah, his brother, would be at the head of affairs before twelve months, as his village already amounted to more than three hundred lodges, and, moreover, he was supported by the bravest men in the nation, among whom were Ink-a-tosh-a-pop, Fibe-bo-un-to-wat-see and Who-sha-kik, who were the pillars of the nation and at whose names the Blackfeet quaked with fear.[26]

"Who-sha-kik" is Washakie, in one of the thirty recorded spellings of the name. He was thus already a noted leader and may even have been a sub-chief. The predicted supplanting of the head chief by the brother did not, however, occur. In the appendix to his work, written probably in 1844, Russell continues:

In the winter of 1842 the principal chief of the Snakes died in an apoplectic fit and on the following year his brother died, but from what disease I could not learn. These being the two principal pillars that upheld the nation, the loss of them was and is to this day deeply deplored. Immediately after the death of the latter the tribe scattered in smaller villages over the country in consequence of having no chief who could control and keep them together.[27]

How long the ensuing anarchy lasted cannot be said. The common need of defense may have soon brought some of the roving bands together under the most competent leader, and the event might have happened many months before Russell, in his distant home, could have heard of it. In 1842 Fremont found the Sioux, the Cheyennes and the Gros Ventres in a most bellicose state, ready to wipe out not only the whites but the Shoshones; and the Blackfeet had not ceased in their recurrent raids from the north. We may safely guess that

---

[26] Russell, *op. cit.*, pp. 114-116.
[27] *Ibid.*, pp. 145-146.

at some time during 1843 the Shoshones who were scattered about the Green river valley had begun to gather around the standard of Washakie and that by the end of the year he was the acknowledged head of a band. It was a year marked by several outstanding events on the frontier. It is the accepted date for the close of the trapping era; for though solitary wanderers continued for some years to hunt beaver, most of the noted characters had left for the settlements and trapping as an organized commercial venture had ceased. It is also the accepted date for the beginning of the emigration era, for though a few families and small caravans had crossed to California and Oregon between 1834 and 1842, it was the year of the first great Oregon emigration – the one in which Marcus Whitman, returning west from his heroic mid-winter journey to the Capital, played so helpful and distinguished a part. Also it was the year in which Bridger, recognizing the close of one era and the opening of another, established his famous trading post and blacksmith shop on Black's Fork of the Green. In all likelihood 1843 also marks the beginning of the chieftainship of Washakie.

The White-top Wagon Road

Washakie's band may at first have remained small. No doubt the average Shoshone warrior deemed the conditions of membership somewhat too exacting. Washakie was not merely a leader, but a ruler, and those who joined knew that they would have to obey. There were other conditions. Horse-stealing, the dearest pastime of the nomadic indian brave, had been banned, at least in so far as the whites were concerned, and with it some other cherished practices. "Washikeek will not permit a horse-thief or a vagabond to remain in his band," wrote Captain Lander in an official report; and though the statement was not set down until 1860, the unblemished repute of these indians shows that it might with equal truth have been written at the beginning. "No instance is on record," Lander writes in the same report, "of the Eastern Snakes having committed outrages upon the whites." [28] "Fit company though few" may well have been the motto of Washakie for the personnel of his band; and though for a time the increase of his following was probably slow, it was steady. Within a few years he appears to have been the acknowledged head of most of the Shoshones who, making the Fort Bridger country their main home, ranged from the Wind river to the North Platte, throughout the Green river valley as far south as Brown's Hole (near the present southern boundary of

---

[28] U. S. Senate Executive Document, 42, 36 Cong., 1 sess., serial no. 1033.

Wyoming) and westward and southwestward to Bear river and Great Salt lake.

Before this time Washakie had met and known only the comparatively few whites who had come to the mountains to hunt and trap and the rarer few who had come as explorers or as missionaries. From now on he was to meet increasing thousands, crossing his lands on their way to the remoter West. The Oregon trail was developing into a broad highway, crowded with the wagons and herds of the emigrants. This thoroughfare, known by the plains tribes generally as "The Great Medicine road of the Whites" and by Washakie and his people as "The White-top Wagon road," was to give him new contacts and responsibilities, and he was to become, in a special sense, the friend and protector of the pilgrims who traveled its winding length.

The earliest westward trails began at Franklin, Missouri. Independence, founded in 1827, soon took the lead as the starting point, but lost it a few years afterward to Kansas Landing and Westport, now parts of Kansas City. But there was at first no single way of striking out for the west and the northwest. Many parties – some by land and some by water – went all the way to the mouth of the Platte or to Old Council Bluffs (now Calhoun, Nebraska) before heading for the interior. The first wagons to reach Wyoming, however, took the route which (probably as far as the present Casper) ultimately became the line of the Oregon trail. They were the wagons of the fur-traders, Smith, Jackson and Sublette, and the year was 1830. The caravan left Saint Louis on April 10, probably passed through Independence, traveled the Santa Fé trail for "about forty miles," then turned north of west to the Platte, followed that river to some point on the Great Bend and then struck off northwest, arriving in July at the place where the Wind river issues from the mountains. It is not supposable that these capable men would have taken wagons over an unknown route, and it is thus probable that the trail had already been well marked by pack trains and horsemen.[29] By the time of the opening of the emigration era this route, as far as the Great Bend, had become the chosen pathway to the West.

From Westport along the Santa Fé trail for some forty miles ran the road. It then struck out to the north of west, reaching the Platte about twenty miles below Grand Island, where it joined the old trail from the mouth of the Platte. It followed the south side of the river, crossing the South Platte near its mouth, and continued to Fort Laramie. From the fort it paralleled the river, though at some distance, to the site of Casper. Here the river was forded, when the road turned sharply to the southwest. Crossing the Sweetwater, it ran somewhat more westwardly as far as Independence Rock, the great landmark which Father De Smet called "the register of the desert," because of the many names and inscriptions which had been cut into its face. From then on, in a generally westward direction, it ran to

29 Smith, Jackson and Sublette. *Letter* to Secretary of War John H. Eaton, October 29, 1830. Reprinted by Alter, *op. cit.*, pp. 110-111. To reach the Rocky mountains, further is stated in the letter, "took us until July 16, and was as far as we wished the wagons to go. . . Here the wagons could easily have crossed the Rocky mountains, it being what is called the Southern pass. . . . It was the first time that wagons ever went to the Rocky mountains, the route from the Southern pass where the wagons stopped, etc." It is thus evident that with pack horses and mules, the fur parties went into the mountains leaving the wagons on the east side of the continental divide. To Captain Bonneville is given the honor of first conducting wagons through South pass from the waters running toward the Atlantic to the streams flowing toward the Pacific ocean. – Simpson, *Explorations*, p. 17.

South pass and down its western slope until it struck
the Big Sandy, which it followed to the Green. From
the farther side of the Green it ran southwestwardly to
Fort Bridger, when it again turned to the northwest,
on to Fort Hall and thence to the junction of the Walla
Walla and the Columbia.[30]

As far as Fort Hall the California and Oregon trails
were for the first few years identical. Soon, however, a
route was established from Fort Bridger to Great Salt
lake, which came to be increasingly used, especially
after the Mormon settlement in 1847, by the emigrants
heading for California. Over a great part of its length –
that is, from Grand Island, Nebraska, to Casper – the
Oregon trail was paralleled by the Mormon trail, along
the north side of the Platte; and in later years it had,
for many miles, a rival in the Overland route. This
route had been traveled by Ashley in his expedition of
1824-1825; by a party of California-bound Cherokees,
commanded by a Captain Evans, of Arkansas, in 1849 –
an episode that gave it the name of the Cherokee trail;
by Stansbury, guided by Bridger, on an eastward journey in 1850, and by various small parties; but not until
the summer of 1862 did it come into general use and
receive the name which ever after it retained.[31] The
Overland branched off from the Oregon trail at the
forks of the Platte, followed the south branch to the
present Latham, Colorado, and then wound its way
northwestwardly and westwardly through Wyoming,
crossing the continental divide at Bridger's pass and
rejoining the parent trail a few miles above Fort
Bridger.

To shorten distances, to avoid steep grades, to make

[30] Hebard and Brininstool, vol. 1: chaps. i and ii.
[31] Hafen, pp. 232, 320.

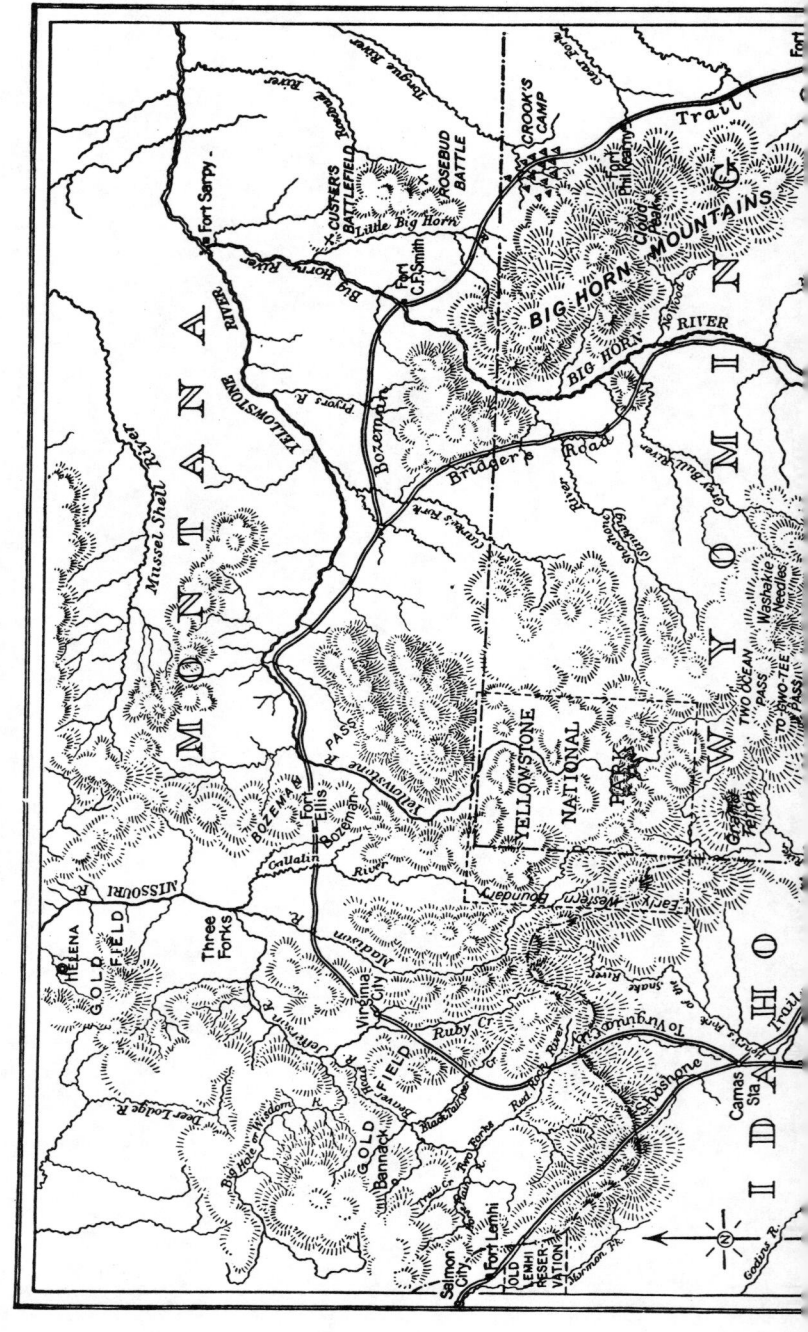

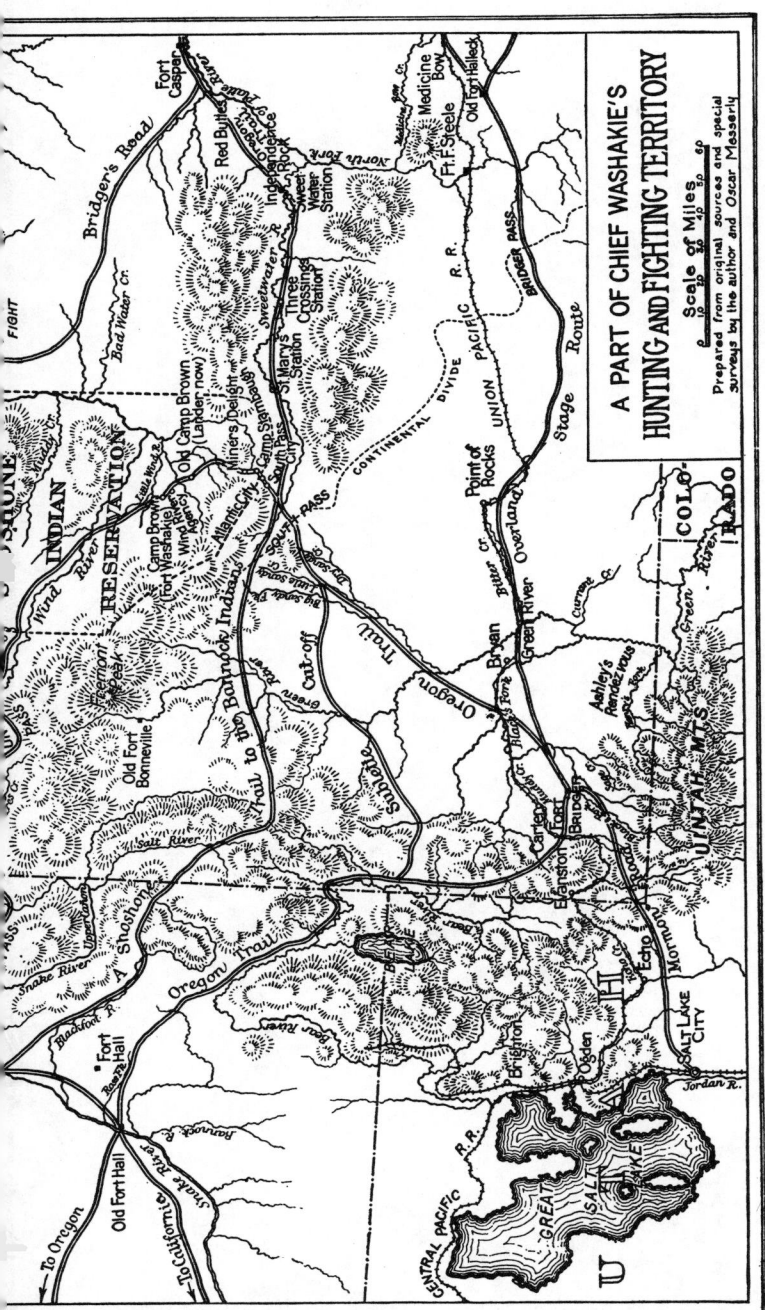

A PART OF CHIEF WASHAKIE'S
HUNTING AND FIGHTING TERRITORY

Scale of Miles

Prepared from original sources and special
surveys by the author and Oscar Messerly

Copyright by The Arthur H. Clark Company, 1930

use of better fords or to evade indians, deviations and cut-offs were made. Some of these were no more than mere shifts of the roadway for a few furlongs or a few miles, but others involved considerable distances. One of these was the Ridge road, in western Nebraska, which connected the routes along the two branches of the Platte. Of the more important deviations the earliest was the Sublette cut-off, or "Dry Drive," sometimes known also as Greenwood's cut-off, which ran from the Little Sandy, near South pass, almost directly west to the Bear river, near Bear lake. By this route the emigrants saved fifty-three miles of travel, though for much of the distance they found no water and missed the opportunity to purchase supplies and obtain blacksmith repairs at Fort Bridger.

To the construction and repair of the main line of the Oregon trail the government never contributed a dollar; nor until the laying out of the Lander cut-off (begun in 1857) did it contribute a dollar to any of its branches or feeders. Yet this great national highway was a wonderful road, the like of which, all things considered, has never elsewhere been seen. The wheels of wagons and the hoofs of horses and cattle had beaten it into shape and transformed it into the semblance of a pavement. To Father De Smet it appeared as one of the world's marvels. Under the date of September 2, 1851, in the vicinity of Fort Laramie, he writes:

We found ourselves on the Great route to Oregon, over which, like successive ocean surges, the caravans, composed of thousands of emigrants from every country and clime, have passed during these latter years to reach the rich gold mines of California, or to take possession of the new lands in the fertile plains and valleys of Utah and Oregon. These intrepid pioneers of civilization have formed the

broadest, longest and most beautiful road in the whole world . . .
which is as smooth as a barn floor swept by the winds.[32]

The indians of the plains noted with wonder and a
growing apprehension the caravans of men, women
and children who were slowly journeying along the
route for the conquest of a land that was empty of
homes and farms. They saw in the movement not only
a present injury but a threat of future extinction. The
remoter West would soon be filled up, and the later
comers would be forced to settle in the regions about
themselves. Game would disappear, and their food supply would become exhausted. Born to the chase, they
knew of no other way by which they could live. The
numbers of these migrating hordes amazed them. They
believed that the country east of the Mississippi was
becoming depopulated, and that all its inhabitants were
moving to the West. The poet Neihardt has well expressed their feeling:

> Were all the teeming regions of the dawn
> Unpeopled now? What devastating need
> Had set so many faces pale with greed.
>   Against the sunset?
>   . . . They did but look
> And whatsoever pleased them, that they took.[33]

The plains indians were stubbornly hostile to this
movement; and though from time to time they made
treaties promising not to molest the emigrants, their an-
tagonism remained deep-rooted and frequently broke
out in acts of plunder and violence.

Among the Eastern Shoshones, on the other hand, no
such feeling is discoverable. They must have suffered
many and great injuries from the impairment or de-

[32] Chittenden and Richardson, *op. cit.*, vol. 2: p. 671.
[33] Neihardt.

struction of their root grounds and the frightening of
game from their hunting fields; but of protest or opposition on their part we have no word. On the contrary,
we have the most positive evidence from many sources
that Washakie and his warriors constantly befriended
the emigrants and aided them with frequent acts of
service. In a later time the old chief was proudly to
cherish a paper, signed by upward of 9,000 emigrants,
testifying to this kindly aid.[34]

The Mormon migration of 1847 planted close to the
domain of Washakie a growing settlement with which
he was long to remain in friendly contact. Toward the
end of June of that year Brigham Young's advance
party of one hundred and forty-eight persons crossed
South pass, and on June 28, at the Big Sandy, met and
conferred with Bridger. It was then and there that the
famous trapper is alleged to have made his frequently
quoted challenge – "Mr. Young I would give a thousand dollars if I knew that an ear of corn could be
ripened in these mountains. I have been here twenty
years and have tried it in vain over and over again." [35]

By easy stages the party continued on its way and on
July 24, reached the site of the future Salt Lake City.
A small detachment had preceded it by three days,
staked off land and turned the water of City creek on to
the soil, and with the arrival of the main party, eight
acres of potatoes were at once planted. Whether President Young met Chief Washakie on the way we do not
know. We know that a few years later they were to
become close friends, but the date of their first meeting
is unrecorded. There is record of a party of Shoshones
appearing at the settlement seven days after the pio-

[34] Lander.
[35] Young, p. 743.

neers arrived, but we can not be sure what kind of Shoshones they were. We learn that they were incensed against the Utes for having traded with the Mormons, an act alleged to have been an invasion of the rights of the Shoshones, who claimed the land as their own and offered to sell it to the Mormons for powder and lead. A conference between the tribes restored peace for the time, and a feast of large "plump crickets," eaten uncooked, restored good feeling.

Distrust of the white-top wagons and their human freight was in a few years to become menacing. Frémont, in the report of his expedition of 1842, had with keen foresight recommended the erection on the Oregon trail of a series of forts, garrisoned by enough soldiers to give the emigrants protection. But congress pondered and delayed, and it was not until May, 1846, that an act was passed authorizing their establishment. Again there was delay, but a beginning was made in the spring of 1849. The first post was Fort Kearney, located three hundred and sixteen miles from the beginning of the trail, at the present Kearney, Nebraska. A few months later Fort Laramie, three hundred and forty miles further west, was bought from the American Fur Company and soon after garrisoned by two companies of mounted riflemen and a company of infantry. This post had been built by the fur company in 1844 to take the place of the original structure, a mile distant, erected in 1834 by Robert Campbell and named Fort Williams for his partner, William L. Sublette. In the same year Fort Hall was purchased and converted into a military post, but for nearly a decade thereafter the program was halted, and these three widely-separated forts were assumed to insure an adequate defense for a trail 2,000 miles long.

Though as a trading post Fort Laramie had been somewhat overshadowed in fame by the original Bent's Fort, on the Arkansas, it came at once, with its conversion into a military establishment, to a place of unique importance. During all the colorful and exciting period from this time on to the close of the Sioux wars, it was the military capital of the frontier. It was the place of councils and futile treaties, the halting place for emigrants, the refuge for fugitives from the persistent attacks of indians; and from it went forth, in all directions, armed expeditions against the savage marauders, and to it, sometimes elated with victory and sometimes dejected with defeat, they returned. Its history has no parallel in American or any other annals.

It was at Fort Laramie that Washakie, so far as the records show, first came into general notice. The occasion was the famous treaty council of September, 1851. This council was planned by the government to establish peace among the warring tribes of the plains and to secure the emigrants from attack. Primarily it was to be a council between the government on the one hand and the Sioux, Cheyennes and Arapahoes on the other. But the government wanted to bring together all the tribes from the Canadian border to the Arkansas and from the Missouri to Fort Bridger, and accordingly indian runners were sent out in all directions to announce the approaching event. Though the Shoshones were not to be a party to the treaty, Washakie decided to attend, and with a party of his followers began the journey. The party had proceeded but a short distance

east of South pass when it was attacked by a band of
Cheyennes, who killed and scalped two warriors before
being driven off.

It was Bridger, now generally known by the honorary title of Major, who announced to the authorities at
the fort the approach of the Shoshones. Appointed a
government interpreter for the occasion, he was detailed as the Shoshone guide and escort, and during the
whole of their stay they had the invaluable aid of his
presence among them. The Shoshones well knew that
they were entering dangerous territory. They had little
faith in the pledges of the eastern tribes, and they were
well prepared for trouble. Every one of them carried a
rifle and a plentiful supply of ammunition.

An eye-witness, Percival G. Lowe, then a corporal
in Troop B of the First Dragoons, gives us an unfor-
gettable picture of the scene of their arrival. Thousands
of indians had already assembled, and most numerous
among them were the Sioux, inveterately hostile to the
Shoshones. A handful of troops, from their paucity of
numbers wholly useless to preserve the peace in case the
indians decided on a killing, were present; and toward
their position, as the designated camping place of the
Shoshones, Bridger directed his wards. Washakie de-
ployed his warriors in battle formation, with the women
and children, well guarded, bringing up the rear.
Steadily the line advanced, Washakie riding somewhat
ahead. Suddenly from the massed ranks of the Sioux a
mounted warrior darted forward, intent upon avenging
the death of his father, slain by Washakie in battle. The
chief, unmoved, kept on and coolly drew up his rifle
for action, while from his followers, as from one man,
came a mighty shout of defiance. In an instant all the

precautions that had been taken by the authorities to assure peace appeared to have come to naught. But before a shot could be fired, a French interpreter among the troops, with rare courage and presence of mind, galloped out, overtook and seized the Sioux warrior and disarmed him, and thus by the narrowest of margins averted a desperate conflict. "Not one out of a hundred Sioux had guns," writes Lowe, "and the Snakes, though not one to five of the Sioux, would have defended themselves successfully, and the battle would have been the most bloody ever known amongst the wild tribes." [36] The incident over, the Snakes proceeded quietly to their camp.

The conduct of his wards elated Bridger, and to Lowe he praised them in the highest terms:

These are the finest indians on earth. . . You dragoons acted nice, but you wouldn't have had no show if the fight had commenced – no making peace then. . . It'll be a proud day for the Snakes if any of these prairie tribes pitch into 'um. Uncle Sam told 'um to come down here and they'd be safe, but they ain't takin' his word for it altogether. . . Awful brave fellows these Snakes; got the nerve; honest, too; can take their word for any thing; trust 'em anywhere; they live all about me, and I know all of them.

Lowe also adds a final summary of the scene, reciting:

The cool deliberate action of the chief, the staunch firmness of his warriors and the quiet demeanor of women and children, who were perfectly self-possessed – not a single outcry from that vast parade save the one cry of defiance that went up spontaneously as the chief raised his gun to take aim at the Sioux. The scene was impressive, as showing the faith that band of warriors had in each other; the entire confidence of their families in them; the self-reliance all through. It was a lesson for soldiers who might never again see such a grand

---

[36] Lowe.

display of soldierly manhood, and the lesson was not lost. Every dragoon felt an interest in that tribe.[37]

Just at this point appears one of those baffling contradictions too often found in frontier chronicles. The episode occurred on either August 31 or September 1. Father De Smet, who arrived on September 2, asserts that the Shoshones present numbered but forty, while Lowe says that they outnumbered the more than two hundred and fifty soldiers. Perhaps both chroniclers are in error. Lowe's account, however, is the more probable. It seems incredible that Washakie, penetrating so dangerous a region, would have taken with him no more than forty warriors, and it further seems incredible that so small a party could have made so profound an impression on the assemblage as that reported by Lowe. The good father is amiss in reporting the council as having lasted twenty-three days, as against a duration of eighteen days reported by Superintendent Mitchell; and his statement that on the break-up of the council the Shoshones moved off to the South Platte for a buffalo hunt, can hardly be true. They had no business in the Arapahoe country, and to invade it would have brought them into immediate conflict.

On the next day orders were given that the council would be held at the junction of Horse creek and the North Platte, thirty-six miles to the southeast, and thither the whole company proceeded. There is a ludicrous disparity in the estimates of the number who gathered there, some persons saying 8,000 and some 60,000. But even with the minimum figure, it was a tremendous convention for the frontier. Representatives of most of the plains tribes were present. The

[37] *Ibid.*

Sioux, the Cheyennes and the Arapahoes came in the greatest numbers, the Crows and Shoshones perhaps next; there were also Assiniboines, Minnetarees or Gros Ventres (Hidatsas), Mandans and Arikaras and doubtless small parties from other tribes. The government was represented by Colonel D. D. Mitchell, Superintendent of Indian Affairs for the Central Superintendency; Thomas Fitzpatrick, the noted trapper and "mountain man," now indian agent for the upper Platte and Arkansas; Colonel Samuel Cooper, Adjutant-general of the army; Colonel A. B. Chambers, editor of the *Missouri Republican*, who acted as secretary, and B. Gratz Brown, correspondent of the *Republican*, who also assisted with the secretarial work. A troop of the First dragoons, two troops of the Mounted rifles and a company of the Sixth infantry, in all some two hundred and seventy men, commanded by Captain R. H. Chilton, represented the military arm of the government. Robert Campbell, the fur trader, and Edmond F. Chouteau were present, and so also, as already stated, was Father De Smet, who to broaden the scope of his missionary work had travelled all the way from his Flathead mission.

When the council session began, the Shoshones demanded that before the peace pipe be smoked, the Cheyennes should return the two scalps taken in the recent attack near South pass. Reluctantly the trophies were returned. Later it was the turn of a Cheyenne woman to demand justice of the Shoshones. The correspondent of the *Republican*, writing from the "Treaty ground near Fort Laramie" on September 8, thus pictures the scene:

A Cheyenne squaw, leading a horse, with a boy, about ten or

twelve years of age, mounted upon him, made her way into the entrance of the council arbor, and commenced her chaunt. The interruption was sudden, and for a few minutes not understood, but soon stopped by the Cheyenne chiefs. The purpose was this. Some years previously, one of the Shoshones, a Snake chief, who was then in the Council, had killed her husband, leaving this boy, then an infant, fatherless. She now came to present the boy and horse to the Shoshonie, by which, according to their customs, the boy becomes the adopted son of the Shoshonie, and entitled to all the rights and privileges of that tribe. The Snake chief had no right, by their customs, to refuse receiving the gift, and upon its s[r]eception became bound to treat the boy in every respect as his own child.[38]

It was perhaps on the same day, and just before the close of the day's session, that Washakie made a brief response to the address of Colonel Mitchell. The *Republican* correspondent thus reports the incident:

Wash-Ah-Wee-Ha, a Shoshone, next spoke: "Grand Father, I have come a great distance to see you and hear you. I threw my family too, away, to come and listen, and I am glad and my people are glad that we have come. Our hearts are full; all our hearts are full of your words. We will talk them over again."[39]

One of the most arduous duties of the commissioners was to fix and grade the rank of the various indian leaders to correspond with the rank of officers in the army. The task accomplished, uniforms, ranging all the way from those of major-generals to those of lieutenants, were distributed, and for the remainder of the session the chiefs and sub-chiefs appeared in this resplendent toggery, further supplemented by swords and medals. Presents of goods were also made and accepted as a quit-claim for all damages so far suffered by the indians through the invasion of their country by the whites. On September 17 a treaty was signed, promis-

[38] St. Louis (Mo.) *Republican*, October 26, 1851.
[39] *Ibid.*

ing the indians an annual distribution of $50,000 worth of goods for fifty years (altered by congress to ten years) and exacting from them a pledge to keep the peace among themselves, to give the emigrants a free passage and to permit the government to build roads in the indian country.[40] The treaty further contained an attempted delimitation of boundaries for the various tribes, though it is not probable that they regarded this feature with great seriousness. One item could not have been other than disappointing to Washakie, for it gave to the Crows the Big Horn country all the way to the Wind river mountains. Representatives of seven tribes signed the document. The work over, the vast assemblage began to scatter. So far as a scrap of paper might give assurance in the matter, the white-top wagons could now move along their way unmolested.

[40] U. S. Report of Commissioner of Indian Affairs for 1852.

Chief Washakie and Brigham Young

With Brigham Young, head of the Church of Latter Day Saints and from early in 1851 to April, 1858, governor of Utah Territory and superintendent of Indian Affairs for the Utah Superintendency, Washakie came into close and long continued relations. He first appears in Young's reports in the fall of 1852. Some of the Utes, under Chief Walker (Wachor, Walkara), had been having trouble with the Shoshones, and in a fight nine of the latter had been killed. In August, 1852, Washakie, with a considerable following, arrived at Salt Lake City and on August 6, with five of his warriors, appeared before Young. He wanted to arrange trade with the Mormons, and he wanted also to conclude a peace with Walker. President Young immediately sought to bring the two chiefs together, but it was not until September 3, that a council could be held. Each chief brought with him about fifty of his warriors. Young asked Walker and Washakie (who appears in the report as "Wash-o-kig") if they wished to make peace and be friends with each other. The answer from both chiefs was "Yes," whereupon Young requested each warrior who was of the same mind to rise and hold up his right hand. The vote was unanimous. "I told them," reports President Young, "that they must never fight each other again, but must live in peace, so that they could travel in each other's country, and trade with each other." The pipe of peace was then produced and offered to the Great Spirit and then passed to the warriors until every one had smoked in token of lasting friendship.

In negotiations regarding trade with the Mormons, Washakie is reported to have made the curious statement that although he and his people lived on the Green river (that is, in the Bridger country), the land did not belong to them, but that their real home was the Wind river valley and the country of the Sweetwater. The statement is obviously a blunder of the interpreter. Washakie well knew that the Wind river country had been awarded to the Crows; he knew also that the Shoshones had occupied the Bridger country for many years before he joined them. He was in later years to assert in the strongest terms the Shoshone ownership of this region and ultimately to cede it to the government in exchange for a reservation. But as for trade with the Mormons, he wanted it eagerly, and he promised that if they would make a settlement in the Green valley his people would gladly visit the place to exchange goods.

For their friendliness to the whites and for the safety in which the emigrants had been allowed to travel through their country, Brigham Young thanked the Shoshones, expressing the hope that this protective care might always continue. After the peace ceremony, Walker promised to Washakie nine head of horses (to be delivered at some future time) as a compensation for the Shoshones that had been killed. He admitted that he had done wrong and said that he was sorry. "I will hear now what Brigham says to me good," he said, placing his hand on his breast; "have been a fool, but will do better in future." One of Washakie's sub-chiefs gleefully declared that "his ears were open wide to

CHIEF WASHAKIE
Advocate of peace, if not — then war

hear; it was good and he felt well; his heart was good."
Ending his report, the President of the Mormons,
writes, "I have been thus explicit in giving the particulars of this interview, as it is the first that has occurred
of a like nature since the settlements were founded, and
it is hoped will result in long continued amity between
the tribes." [41] The hope was, however, a delusive one,
for within a year Walker with his Utes was ravaging
the Mormon settlements far and wide.

The Bridger valley was then a part of Utah. The
Mormon authorities had become antagonistic to Bridger. They alleged that he was in league with the indians
hostile to them and had become a menace to the safety
of the colony. The friends of Bridger, on the other
hand, maintained that the charges were untrue. Be that
as it may, in the fall of 1853, on affidavits asserting that
he had been selling powder and lead to the indians with
which to kill Mormons, a posse was sent out from Salt
Lake City to arrest him and confiscate his property.
Bridger was shrewd enough to keep out of the way of
the posse, but the remainder of the program was carried out effectively. He was driven away and his property was taken. On November 2, a colony of thirty-nine
Mormons was sent to occupy the region about the fort,
and two weeks later a party of fifty-three followed.
Finding Fort Bridger in the hands of a number of
"rough mountain men," the first party did not attempt
to gain possession, but moved twelve miles southwest,
where they established a post afterward known as Fort
Supply. Other Mormons coming later occupied Fort
Bridger.[42]

Fort Supply was the first agricultural settlement in

---

[41] Young. Report for 1852.
[42] Alter, *op. cit.*, pp. 233-263.

Bridger valley. Its site was on Willow creek, a tributary of the Smith Fork of Black's Fork of the Green, near the present Robertson, Uinta county (Wyoming). At the height of its prosperity it consisted of twenty-five buildings, corrals and a stockyard, inclosed in an area of ten acres by a double row of pointed pickets eighteen feet long and about one foot thick. The colonists brought with them many wagons, oxen, horses, mules, milk cows and beef cattle, farm implements, grain and miscellaneous supplies, for the colony was intended to be not only the headquarters and distributing point of the Mormons in that region but also a trading post for the emigrants. Some time later it was made the county seat of Green county, Utah.

To enable them to converse with the members of Washakie's band, then camped nearby, the colonists assiduously studied the Shoshone language, a labor in which they were greatly aided by Elijah B. Ward, a trader and trapper who had married a Shoshone woman. The Shoshones watched with great interest the planting, cultivating and harvesting of crops, and some of them began farming on their own account. One of these was Bazil, a sub-chief of Washakie's and the adopted son of Porivo or Wadze-wipe, the noted Shoshone woman, Sacajawea, the interpreter of the Lewis and Clark expedition. That he had profited by following the example of the colonists is shown by a statement made by Elder Isaac Bullock, in the *Deseret News* for October 1, 1856:

Baziel, one of the Snakes who had lived in the fort with us during the last year, has raised about thirty bushels of wheat and some vegetables. He and his squaws have harvested it clean and neat, and appear to feel well satisfied with their prospects for bread this winter.

At the Pioneer Day celebration at Fort Bridger, on July 24, of the same year, Bazil had enthusiastically commended the agricultural experiment:

I feel well to see grain growing on the Snake land, for their children can get bread to eat, also butter and milk. Before you came here our children were often hungry, now they can get bread and vegetables when not fortunate in hunting meat.

And another Shoshone, John, had added his approval:

I like to see wheat, potatoes, beets and peas growing, for it makes my heart feel good to see our children eating the bread you raise on the land; you treat us as friends; when we come to your houses hungry, you give us something to eat. I am glad to see the good things that you raise around the fort, for they did not grow before you came.

Thus Shoshonean agriculture had its beginning, and its benefits were to be remembered when the band was placed on a reservation.

From the agricultural work of the Mormons coming under the observation of Washakie, while living in Bridger valley, he learned well the value of reclaiming arid lands through the process of irrigation, thus putting into operation the methods he had learned by observation from his Mormon neighbors on his beloved reservation, knowingly preparing for the day when the abundance of game no longer was a part of his choice selected lands.

One of the colonists of the first party was James S. Brown, who came to know Washakie well, and who in his book, *Life of a Pioneer*, has left a record of several meetings with the chief. In the spring of 1854, having acquired some knowledge of the Shoshone language, he visited, with three companions, Washakie's camp. To his proffer of friendship the doubting chief responded:

Who are you, from where do you come and what is your errand
to my country? Tell me the truth, do not tell me any lies, nor talk
any crooked talk.

Brown informed him that the Mormons had journeyed to his country because they and the indians had
one father, who was disturbed that his children should
fight. They came, they said, to tell the chief that it
would not be many snows before the game in his country would all be destroyed and there would be no food,
and that therefore it was believed wise for the indians
to learn how to build houses, to plow the soil and to
raise livestock just as did the white man. To this explanation Washakie replied: "Wait a while. My little
children are very hungry for some of the white man's
food, and they want some sugar." Brown and his companions then gave all their bread and sugar to Washakie, who handed it to his wife, who in turn distributed
it to the hungry little ones. The gift made the visitors
welcome.

A council was held in the evening, when Washakie
explained the purposes of the visitors, and after listen-
ing to the views of such of his warriors as chose to
speak, summed up the subject in a few pointed words.
He also, according to Brown, complained that he was
no longer head chief of the Eastern Shoshones. The
power, he said, had been taken from him by the Indian
agent at Fort Laramie and given to a man of small consequence, whom the Shoshones refused to recognize
and whom in derision they had dubbed Tavendu-wets
(White Man's Child). The statement is not credible
since it is inconsistent with what we know of Shoshone
history, with the prestige won by Washakie at Fort
Laramie in 1851, and with the fact that the Indian

agent at the time was that most capable judge of men, Thomas Fitzpatrick. Doubtless there was a Tavenduwets, since Brown reports having visited him at his camp; but he could hardly have been more than the head of a short-lived faction of seceders from Washakie's band, and his support among the whites was probably confined to some of the semi-outlaws who had begun to infest the Green river valley. Brown could at that time have had but a smattering of the difficult Shoshone language, and doubtless misunderstood much of what he heard.[43]

The statement is further inconsistent with Brown's account of a visit to Washakie's camp in the following year, since at this time the chief is apparently in full control of the situation, and the mysterious Tavenduwets has faded into oblivion. The camp was on Horse creek, in the upper valley of the Green, near the site of Fort Bonneville and also the site on which Father De Smet held his first high mass in Wyoming.[44] Here Washakie had more than three thousand of his people, with "a pony for every soul; they were well supplied with rifles, Colt's revolvers, bows, arrows, shields and some cutlasses and large heavy knives. They were excellently mounted, and their discipline could not well be improved for the country they were passing over and the force they were most likely to fall in with."

In council with the warriors the missionaries told of the messages President Young had sent to Washakie and of his desire to help the chief and his people, even to furnishing them with seed and tools and some capable men to instruct them in putting in their crops. The

[43] Brown, James S.
[44] This site was marked July 5, 1925, by a monument erected by the Knights of Columbus.

Book of Mormon was presented to Washakie. Though not being able to read a word, he opened it as if scanning its contents, and then said, "It is no good for my people; it is very good for the white man." The book and the pipe were passed around the council circle twenty-one times, and several warriors gave their views. One said: "This book is of no use to us. If the Mormon captain has nothing better to send than this, we had better send it, his letter and these men, back to him, and tell him that they are no good to us, that we want powder, lead and caps, sugar, coffee, flour, paints, knives and blankets, for those we can use." Another said: "We have no use for this book. If the paper were all cut out and thrown away, we could sew up the ends and put a strap on it, and it would do for the white man's money bag; but we have no use for it, for we have no money to put in it."

Washakie, closing the discussion, then spoke:

You are all fools; you are blind, and cannot see; you have no ears, for you do not hear; you are fools, for you do not understand. These men are our friends. . . They talk straight, with one tongue, and tell us that after a few more snows the buffalo will be gone, and if we do not learn some other way to get something to eat, we will starve to death. . . We can make a bow and arrows, but the white man's mind is strong and light.

Picking up a Colt's revolver, the chief continued:

The white man can make this, and a little thing that he carries in his pocket, so that he can tell where the sun is on a dark day, and when it is night he can tell when it will come daylight. This is because the face of the Father is towards him, and His back is towards us. But after a while the Great Father will quit being mad and will turn His face towards us. Then our skin will be light, then our mind will be strong like the white man's, and we can make and use things like he does.

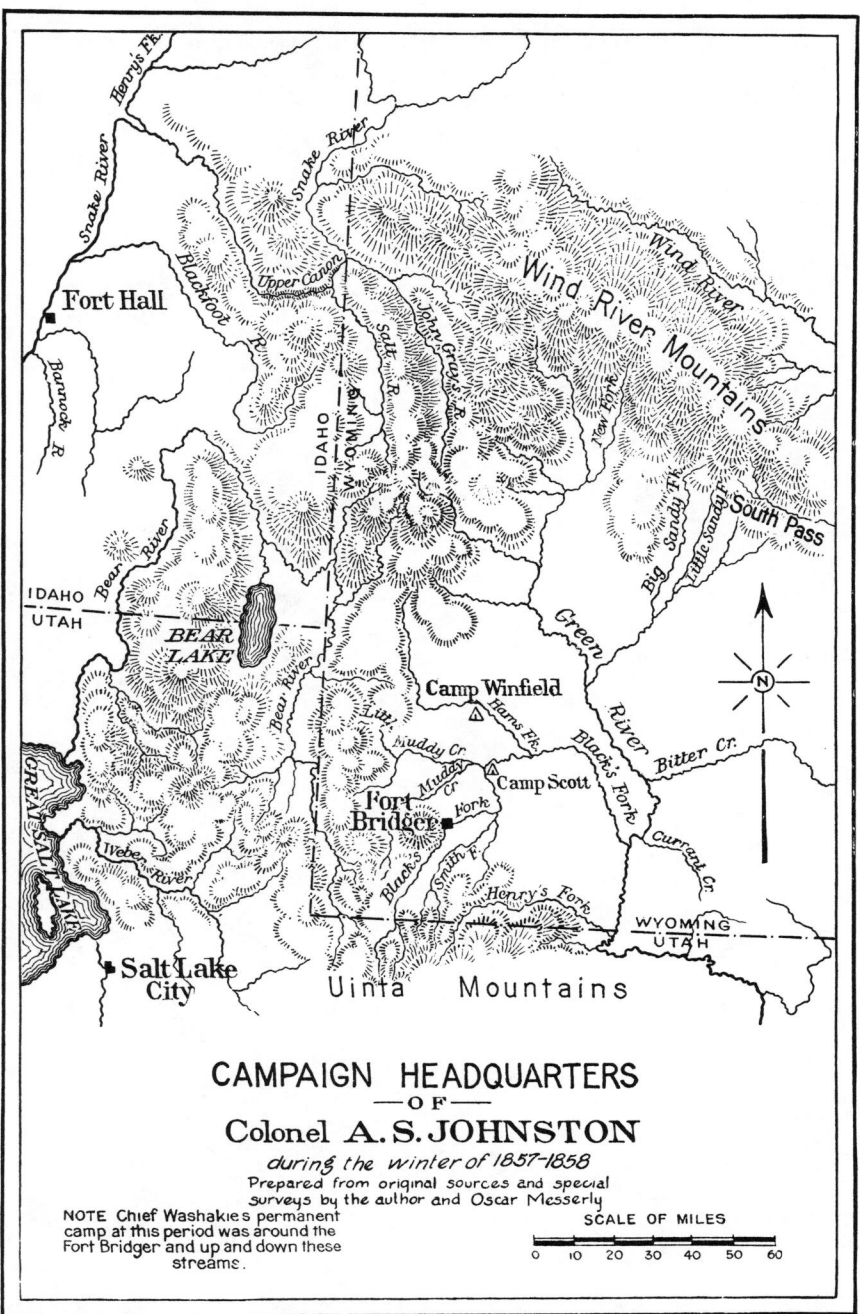

CAMPAIGN HEADQUARTERS
—O F—
Colonel A. S. JOHNSTON
during the winter of 1857-1858
Prepared from original sources and special
surveys by the author and Oscar Messerly

NOTE Chief Washakie's permanent
camp at this period was around the
Fort Bridger and up and down these
streams.

SCALE OF MILES

0   10   20   30   40   50   60

On the following morning the missionaries departed, deeply gratified that their book had been accepted and carrying with them an ineffaceable impression of the sachem. "Chief Washakie," writes Brown, "was a bold, noble, hospitable and honorable man. As an orator I think he surpassed any man I ever met." [45]

With the year 1857 Washakie had to meet a new and momentous situation – nothing less than civil war among the whites. To both sides in the controversy he was friendly and so could only look on with what in high diplomatic circles is known as "benevolent neutrality." Difficulties between the Mormon church and the National government had gradually become acute. Federal officers returning from Utah asserted that their authority had been defied and their lives endangered and that the territory was in a state of open revolt. In May, President Buchanan revoked the appointment of Brigham Young as governor and indian superintendent, appointed a new set of officials, headed by Alfred Cumming, of Georgia, as governor, and ordered an army of 2500 men to proceed to Utah. By explicit orders the soldiers were not to use arms except in self-defense or when called upon by the civil authority to preserve the peace and to execute the laws. The army assembled at Fort Leavenworth, and in detachments began its march across the plains. It was at first commanded by General W. S. Harney, but on the eve of his intended departure he was transferred. General P. F. Smith was then assigned to the command, but died shortly after his appointment, and not until most of the army was half way along its journey was the place given to Colonel (afterward General) Albert

---

[45] Brown, *op. cit.*

Sidney Johnston. With Johnston went the newly appointed officials. At Fort Laramie, in July, one of the early detachments found Major Bridger, who was at once engaged as a guide and who continued to serve until the end of the campaign.

News of the President's action reached the assembled Mormons at their celebration of the tenth anniversary of the founding of the colony, on July 24, and created intense excitement. Their first determination was to resist what they termed the invasion. "The Mormon militia, numbering probably 6000 men," says Alter, "began intensive training and defensive activities, while the faithful Mormon women and children devoted themselves unselfishly to the work of the fields, the gardens, and to the making of clothing for the prospective campaign against the United States army in the Wasatch mountains." [46] The colonists at Fort Supply and Fort Bridger evacuated their homes, destroying the buildings and all the property they could not carry, and removed to Salt Lake City. On September 15, Young issued a proclamation forbidding the army to enter the territory and declaring that "all the forces in said territory would hold themselves in readiness to march at a moment's notice, to repel any and all such invasion, and that martial law is hereby declared to exist." Shortly afterward he dispatched an order to the "Officer commanding the forces now invading Utah territory," declaring himself still to be governor and commanding that officer to retire forthwith by the route by which he had entered.[47] Mormon light cavalry attacked the scattered wagon trains of the army, and

[46] Alter, *op. cit.*, 281-282.
[47] *Ibid.*, 286-288.

though refraining from the use of arms, captured the supplies and stock and burnt the wagons.

Slowly the army concentrated about Fort Bridger, where it established Camp Scott. Cooped up by the intensely cold weather, by heavy snowfalls and by lack of supplies and stock for transport, it remained there throughout the winter. But the war, despite all the preparations made for it, was never fought. A Philadelphian friendly to the Mormons, Thomas L. Kane, journeyed by way of Panama to Utah and after conferring with Young visited Camp Scott and talked with Cumming. In April the newly appointed governor hurried on to Salt Lake City, where he assumed office. More than two months later the army marched unopposed to Salt Lake City and on to a point forty miles south, where it established Camp Floyd. Not a gun was fired.[48]

Washakie, with some 2000 reported followers, saw a considerable part of this drama. His band seems to have been in the Green valley all the summer and fall, and it wintered at the crossing of the Green, though a part of it moved into the mountains for a time to be nearer game. The chief is said to have been asked by General Johnston to join with him in the invasion of Utah and to have declined on the ground that he had taken a vow never to war with the whites. We may be sure that this would have been his response if the request had been made, but the incident is unverified.

The new indian superintendent for Utah, Doctor Jacob Forney, set up his office with the army at Camp Scott, and to him, during the hard winter, came many parties of Shoshones. One of these bands, from the ter-

---

[48] *Ibid.*, 303-314.

ritory west of Washakie's domain, headed by Little
Soldier, the chief, and Benjamin Simons, a sub-chief,
arrived on December 10, with a demand to know the
object and destination of so many soldiers in the country and the reason why so many whites were occupying
the indians' lands under grants given them as "herd
grounds." They seemed to be satisfied with the explan-
ations offered and after receiving some presents left
for their homes. Speaking generally of the Shoshones,
Forney reported that no tribe in the territory had been
so discommoded by the incursion of a white population
among them, but that they had shown no evidence of
hostility.[49] Colonel (afterward General) Fitz-John
Porter, on the other hand, reported that "an expedition . . . was sent into the Snake indian country to quiet
the indians, and prevent their employment by the Mormons." [50] There is no indication, however, that the difficulty was serious.

On May 13, 1858, Forney, still at Camp Scott, was
able to patch up a peace between the Eastern Shoshones, represented by Washakie and his five sub-chiefs,
and a band or sub-tribe of Utes, represented by White-
Eye, Son-a-at and San Pitch. These indians, he reported, had been "at enmity for years fighting and
killing each other and endangering the lives and property of whites." Washakie, for the first time so far as
known, indicated to a government official his wish for
a reservation, making choice of the valley of Henry's
Fork, about forty miles south of Fort Bridger, and
asking that a farm be opened there. His band, reported
the agent, numbered about 1200 souls, and "he has per-

---

[49] Forney. *Report*, September 6, 1858.
[50] Alter, J. Cecil. Quoted *op. cit*, p. 304.

fect command over them, and is one of the finest looking and most intellectual indians I ever saw. He prides
himself that neither he nor any of his tribe ever molested a white." [51] Some Bannocks attended the council,
but took no part in the "talks." In the following year
this band received governmental permission to make
their home in the region claimed and inhabited by
Washakie's band, and for several years the two peoples
lived either together or closely adjacent. The object
of this permission was doubtless to put the Bannocks
under the watchful eye of Washakie. But it failed to
bring the benefits expected, for there was a further increase of depredations against the emigrants.

[51] Forney. *Report, op. cit.*

Fort Bridger and Indian Depredations on the Oregon Trail

One outcome of the difficulties with the different classes of emigrants who utilized the Oregon trail was the construction of a new emigrant highway through Shoshoneland. It was a cut-off from the Oregon trail, and it became known as the Lander road, from Captain Frederick West Lander, its chief engineer and later its superintendent. Surveying began on the Sweetwater in 1857, and the route was opened in time for the emigration of 1859. It was a government road, the first of its kind in the far West; and the cost was heavy, since to cut this way through the rough country required many excavations, the removal of thousands of tons of rock and the clearing away of much timber. Instead of traversing South pass, the road ascended the Sweetwater twenty miles further north and crossed the divide by a pass a thousand feet higher. Descending into the upper Green valley, it followed a generally westward course to the junction of the Bannock with the Snake, thence continuing along the Snake to a point known as City of Rocks, somewhat beyond the mouth of Raft river – a total distance of three hundred and forty-six miles.

Traders and other materially interested persons to the south, incensed that the flow of emigration should be turned away from them, vigorously denounced the project and declared the road a dangerous thorough-

fare which would not be traveled at all but for the mis-
representations made in its behalf by Lander's agents.
Lander, however, was able to reply that the only mis-
representations of which he was aware were those made
by its enemies; that by official orders no efforts were
directed toward inducing anyone to choose it, and that
in spite of that fact thirteen thousand emigrants had
traveled it during the season of 1859 and had signed
statements expressing their satisfaction with it. The
road continued to be traveled by thousands during the
emigration era and is still in use today. Over it hundreds of cattle are annually driven to market from the
Green river valley, and the money spent on its repair
has made it available as a highway for automobiles.

Lander became closely acquainted with Washakie
and has given us many interesting glimpses of the chief
and his people. In July, 1858, newly promoted to the
post of superintendent of the road, he came upon Washakie and his band near South pass. He writes in his
report to the commissioner of Indian affairs:

After leaving the South pass . . . I met the whole of the great
tribe of the Eastern Shoshones, under the direction of the celebrated
Wash-i-kee. They were on their annual hunt near the headwaters of
the Green river, surrounding antelope. . . [I] talked with him upon
the subject which brought me to the country. . . He remarked that it
was never the intention of the Shoshonee tribe, at least his portion of
it, to fight the whites; that he had himself been fired upon by emigrants, but had always taught his young men that a war with the
"Great Father" would be disastrous to them. He said, before the emigrants passed through his country, buffalo, elk and antelope could be
seen upon all the hills; now, when he looked for game, he saw only
wagons with white tops and men riding upon their horses; that his
people were very poor, and had fallen back into the valleys of the
mountains to dig roots and get meat for their little ones. . . He said
he did not even propose to fight, notwithstanding the building of this

new road would destroy many of their root grounds and drive off
their game. . . Although Wash-i-kee declares his intentions to be
friendly, the Snakes will be much injured by the passage of the new
road by emigrants.[52]

Lander promised recompense for damages that
might be inflicted and rewards for friendly coöperation.
The first payment was made on July 2, of the following
year, in the presence of a large number of emigrants,
at the crossing of the Big Sandy, about forty miles west
of the pass. Subsequent payments were made to small
parties of the band as the expedition proceeded. The
goods distributed were given both as a reward for the
good behavior of these indians in the past and as a payment "for the destruction of their root and herding
grounds by the animals of the emigration." It is in this
report that Captain Lander makes the statement quoted
in a previous chapter: "No instance is on record of the
Eastern Snakes having committed outrages upon the
whites." Not only had they abstained from molesting
the emigrants, but they had rendered most valuable
service by recovering lost stock and by aiding the trains
in passing the dangerous ford of the Green. The personality of the chief interested Lander greatly. He continues:

Washikeek [elsewhere spelled Washikee], the principal chief of
the tribe, is half Flathead. He obtained his popularity in the nation
by various feats as a warrior and, it is urged by some of the moun-
taineers, by his extreme severity. This has, in one or two instances,
extended so far as taking life. . . "Push-i-can" or "Pur-chi-can," another war chief of the Snakes, bears upon his forehead the scar of a
blow of the tomahawk given by Washikee in one of these alterca-
tions. Washakee, who is also known by the term of "the white man's
friend," was many years ago in the employment of the American and

---

[52] U. S. House Executive Document, 108, 35 Cong., 2 sess., serial no. 1008,
pp. 68-69.

the Hudson's Bay fur companies. He was the constant companion of the white trappers, and his superior knowledge and accomplishments may be attributed to this fact.

He is very light colored, remarkably tall and well formed, even majestic in appearance, and, in my own opinion, an undeniable half-breed. He is desirous of visiting Washington with the principal warriors of his tribe, never having been further east than Fort Laramie. . .

Washikee expresses himself in favor of the reserve system, and has named a section of country near the Medicine Bow butte, on the border lands of his tribe, as a suitable place for farming purposes.

Lander was skeptical, however, about the agricultural ambitions of the remainder of the band, since an offer of seeds and utensils made by him was not well received. Toward herding they were better disposed, and he believed that by appointing suitable agents to reside among them they "might be restrained to habits of discipline and self-denial." The Salt Lake Diggers, he says, "inter-marry with the Eastern Snakes and are on good terms with them," though among these Diggers "are some of the worst [indians] in the mountains." "Washakie," continues Lander (in a passage quoted in a previous chapter) "will not permit a horse thief or a vagabond to remain in his band." Indians from the Mormon region, however, go about the country with minor chiefs calling themselves Eastern Snakes, and their depredations are sometimes laid to their peaceful kinsmen.[53]

Of Washakie's severity, to which Lander refers, a number of tales are related. One tale has to do with Six Feathers, a warrior who was in the habit of unmercifully beating his wife. Called to account by an army officer for permitting this form of punishment,

---

[53] U. S. Senate Executive Document, 42, 36 Cong., 1 sess., serial no. 1033, pp. 121-123.

Washakie replied, "Oh, sometimes we beat them [the wives] when they do not obey." On being told that the wife-beater's cruelty showed that he did not have his men perfectly under control, Washakie asked, "What should be done?" The officer suggested that the matter of discipline be left in the chief's hands. After a few days Washakie reported, "No more beat his wife, me fix him."

"How did it happen?" asked the officer.

"Oh," responded Washakie, "Me kill him. Me find him beating her, me tell him white man say stop. Two sleeps go by. Me find him beating her again. Me shoot him and drag him out to the rock."

At another time a medicine man, in attempting to cure an injured leg of Washakie's adopted boy, bungled the job. All excuses were futile. The chief burst into a fury, exclaiming, "I don't want any more of your lies. If this boy had died, I would have had you tied to the tail of a wild horse and let him kick and drag you to death. Now, go, and don't let me see you any more, for you are hated by every indian, squaw and papoose in this camp." [54]

But though quick-tempered and sometimes severe in his punishments, his nature was kindly, and he delighted in acts of personal helpfulness. Mrs. Jeannette Young Easton, a daughter of Brigham Young, in a recent letter to the author, tells of his rescue of a party of freighters. She writes:

As I remember Washakie he was the ideal type of indian, not extremely tall, but majestic in his bearing. He was not a talker, very quiet, but when he spoke, people listened. I saw him many times in father's office, where he was treated with utmost kindness. Father's policy with the indians was "to feed them, not fight them," although

---

[54] Wilson, p. 145.

our people had several skirmishes with Walker's and Arapeen's bands. Washakie, I remember, was at one time located near the Sweetwater mining country at the time two of my uncles were Pony Express riders, and as a child I heard them say many times, when the indians were bad on the trails, "If we can only make Washakie's camp we are safe." Once when some of our boys were freighting, the heavy snows and bad roads, together with ice and snow, had reduced them almost to starvation. They were in a pitiful condition, besides being harassed by indians. Washakie's braves were out skirmishing, and word was sent to the chief that white men were being pursued. He lost no time in coming to their rescue, keeping the boys for days in his "wickiup," showing every courtesy in his power.

During a blizzard some Mormon freighters came into Washakie's camp, carrying one of their men whose feet were so frozen that he could not walk. Not knowing what measures to take in so severe a case, they appealed to Washakie. The chief left the group immediately and returned with one of the women, saying, "My squaw make well." "See," he said, cutting the boots from the feet of the freighter and making him place them against the breasts of the woman. A gradual thawing resulted, and in twenty-four hours the feet were restored to their natural condition.

Washakie had a deep affection for his numerous children. On the journey home to Fort Bridger from a successful buffalo hunt in the Big Horn mountains, in the fall of 1866, he established a night camp on the Sweetwater river in the immediate vicinity of South pass. At daybreak the following morning the camp was attacked by a party of two hundred Sioux. Rallying his hundred warriors, Washakie countercharged, driving the enemy back into the timber. A Sioux, slain by Washakie, was the first victim of the combat. While Washakie and a group of his warriors were examining the dead man, the chief's oldest and idolized son, Nan-

FORT BRIDGER

Reproduced from an original painting of 1870. Today one of the best preserved of the extreme frontier military posts. Situated on the Oregon trail. In 1849, on Fremont's advice, purchased and used as a military post. Here Jim Bridger in 1843 established a black-smith shop and supply station. Later a central meeting place of traders and trappers. In 1929 purchased by the state of Wyoming

nag-gai, rode into the camp. Angered that the boy should not have taken part in the skirmish, the father reproved him, saying, "I, an old man, have killed this Sioux our enemy, while you, like a squaw, come into camp after the fight is over."

Indignant over the reproof, for Washakie had given him permission to leave camp, Nan-nag-gai wheeled on his horse and calling aloud to his father, "I will make for myself a name as great as is yours, or die in the attempt," dashed toward the Sioux, who were hiding in the grove. He killed and scalped several of the enemy, but was finally slain, and his body was scalped and hacked into pieces in sight of his father, who had followed after him.

All day long Washakie with his men fought the Sioux to avenge the death of his cherished boy, and with the coming of twilight the enemy was forced to retreat, with the loss of a number of their braves. The war-whoop of the sunrise now became the doleful wail of death, and Washakie realized that he was himself responsible for his bereavement. The story runs that overnight his hair turned white. Never afterward did he speak of this son without great emotion.

Fort Bridger had been destroyed by the Mormons in the fall of 1857, and nothing remained of it but a cobble-stone wall inclosing an area a hundred feet square. It was a good piece of masonry, which had been built by the Mormons, and a part of it is still standing. General Johnston, during the winter, added another wall and two lunettes to make the place defensible, and from this beginning was to come a resurrected Fort Bridger. On November 18, 1857, papers were signed by James Bridger and Captain and assistant Quartermaster John

H. Dickerson, leasing the property to the government at a yearly rental of six hundred dollars, with the privilege of purchase for ten thousand dollars. No money, however, was to be paid until Bridger could prove title, and as this proof was not produced, he never received a penny. In June of the following year, when most of the army departed for Utah, the place was left in charge of Major William Hoffman, who began the erection of new buildings, and this work was continued by Lieutenant-colonel (afterward General) E. R. S. Canby, who assumed command on August 17.[55]

Bridger was henceforth to be a stranger to the fort he had established and made famous. John Robertson, trapper, trader and farmer, known generally as "Uncle Jack Robinson," who had preceded even Bridger as a resident in the region, stayed on to become noted later as the patriarch of the community and the first permanent settler in Wyoming. But the man who, next to Bridger, was to become most widely famous for his connection with the fort and the surrounding country was a newcomer, William A. Carter. He was born at Pittsylvania, Virginia, April 15, 1818. When eighteen years old he enlisted in the Second Dragoons. He fought in the Seminole war, and while on this service he became well acquainted with General Harney, who took an unusual interest in him. After four years in the army he was honorably discharged. Returning to his home, he was married, November 2, 1848, to Mary E. Hamilton, also a Virginian. The young couple moved to Boone county, Missouri, where for two years they made their home on a farm. With his brother Richard and brother-in-law Richard Hamilton he trekked to

---

California in 1850, all three eventually returning home by way of Nicaragua.

When Harney received orders to march to Utah he sent for Carter and offered him the place of post-sutler at the post to be established at Fort Bridger. Carter accepted, and as Johnston confirmed the appointment, accompanied the troops to Camp Scott and in the following year to Camp Floyd. In the same year (1858) he returned to Missouri and brought back to Fort Bridger his wife and their two daughters. The specially built trader's residence which, with the postoffice, adjoined the officer's building, became his home. On this border of civilization it was a center of culture and refinement. He had an excellent library, rich in works of literature, and in 1864, a lumbering ox-team brought out to him from the Missouri a piano, the first in that part of the West.[56] The Carter children were privately educated in a little school house adjoining the home. It is so well preserved that it is today one of the main attractions for visitors; and though the sutler's store long ago disappeared, the tall wide chimney of the fireplace still stands.

As new army posts were from time to time established, Judge Carter became successively post-trader at Camp Floyd, Fort Brown, Camp Stambaugh and Fort Washakie. But his home remained at Fort Bridger, and here he became the local autocrat and merchant prince. He was not only the post-trader, but the probate judge, the postmaster, a special agent of the Postoffice Department and a United States Commissioner, besides serving from time to time various incidental roles, such as that of a witness to the Great Treaty of July 3, 1868.

[56] Many of these books and the well-preserved piano were donated by the Carter family in 1926 to the University of Wyoming.

Superintendent Forney, in accompanying the troops to Utah and establishing his headquarters in Salt Lake City, had not forgotten Washakie and the project of a reservation. On June 22, of that year (1858) he wrote the commissioner of Indian affairs that he would station Agent Craig temporarily at Fort Bridger, "with directions to examine the several small valleys and streams running into Green river, with a prospective view of locating for agricultural purposes the Snake tribe, under Chief Wash-A-Kee." Nothing came of the action. At the end of 1859, Forney was succeeded by James Duane Doty. In 1861, a regular agency was established at Fort Bridger and on December 19, its first agent, Luther Mann, jr., arrived and assumed office. The Civil war had drawn off nearly the whole garrison, and during the greater part of 1862 the fort was held by a sergeant and a few privates. In this emergency Judge Carter organized a company of volunteer mountain men who remained under arms until the arrival, in December, of Captain M. G. Lewis, who assumed command, later bringing in several other companies of volunteers.

With the spring of 1862, indian outrages along the Oregon trail, which to some degree had lessened during the previous year, became more frequent. The trail was now a highway more difficult than of old to guard. Emigrants, when massed in large companies, could successfully withstand attacks, but for the lesser parties that now also traveled the route and the few guards and helpers at the various stations that had been established, there was an ever-present peril. The daring riders of the Pony Express, which had begun operations on April 3, 1860, had done their work and passed on to other fields, for with the completion of the through telegraph line on October 24, 1861, the service was abandoned. But the daily stage coach mail, which had begun in July, 1861, had become, in the hands of Ben Holladay, who purchased it on March 21, 1862, an important and dependable service. The stage coach with its passengers, the stations with their few guards and helpers, traveling linemen and various small parties that occassionally tempted fate by journeying along the route offered to the red brigands a tempting opportunity for scalps and plunder. On April 4, the four stations immediately east of Fort Bridger were attacked, several men were killed, coaches and mail were destroyed and sixty head of horses were taken. Thirteen days later a mail party of nine men with two coaches was attacked on the Sweetwater, and five men were wounded, while at the station of Three Crossings, eight miles away, all the mules and eight of the cattle were run off the previous night.

West of Fort Bridger other raids occurred. To the secretary of war, on April 11, a message signed by the governor of Utah, the chief justice and the officers of the Overland Mail Company and the Pacific Telegraph Company was sent to Washington, declaring that the indians in Utah were robbing the Overland Mail Company of its horses and provisions, destroying its stations and boasting that the "paper wagons" (the mail) would all be stopped in two weeks. It would be necessary, said the message, to have at once a regiment of mounted rangers organized from the inhabitants of the country menaced by the raids. Brigham Young, on the other hand, stated that the indians were unusually quiet. "If the traders," declared Young, in a letter to

Washington, April 14, 1862, "on the eastern road, who are buying up stock for the Salmon river mines, were all gibbeted, there would be less, if any at all, loss of mail stock." Nevertheless he telegraphed to the Utah delegate, in Washington, that "the militia of Utah are ready and able as they ever have been to take care of all the indians, and are able and willing to protect the mail if called upon to do so," and on April 24, a detachment of the Nauvoo Legion militia was sent out to guard the eastbound stage. On April 28, on news of the attack, eleven days earlier, on a mail party near the Sweetwater, President Lincoln called upon the ex-governor to raise a company of one hundred men for ninety days' service in the vicinity of Independence Rock. The company was promptly organized and dispatched, but found no indians.[57]

The Holladay mail and passenger coaches were withdrawn from the Oregon trail in July and transferred to the Cherokee trail, which gradually thereafter became known as the Overland trail. Other traffic, however, as well as the telegraph service, continued along the former route, and soldiers were brought in to protect both lines. In August rumors began to be circulated that Washakie had been set aside and Pash-e-go (Pa-chi-co), a Bannock and "a man of blood," elected in his place; that the Shoshones and Bannocks were killing the emigrants and had driven off one hundred and fifty horses and mules at Fort Bridger; that they were moving their families to the Salmon river country to get them out of danger, and, that when the leaves turned yellow and began to fall there would be a general massacre of the settlers. Agent Mann, in his first report,

[57] Hafen, *op. cit.*, pp. 245, 247.

September 20, of that year, confirmed some of these rumors and refuted others. He wrote:

Large numbers of the Shoshones, in conjunction with the Bannocks, who range along the southern boundary of Washington territory, have been committing upon the emigrants travelling to California and Washington some of the most brutal murders ever perpetrated upon this continent.

I am glad to say, however, that Washakie, the head chief of the Shoshones, and his band, have abstained from any acts of violence or theft, which have characterized a large portion of the tribe.

From talks with Washakie, however, he was apprehensive of a general indian outbreak. Failure to chastise the savages for their previous acts of violence had emboldened them to a degree which promised further outrages. He recommended that Fort Bridger (then almost entirely unguarded) be garrisoned by three or four companies of troops, and he further recommended that Washakie's band be placed on a reservation, naming three possible locations. The first was the Wind river valley, the next the valley of Smith's Fork and the last the region about the junction of Henry's Fork and the Green.[58]

The depredations continued. For better protection of the Overland trail, Fort Halleck had been established, on the north base of Elk mountain, in the fall of 1862, and troops from this center were scattered along the trail at various points. West of Fort Bridger the routes were not so well guarded, and the Bannocks and outlaw Shoshones continued their attacks. They were soon, however, to meet with a staggering punishment. Colonel Patrick E. Connor, with the Third California volunteers, reached Salt Lake City on August 6, and on a height overlooking the city established Camp Doug-

[58] Mann, Luther, Jr. *Report*, September 20, 1862.

las. Various small patrolling and scouting expeditions
were sent out, but the main body of the marauders was
not encountered. Learning in January, 1863, that it was
camped in a rocky fastness on Bear river, near the
present Franklin, Idaho, he set out with a force of
about three hundred men. The weather was bitterly
cold, the snow was deep, and the men suffered greatly.
On the early morning of January 29, Connor attacked
the village. After a hard-fought battle, in which the
whites suffered heavy casualties, the village was destroyed, nearly all the warriors were killed and one
hundred and sixty women and children were captured. The victory brought at least a temporary peace
and opened to settlement a region that had been dom-
inated by hostiles for fifteen years. On March 30, Connor was made a brigadier-general of volunteers.

There is little doubt that during the period immediately preceding this battle Washakie's authority had
declined and that his following had decreased. Many
of the warriors in this party, as well as others then on
the warpath, are believed to have been renegades from
his band. There is a story that he followed one band of
renegades, attacked and defeated them and brought
them back to the vicinity of Fort Bridger. There is
another story, somewhat more plausible, of a survivor
of the Bear river battle who returned of his own accord to Washakie's village. Upon seeing him, the chief
asked, "Who are you?" "I am a Shoshone," was the
reply. Shaking his head, Washakie answered, "You
have been whipped. Shoshones are never whipped.
You are no Shoshone." Obviously, the penitent's return
was not welcomed. It would be, however, too much to
assume that against all the wayward spirits of his band

Washakie maintained an inexorable rule. Doubtless many of them, after giving sufficient evidence that they had learned a needed lesson, were taken back into the fold.

Though for a time there were further indian disturbances, they were mostly to the south and west of Salt Lake City, the work of Utes and Diggers, and the operation of the mail service for 1863 was in general satisfactory. In the summer and fall five peace treaties were signed – with the Eastern Shoshones on July 2, with the northwestern Shoshones on July 30, with the western Shoshones on October 1, with the Goshutes (a mixed band of Utes and Shoshones) on October 12, and with the Bannocks and Shoshones on October 14.

The most important of these treaties was that made with the Eastern Shoshones at Fort Bridger on July 2. According to Superintendent Doty, who with General Connor, as special commissioners represented the government, a thousand indians "were present at, or immediately after, the conclusion of the treaty," and the chiefs in council represented between three and four thousand souls, or "nearly the whole nation." Washakie, "the principal chief of the nation," was there as the head of his own band, and with him were ten other chiefs or sub-chiefs, including Bazil and San Pitch, each the leader of a more or less independent following.[59] Why San Pitch, a Ute, should have been included in the company as a Shoshone, is not explained.

The treaty, of course, provided for lasting peace among the signatories. It granted to the government the right to use the lands of the Shoshones for roads and

[59] Doty, James Duane. *Report*, to the Commissioner of Indian Affairs, November 10, 1863.

travel, for military and agricultural settlement and for military posts thereon; to establish ferries over the rivers and to erect houses and to found settlements at stated points from time to time as the country might develop, and to operate telegraph and overland stage lines as well as a railroad. It further defined, though vaguely, the boundary of the Eastern Shoshones territory, and it promised annuities of goods to the value of $20,000 (reduced by congress to $10,000) for twenty years, with the understanding that they were "for the benefit of all the bands of the Eastern Shoshone nation who might give their assent" to the terms.

The goods, however, were slow in arriving. More than a year later – that is, on September 26, 1864 – O. H. Irish, who had become head of the Utah superintendency on the appointment of Doty to the governorship, wrote to the commissioner of indian affairs that the annuities had not been paid and that he had sent to Washakie to come and consult with him. Washakie rode in a stage from Bridger to Salt Lake City in order to meet the superintendent. He told Irish that he would not go on his annual hunt that year, because it was too late in the season and too cold to take his women and children into the mountains, and further, his warriors were afraid of their hereditary enemies, the Sioux. Instead, he would hunt in the neighborhood of Fort Bridger, leaving his family near the fort for safety. He appealed to the superintendent in the name of justice, saying that his people depended upon their Great Father to help them to live now that the white men whom he would not fight had driven off his game. Provisions must be given to him or his people would die. This plea, as the superintendent reported, was presented without the slightest intimation of an unfriendly spirit.

Doubtless the goods eventually arrived. From the next information we have of Washakie's people we learn that conditions had greatly improved. Agent Mann, in his report for September 28, 1865, says that everything is peaceful, and the band, now increased to about 1800 souls, had become prosperous. The hunters were finding buffalo, and the hides found a ready exchange for horses, clothing, firearms and ammunition. Irish, in his report for September 9, estimates the total number of Eastern Shoshones and mixed bands of Bannocks and Shoshones at 4000, and says of them: "These bands are under the control of Wash-a-kee, the finest appearing indian I have ever seen."

Agent Mann further recommended that the Wind river valley, unless it should prove to be rich in gold and silver or "springs of petroleum," might well be chosen for Washakie's reservation. The chief himself had become convinced that this was the best territory. Though the treaty of 1851 had specifically allotted it to the Crows, there is nothing to indicate that the Shoshones paid any attention to the provision. For generations they had hunted there, and in spite of occasional brushes with the Crows they continued to visit it at least annually. Moreover, a new situation had arisen. The pressure of the Sioux, which became especially severe with the beginning of 1865, had forced the Crows westward and northwestward and had tended to make them allies of the Shoshones in the effort to resist the Sioux advance. It was thus unlikely that they would object to the settlement of the Shoshones as their nearby neighbors.

Sioux attacks along the Oregon trail, particularly on the North Platte, had become frequent, and Washakie had offered his services in the effort to repel them. The commissioner of indian affairs, in his report for 1865, makes this statement:

Washakee recently asked permission to take part in the campaign against the western Sioux, and this was granted, subject to the arrangements to be made with the military commander of the district of the Upper Platte.

Nothing came of the offer for the time. But the commissioner's recommendation, in the same report, that a medal and presents be given to Washakie was shortly afterward fulfilled. The medal was a large silver one, bearing the likeness and superscription of the "Great Father," who at the time happened to be Andrew Johnson. Washakie accepted it and wore it suspended from his neck. A photograph of the chief thus decorated was taken and sent to Washington, eliciting from the commissioner the following letter, September 1, 1866, to the superintendent at Salt Lake City:

When you are able to communicate with Washakee you will say to him that his Great Father at Washington is pleased to be able to look upon the friendly face of so good a man.

In the spring of 1866 Superintendent Irish was succeeded by F. H. Head. The new superintendent became closely acquainted with Washakie and in his official reports praised him in high terms. It is from Superintendent Head that we have the most authoritative word of Washakie's relations with Kit Carson. In his report for September 20, of that year he writes:

During the year these indians (the Eastern Shoshones) have been entirely friendly. Washakie, the chief, is the noblest indian, both in act and appearance, that I have ever known. When young he spent

much of his time for many years in company with the famous Kit
Carson, then an adventurous trapper among the Rocky mountains.
Carson and his companions had frequent skirmishes with the hostile
savages, and the familiarity which Washakee thus acquired with the
arts of civilized warfare enabled him to rise to the chieftainship of
his tribe. It is his boast that he has never shed the blood or stolen the
property of a white man.

This was the year in which the government, deter-
mining to keep open the Bozeman trail, established
three forts along the line and manned them with troops.
This route, known also as the Powder river road, running from Fort Sedgwick, on the South Platte, along
the North Platte to Fort Laramie and to the northwest
paralleling the eastern base of the Big Horn mountains to the Yellowstone and thence westward to Virginia City, Montana, cut through the hunting grounds
of the Sioux, the Cheyennes and the Arapahoes and was
regarded by them with especial hatred. In the previous
year the government had attempted to clear the region
of hostiles and had sent in three columns of troops to
effect a juncture on the Powder river, but the whole
movement had resulted in a fiasco. This new program
the hostiles accepted as a challenge, and opposed it with
all the forces at their command. The three forts – Reno,
Phil Kearney and C. F. Smith – were menaced by savage hordes at all times, and one of them, Phil Kearney,
which occupied the center of the line, remained in a
state of virtual siege throughout the two years of its
existence and was the scene of one of the outstanding
tragedies of the frontier, the Fetterman fight of December 21, 1866.

Washakie, though an inveterate enemy of these hostile tribes, could yet see and appreciate their side of the
controversy. To Superintendent Head, who then wrote

of him as "undoubtedly the most sagacious, honorable and intelligent indian among the uncivilized tribes," he talked freely on the subject. The country from the settlements to the Wind river mountains, he said, had always been claimed by the four principal tribes – the Sioux, the Cheyennes, the Arapahoes and the Crows. Abounding in game, it supplied them with food as well as with large quantities of skins and furs from the sale of which they could obtain the goods they needed. They were contented, and they entertained toward the whites the most friendly feeling until the opening of the road. They objected strongly to the road, for experience had taught them that travel along it would cause their game to disappear; but they did not for a time begin hostilities because they had been informed by the whites that there was no other way to reach the Montana mines. They found this statement to be untrue. Forts were built, soldiers were sent in, and the trains that used the road were not the trains of emigrants but of the military with supplies for the troops.

Thus gradually these hostiles, according to Washakie, came to believe that the road was built only to afford employment to the soldiers and to destroy the game. They thereupon decided that as they were likely to starve within a few years, it was as well "to die fighting as by starvation," and they took up arms with the resolve to drive out the invaders or to perish in the attempt. Asked by Head if the white traders had in any way aided in bringing about this state of affairs, Washakie said, "No." The regular traders, licensed by the government, were good men. There were, however, great numbers of white men – thieves and murderers outlawed because of their crimes – who had come to

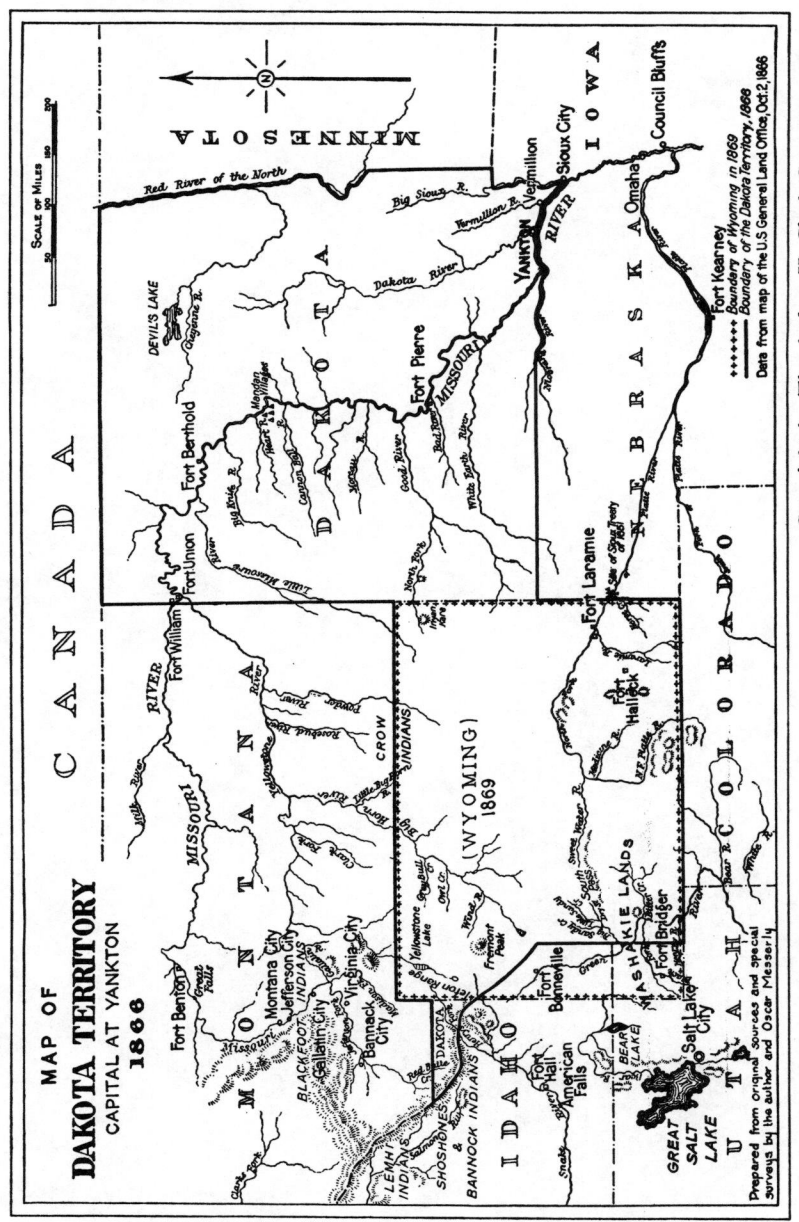

MAP OF
DAKOTA TERRITORY
CAPITAL AT YANKTON
1866

SCALE OF MILES

+++++++ Boundary of Wyoming in 1869
+++++++ Boundary of the Dakota Territory, 1866
Data from map of the U.S General Land Office, Oct 2, 1866

Prepared from original sources and special
surveys by the author and Oscar Messerly

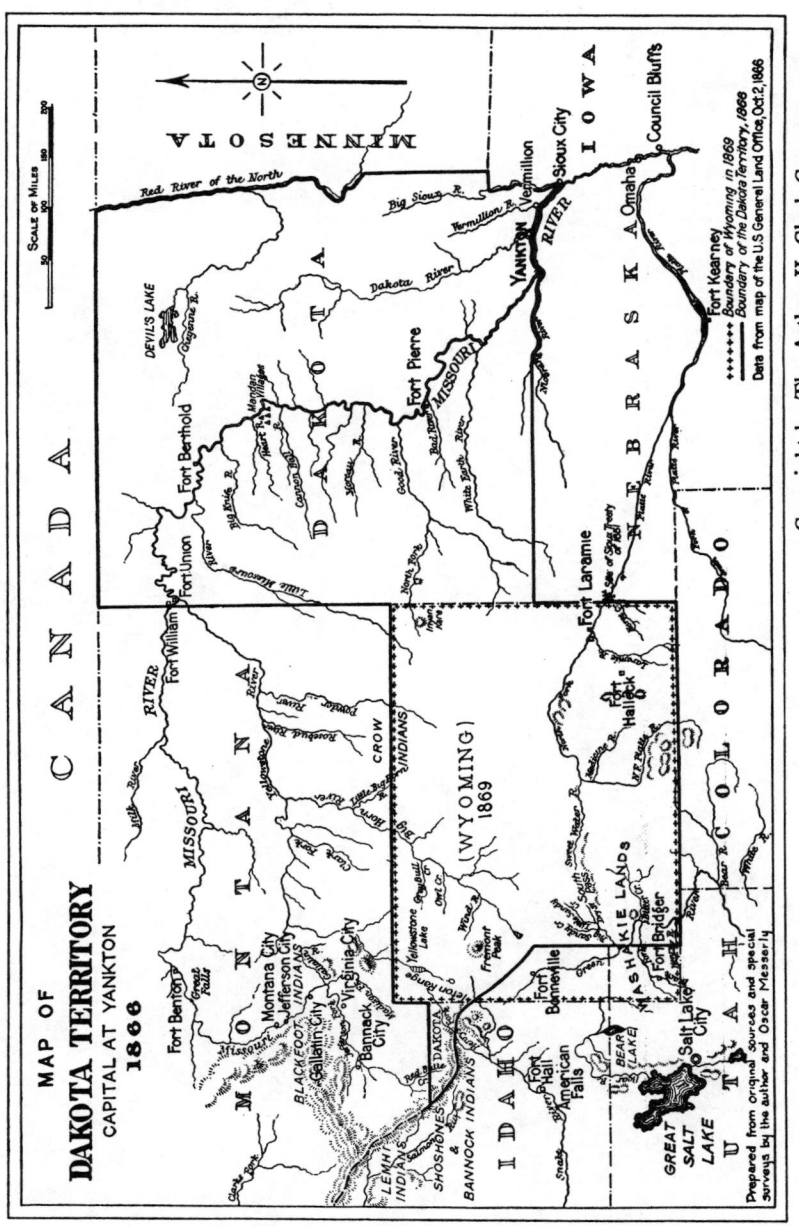

MAP OF
DAKOTA TERRITORY
CAPITAL AT YANKTON
1866

Prepared from original sources and special
surveys by the author and Oscar Messerly

Boundary of Wyoming in 1869
++++++ Boundary of the Dakota Territory, 1866
Data from map of the U.S General Land Office, Oct 2, 1866

Copyright by The Arthur H. Clark Company, 1930

live with the indians and who were always inciting them to violence and sometimes leading them in their forays.[60]

It is not likely that either Washakie's or Head's views on the subject exerted much influence in Washington. For various reasons, however, the government decided to discontinue the contest; and by the Fort Laramie treaty of April 29, 1868, agreed to abandon the forts and to forbid the whites to enter the region north of the North Platte. In the fall the troops withdrew. At Fort Phil Kearney, the most substantial of the posts as well as the one most hated by the indians, Old Little Wolf, one of Red Cloud's chiefs, applied the torch, and the structure was on fire before the soldiers were out of sight.

The Eastern Shoshones had during these last few years become increasingly prosperous. Agent Mann reported that their winter hunt of 1865-1866 had produced a larger stock of hides and furs than ever before and also a plentiful supply of dried meat. They did even better the following winter, though before they could lay in a store of meat they were forced out by the Sioux and the Cheyennes, and they were almost destitute of provisions when they arrived at the agency. They were reported as being still faithful to the treaty of 1863, and so also were the mixed bands of Shoshones and Bannocks. These bands, that constituted a loose confederacy under Chief Taggee, had not been so prosperous. Through Agent Mann, Taggee sought to induce Washakie to share with them the government annuity, but Washakie peremptorily refused, on the ground that it was little enough for his own band and

---

[60] Head, F. H., Superintendent. *Report*, July 25, 1867.

that it was Taggee's business to get an annuity from the
government – an action and argument in which he was
supported by Head. Another branch of the great Shoshonean family also at this time (1867) became somewhat solicitous about government aid. Its members
were known as Tukuarikas, or Sheepeaters, from the
fact that their main food was the Rocky mountain big
horn. They were a timid and fugitive people, who lived
in the most inaccessible part of the Absaroka, Ten Sleep
and Teton mountains, and who, in their rare contacts
with the whites, showed themselves generally friendly.
Ultimately the Sioux penetrated to their recesses and
virtually exterminated them. Of their history we know
little, for though they left on the mountain walls many
gravings and bright-colored paintings that may tell
their story, the characters have never been interpreted.

In the fall of 1867 Washakie, through Agent Mann,
renewed his plea that the Wind river valley be set aside
for a reservation for the Shoshones. The next year
brought action. The indian peace commission, which
sat at Fort Laramie in April and May, 1868, after fin-
ishing up its other business, directed Brevet Major-
general C. C. Augur to proceed west to Fort Bridger,
there to make arrangements with "the Snakes (Shoshones), Bannocks and other indians along the line of
the Union Pacific railroad in Utah." The authority was
understood to include the power to locate a reservation
and was so acted upon. At last, after years of patient
waiting, of fidelity to the whites and of loyalty to their
government, Washakie had won and his dreams were to
be realized.

The Great Treaty of July 3, 1868, Giving the Union Pacific Railroad A Right of Way

About the first week in May, 1868, a call went out from Fort Bridger summoning all the Eastern Shoshones and the Bannocks to assemble at the fort on June 4. General Augur was to be there and treat them on the matter of a reservation. The enterprising Taggee, with eight hundred Bannocks, arrived about May 15, and settled down to await developments. But the wagon trains which were to bring food and presents for the indians were delayed by bad roads, and half of his force scattered to their fishing and summer resorts. The Shoshones, led by Washakie, came in more slowly, and when once there, most of them remained. Augur did not arrive until June 15. But even then the wagons were still on their way; and the indians, not wholly assured of their coming, wanted to see them before taking part in a council.

With Washakie and Taggee, however, General Augur held informal conferences. He learned that Washakie claimed as the country of his people all the region "between the parallel of the highest point of the Uinta mountains and that of the Wind river valley and between the meridian of Salt Lake City and the line of the North Platte river to the mouth of the Sweetwater." Taggee, for the Bannocks, claimed all the Idaho country about Soda Springs and the Portneuf river and the great Kamas prairie to the northwest of it. Washakie, however, was willing to relinquish the Green valley for the "warm valley" of the Wind river and the region immediately to the south of it, and this willingness accorded exactly with the views of the commissioner. The Union Pacific railroad was approaching the Bridger country; it had entered Cheyenne on February 17, 1867; it was at this time crossing the Laramie plains and by November was to reach the neighborhood of the fort. White settlers would be coming in, and it was desirable to locate the indians in a region which they could have for their own. As for the Bannocks, Augur wished them for the time to settle with the Shoshones.

On July 3, the wagons having arrived and the goods having been distributed, a great council was held. According to Shoshones still living who attended it, women were present, and one of them addressed the gathering. This was Porivo or Wadze-wipe, the woman known as Sacajawea, the interpreter of the Lewis and Clark expedition. Augur, through his interpreter, J. Van Allen Carter,[61] told the indians that the Great Father desired to give them a land into which no white man would be permitted to go. To this reservation he wished them to move as soon as possible and to make it their permanent home, but with permission to hunt wherever game was to be found. "In a few years the game will become scarce," he told them, "and you will not find sufficient to support your people. You will then have to live in some other way than by hunting and fishing. [The Great Father] wishes you, therefore, to go to this reservation now and commence to grow wheat

---

[61] Carter, J. Van Allen, often served as Washakie's interpreter, married a daughter of William A. Carter. Though their surnames were identical, they were not related by blood.

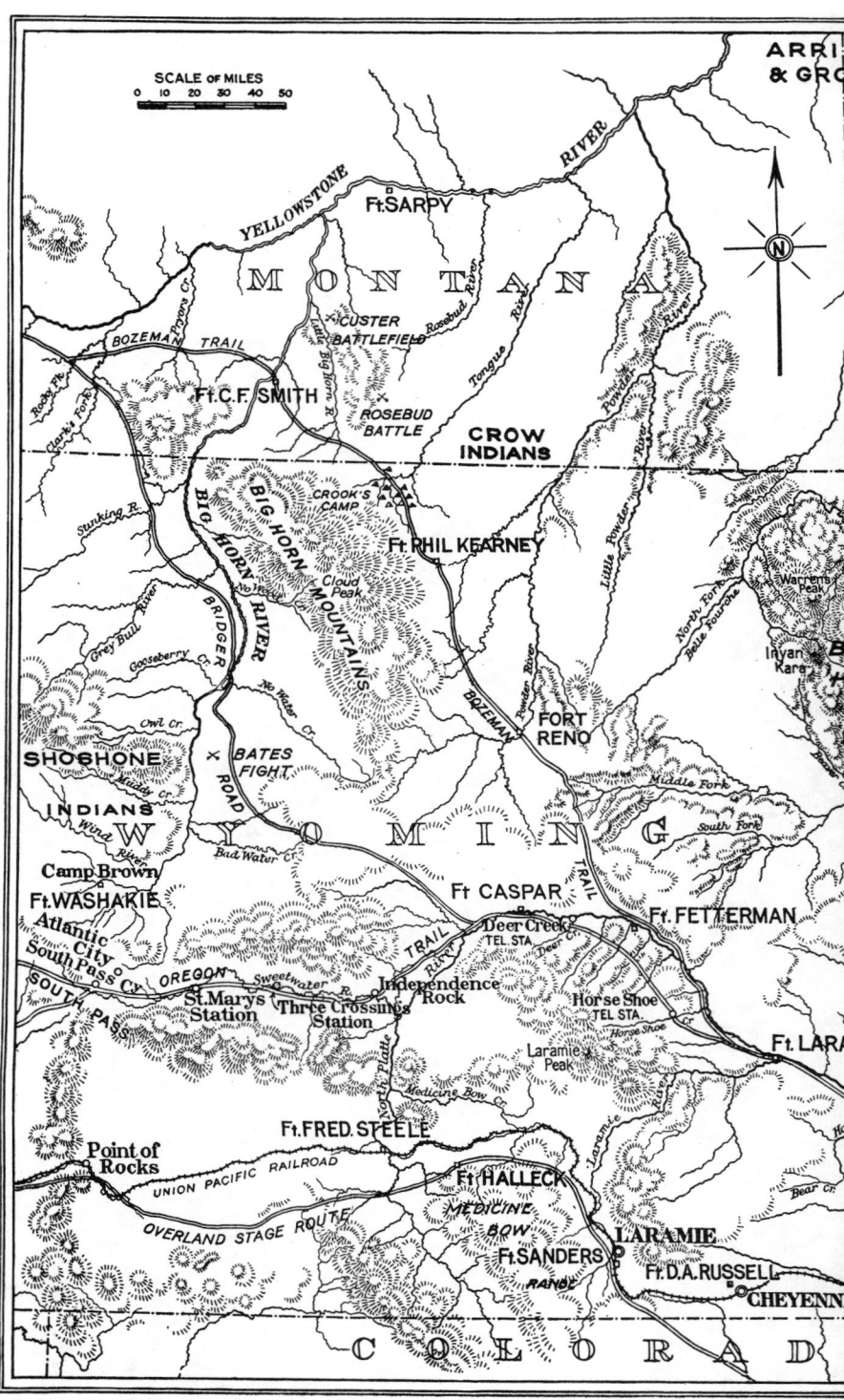

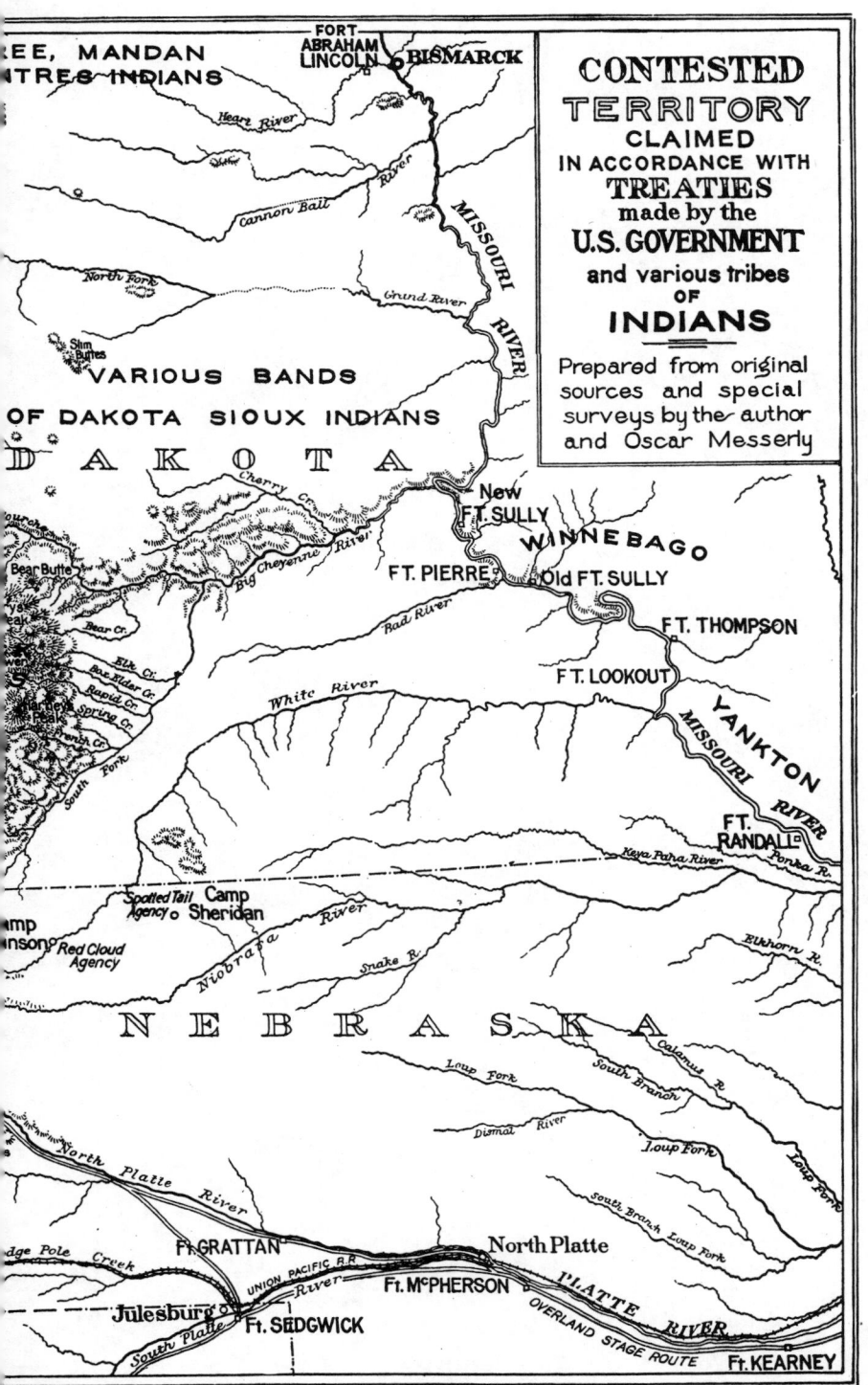

and corn and raise cattle and horses, so that when the game is gone, you will be prepared to live independently of it. . . Your Great Father desires . . . that you should remain at peace, not only with white men but with all other indian tribes. . . He wishes the Shoshones and Bannocks to be together where you can have one agent to attend to you."

Washakie, assured of obtaining his cherished Wind river valley, said in reply:

I am laughing because I am happy; because my heart is good. As I said two days ago, I like the country you mentioned then for us, the Wind river valley. Now I see my friends are around me, and it is pleasant to meet and shake hands with them. I always find friends along the roads in this country, about Bridger; that is why I come here. It is good to have the railroad through this country, and I have come down to see it. When we want to grow something to eat and [to] hunt, I want the Wind river country. In other indian countries there is danger, but here about Bridger all is peaceful for whites and indians, and safe for all travel. When the white man came into my country and cut the wood and made the roads, my heart was good, and I was satisfied. You have heard what I want. The Wind river country is the one for me. We may not for one, two or three years be able to till the ground. The Sioux may trouble us. But when the Sioux are taken care of we can do well. Will the whites be allowed to build houses on our reservation? I do not object to traders coming among us, and care nothing about the miners and mining country when they are getting out gold. I may by and by get some of that myself. I want for my home the valley of Wind river and lands on its tributaries as far east as the Popo-agie, and want the privilege of going over the mountains to hunt where I please.[62]

Taggee then said: "As far away as Virginia City our tribe has roamed. But I want the Port-Neuf country and Kamas plains."

Asked by the commissioner why the Shoshones and

[62] Augur, C. C. *Letter*, October 4, 1868, to the President of the Indian Peace Commission.

Bannocks might not live in peaceful relations on the same reservation, the chief answered, "We are friends with the Shoshones, and like to hunt with them; but we want a home for ourselves."

The commissioner next asked, "If you have a separate home, can you and the Shoshones get along with one agency and come to the Shoshone reservation for your annuities, etc.?"

"We want," he replied, "to receive anything that is for us on our own ground."

Augur then said that he was not sufficiently acquainted with the country to locate a reservation for them, but that when they were ready to go on a reservation some one would be sent to lay it out. He told all the assemblage to return to the council the next day, when the formal treaty would be read to them, and in closing the session, paid tribute to Washakie:

> The Great Father at Washington and the grand council have always known Washakee as a good friend of the white man and look upon him as chief of the Shoshones and good adviser of all the peaceful tribes about here. He always gives them good advice, and we hope they will always follow it.[63]

It is to be noted that from this time on we hear no more of the "mixed bands of Bannocks and Shoshones." Superintendent Head had used the term, Agent Mann had used it, and so had almost every one else who wrote anything on conditions among the Shoshones. But Augur, on the authority of both Head and Mann, asserted in his report to the president of the peace commission, that the term was a misnomer and had no basis of fact. The followers of Taggee were to be considered as Bannocks and nothing else. Just how there could

---

[63] *Ibid.*

have been so complete and persistent a misapprehension regarding these bands is nowhere explained.

On July 4, the treaty was interpreted to the indians, article by article, agreed to without dissent and signed by all the chiefs present. Though officially entitled "the treaty with the Eastern Shoshoni and Bannocks," it is more generally known in the West as "the Great Treaty of July 3, 1868." Its first provision, after the customary declaration of lasting peace between the white and red men, promised that the government would assist in the arrest and punishment of "bad men among the whites" who might commit depredations upon the property or person of indians or whites. If granted to the Shoshones, in lieu of the land on which they were then living, a tract in the Sweetwater river and Wind river mountains country, to be known as a reservation, and it stipulated that until a special tract be set aside for the Bannocks that tribe should share the reservation with the Shoshones. The latter were to make it their permanent home, but as long as there were unoccupied government lands within reach on which game could be found, they could, under certain conditions, use such lands for hunting. An agency was to be established; a circular sawmill, a grist mill, a school and various other buildings were to be erected, and farm implements, seeds and a teacher in farming furnished. One of the most important provisions was that contained in Article XI, which read:

No treaty for the cession of any portion of the reservation therein described which may be held in common shall be of any force or validity as against the said indians, unless executed and signed by at least a majority of all of the adult male indians occupying or interested in the same; and no cessions by the tribe shall be understood or construed in such manner as to deprive without his consent, any individual member of the tribe of his right of any tract of land selected by him.[64]

The reservation, containing approximately 2,774,400 acres, was described as being within the following boundaries: Commencing at the mouth of Owl creek and running due south to the crest of the divide between the Sweetwater and Popo Agie rivers; thence along the crest of the divide and the summit of the Wind river mountains to the longitude of North Fork of Wind river; thence due north to the mouth of said North Fork and up its channel to a point twenty miles above its mouth; thence in a straight line to the headwaters of Owl creek and along the middle of its channel to the place of beginning.

So Washakie at last had his reservation. It was a princely domain, almost as large as the state of Connecticut, though it was later, by the cessions of 1872, 1896 and 1904, to be reduced to less than one-fifth the original area. To have, however, was not for the time to hold. Washakie and his people declined to move to their reservation until the region was cleared of hostiles. The Fort Laramie peace treaty of the preceding May 9, had decreed peace when there was no peace, and numbers of the unruly tribesmen of the plains continued to raid the country north and west of the Platte. In the spring of this year, when Washakie and his following were making their way to the Bridger agency, a band of three hundred Sioux, Cheyennes and Arapahoes, led by a son of the famous Oglala chief, Red Cloud, had attacked them, and though losing their leader and several other warriors, had killed four Shoshones, wounded a number and captured eighty

[64] Kappler, treaty of July 3, 1868, also of July 2, 1863, and September 26, 1872.

horses. This band had also killed several prospectors in the Wind river valley and committed a number of atrocities along the Union Pacific railroad [65] and the route from Benton to South pass. The Crows also had shown recent hostility to the Shoshones, and though their subsequent expression of a desire for peace had been met by Washakie with a consent to a conference provided a government official were present, conditions were too unsetttled to assure the Shoshones of a peaceful occupancy of their new home. Accordingly they kept to the Green river valley, and though continuing their occasional hunting trips to the Wind river, waited to see what the government would do. Superintendent Head, in his report of September 18, 1868, expressed confidence that the chief would move his people as soon as he could do so with safety, and added:

Chief Washakie retains the same upright and manly character he has ever sustained from the first settlement of Utah. His control over his indians is more absolute than that of any other chief within the superintendency, and such influence is uniformly exercised wisely and for the best interests of his indians.

After the signing of the Great Treaty, Augur marched from Fort Bridger with an escort of soldiers to visit the new Sweetwater (South pass) gold placer mines thirty miles south of the reservation. The miners were found to be entirely satisfied that the Shoshones should be placed near them, for they felt that these indians would be a protection to them against the hostiles. Here, within a few miles of one another, were three populous mining camps – South Pass City, Atlantic City and Hamilton – the last-named, by reason of its principal mine, soon becoming known as Miners' Delight.

<hr>

[65] Ghent, W. J., chap. xii: Perkins, chap. xiii.

As early as 1842 an employee of the American Fur Company had discovered gold in paying quantities north of the South pass, though little mining was done at the time. In 1857 the entire length of the Sweetwater river was explored by a party of forty prospectors, and gold was found in many places. Along Willow creek, a northern branch of the Sweetwater, in 1861, about sixty men located claims in a camp that was soon to grow into South Pass City, located about twelve miles north and east of the famous pass. In 1863 prospectors from Pike's Peak and from the gold fields of Montana, Nevada, Utah and California, flocked to this region. It was during this year that the first placer mining was done in the Carissa gulch, South Pass City, which proved to be one of the district's greatest mines and in which the pumps have ever since been working.

By the fall of 1867 the stampede for the gold fields of this country became noticeable. Emigrants on the road to California abandoned their hopes of riches in the far West, unharnessed their horses, removed the yokes from their oxen and used their bread pans for placer mining along the banks of the streams. Even some of the indians caught the spirit of the white man and dug for gold. They brought nuggets and quartz to Fort Bridger, showing them to the Mormons living farther to the west, and thus increased the feverish rush to the fields. First among the whites to bring gold to Fort Bridger was the noted John Robertson, "Uncle Jack Robinson," who returned from the placers in 1867.

South Pass City grew rapidly and soon had, in addition to its many saloons, a postoffice, a Masonic Temple, a schoolhouse, stores and hotels. Though there was no

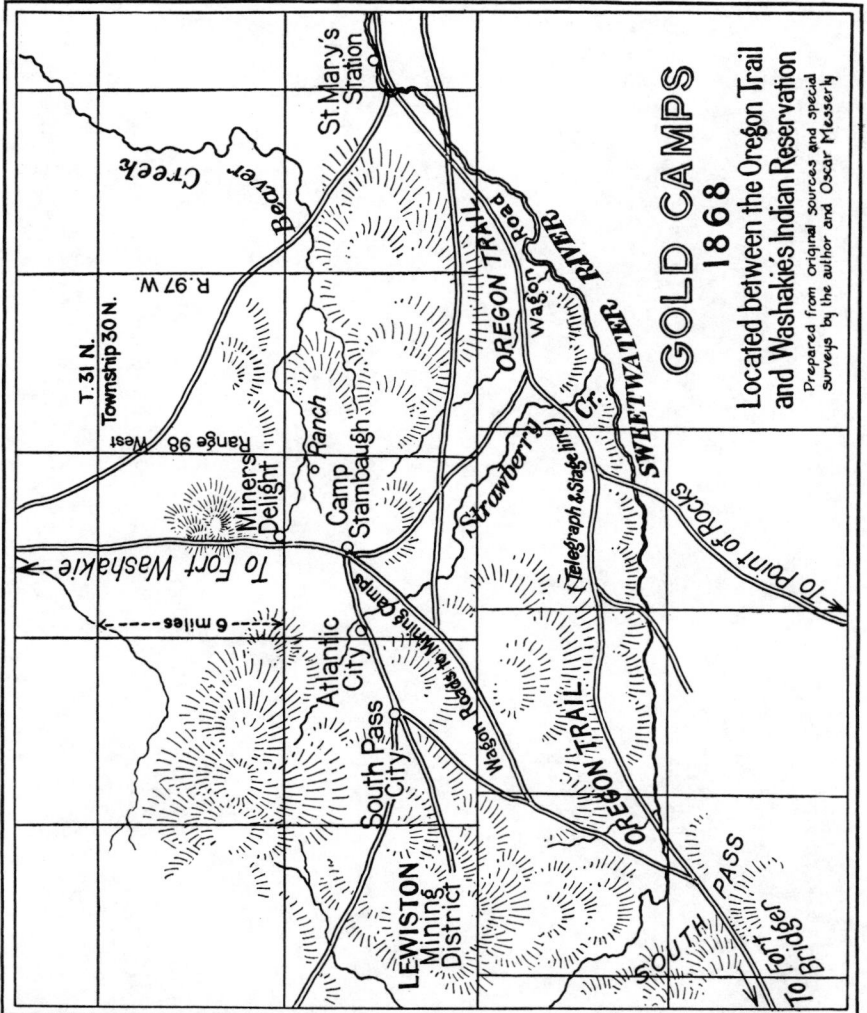

GOLD CAMPS
1868

Located between the Oregon Trail
and Washakie's Indian Reservation

Prepared from original sources and special
Surveys by the author and Oscar Messerly

Copyright by The Arthur H. Clark Company, 1930

established church, occasional religious services were conducted by some itinerant minister of the gospel. Streets were platted following the course of the creek, Main street having a line of compact houses on each side for half a mile. The population in 1867 approximated 3000 persons. During 1868 there were at least 5000 new arrivals. It was the most prosperous year for the city and also for the outlying district. Other towns sprang up. Atlantic City, four miles to the east, was started and soon reached a population of 3000 souls. Hamilton, later Miners' Delight, a few miles further east, had its beginning the same year. In this camp an experienced California miner assisted in operating a gold mine which in six months yielded $300,000 and which during its life yielded $1,200,000. With the coming of the early spring of 1869 every road and trail running north of the Union Pacific railroad teemed with human beings, some on foot, others with pack horses, many in wagons. Some of the more eager ones, not waiting for spring, plowed their way to this El Dorado through deep and dangerous snow. But the boom times were passing, and the new arrivals gradually scattered to other locations. The census of 1870 revealed only 2106 persons in this entire valley, against an estimated 9000 two years earlier.

On July 25, 1868, the act of congress granting the creation of the territory of Wyoming was approved by President Johnson, and in the following year, shortly after his inauguration, President Grant appointed John A. Campbell, of Ohio, as governor and superintendent of indian affairs. Campbell was born at Salem, Ohio, October 8, 1835. After leaving school he studied law and became a practising attorney. He served for three

years in the Civil war, first as a lieutenant, and then as
a major of the company he had organized. At the end
of the war he was promoted to the rank of colonel and
brevetted a brigadier-general "for courage on the field
and marked ability and fidelity." Resigning his position in the army, he accepted the position tendered him
by the president.

Governor Campbell arrived in Cheyenne, the capital, toward the end of March, and the machinery of
government was perfected on April 7, when the last
official was sworn in.[66] His first official act as indian
superintendent was on May 10, when he issued a call
for troops to be used to suppress a war party of Sioux
who were raiding the Wind river valley and had killed
four white men and taken a number of horses and mules
belonging to the white settlers. An utterly inadequate
force of a company of infantry and another of cavalry
was sent by the department commander into the field.
On July 3, another raid was made and more stock stolen,
and on September 14, a third foray was made. This
time four whites were killed, but the troops were near
enough to go to the rescue, and the indians were driven
off. On September 28, three miners were killed while at
work near Atlantic City. The indians then started to
make a raid on the mining settlements, but as the governor had been able to supply arms and ammunition to
the miners, the raiders, discovering the fact, withdrew.

With the organization of Wyoming into a territory,
Fort Laramie, the Powder river country, the Oregon

---

[66] Campbell, Governor, after serving for four years, was re-appointed in
1873. In 1875 he resigned, to accept the office of Third Assistant Secretary
of State under Secretary Hamilton Fish. He was later appointed to a con-
sular office in Switzerland, but served for only a short time, ill-health com-
pelling his return to the United States. He died in Washington, D. C., July
15, 1880.

trail along the North Platte and Sweetwater rivers, South pass, the Green river valley, Fort Bridger and Washakie's lands came under the jurisdiction of Governor Campbell. He was thus faced at once with the problems of suppressing the hostile indians and of settling Washakie's people on their new reservation. His first report as superintendent of indian affairs is the following:

Wyoming Territory, Executive Department, Cheyenne,
June 10, 1869.

Hon. ELY S. PARKER,
Commissioner of Indian Affairs, Washington, D. C.

GENERAL: I have the honor to acknowledge the receipt of your letter of the 31st ult. and would state in advance of the full report in relations to the Shoshones and Bannocks (for which I have called on the agent for those Indians), that they are not on the reservation set apart for them by the treaty of the 3rd of July, 1868. I am informed to-day that their chief, Washakie, states that he will not go to the reservation until his named time – early next winter. Mr. Mann, the agent, will tomorrow leave Fort Bridger for the Wind river valley, where he will establish his agency. General Augur has sent a company of infantry to protect the agency and the settlers in the Sweetwater mining district from further depredations of the Sioux, which in April defeated a party of Washakie's Shoshones, killing twenty-five, and coming down to the entrance of the valley murdered four white men.

It is very desirable that these indians be induced to settle on this reservation, not only in order that they may be prepared to carry out their part of the treaty, but also because the presence of these indians will serve to assist in protecting the Wind river valley and the miners on the Sweetwater from the Sioux. In view of these facts, I respectfully recommend that if possible, a greater sum than the $20,000 you have estimated for, be set apart for the indian service in this territory in order that we may as far as possible, carry out our treaty with them – or give them some evidence that we intend to do so. I do not think it advisable to give further presents, food or articles of any kind to these indians until they return to their reservation.

I shall start to-morrow for the Wind river valley and Fort Bridger, and on my return will be able to make a more definite report in relation to this matter. Very respectfully, Your Obt. Sevt.

J. A. CAMPBELL, Govr. and *ex off*. Supt. Indian Affairs.

There is no official record, so far as can be ascertained, to show that the governor made his proposed official visit to Washakie's reservation on the date indicated. Washakie was still obdurate in his refusal to move his people into the Wind river country, protesting that the government had not furnished them protection. In the spring of this year (1869) a party of fifty of Washakie's best warriors, before leaving their Wind river hunting ground, had attempted to recover some horses stolen by the hostiles, but had been attacked by a superior force, with a loss of thirty men killed, all the remaining twenty having been wounded. Depleted in his fighting force, Washakie was greatly dispirited. Much of his following shared his feeling, and the effort to obtain a company of Shoshone scouts to remain on duty at the reservation proved a failure. Taking advantage of the situation, a strong party of his men separated from him, joining with a crafty and ambitious half-breed, thus further weakening his force.

The government was at last moved to act, and on June 28, it established Camp Augur on the site of the present town of Lander, with a garrison of one hundred men commanded by Lieutenant P. H. Breslin. There was not much that a force of one hundred soldiers could do toward making the reservation secure from molestation, but they at least furnished an indication of a change in the government's policy. Washakie in the meantime had received offers of a new alliance. In May information from General Augur was received by

Washakie at Bridger agency that one hundred lodges of northern Arapahoes under Friday Sorrel Horse and Medicine Man had expressed a desire to form a treaty with him and to go with him and live on the Wind river reservation. When Washakie, away from the reservation, was located, for he was not as yet established and making his camps on the reservation, in the earlier days of June, he was told of the Arapahoes' ambition, to which he replied, "I have lately perfected a treaty with the Crows, because I need to strengthen my warriors by any reliable allies. I do not understand why the Arapahoes, who have for many years allied themselves with my enemies, the Cheyennes and Sioux, and battled against me, should so suddenly wish to join me. Because Friday Sorrel Horse was a friend of my youth I am willing to have council, for when I see their faces I can understand their intentions."

Nothing for the time was done in the matter. Washakie was experiencing difficulty with his band, who would not leave Fort Bridger to go upon the reservation and were demanding that the annuities be distributed at the fort. Being told of the desirability of having council with the Arapahoes and the government, Tab-en-shen, one of the lesser chiefs, became very independent, declaring that after he had drawn his rations he would leave Washakie's band and go over to the Crows. Norkuk, a half-breed, another chief, one of the signers of the Great Treaty and a competent interpreter, said, "I am also leaving. I might return next spring when my people desire annuities in the form of powder, balls, pistols, lead, brass wire, paint and ornaments." When the agent informed him that the gifts would not be distributed, Norkuk replied, speaking fluently in good

English, "The only way to receive presents is to steal a few horses and kill a few white men."

The authorities at Fort Bridger three different times sent for him, urging the necessity of a talk. To all of these requests, Washakie sent the word, "I am sick. I am cold. My reservation has been invaded many times by my enemy, the Sioux." It was about this time, September 14, that a band of one hundred and forty Sioux made an attack on a company of the Second United States cavalry, then stationed at Camp Augur. It was a mere skirmish, for no soldiers were injured and the indians lost but one of their number, but it served further to dissuade the Shoshones from moving to their reservation.

On October 8, Governor Campbell issued instructions to Lieutenant Breslin to proceed at once to Fort Bridger and perfect, if possible, arrangements for the proposed council with the Arapahoe chiefs, Medicine Man, Friday Sorrell Horse, Little Wolf and Cut Foot, by which, it was hoped, a treaty would be made placing the Shoshones and Arapahoes on the same reservation. Arriving as promptly as the long and difficult journey permitted, Breslin held a conference with Captain J. H. Patterson, who had succeeded Luther Mann, jr. as indian agent of the Shoshones. Chief Washakie having failed to arrive, a plainsman, Cruch, was employed to scout along the Shoshone trail and try to find him. After an absence of twelve days the runner returned with the statement that neither the chief nor any of his following could be located, nor could any information be obtained as to their whereabouts. Tired of waiting, and believing that there would be no council, or, if one were had, it would amount to nothing, the Arapahoes in disgust took their departure to their home camp, at this time about eighty miles north of Fort Fetterman. Lieutenant Breslin returned to Cheyenne.

When Washakie returned to his camp he found the younger men grumbling about their chief's alleged inability to fight and openly hinting that he was too old to win victories in battle, that he was too civilized to scalp his victims and that war blood had ceased to flow through his veins. They remembered the stories of his earlier exploits, and they asked: "Were these deeds of valor no longer to be performed? Why does Washakie not do these brave and daring things now?"

Washakie, whose hearing remained keen, overheard his younger warriors arguing among themselves as to which one of them would succeed him. Giving no evidence that he had heard them, he mounted his horse and disappeared, no one knew where. After an absence of two "moons" he reappeared with seven scalps. He told his warriors that he had been out on the warpath single handed to test his skill, that he had come across a band of hostiles and that each scalp was his own trophy. "Let him," he said, holding high the scalps, "who can do a greater feat than this claim the chieftainship. Let him who would take my place count as many scalps." No further questions were raised by the warriors, and from that time to his death he was the unchallenged leader and chief of the Eastern Shoshones, old and young.

Washakie and the Arapahoe chiefs were, after many efforts, brought together at the reservation agency on February 7, 1870. The Arapahoes were represented by Medicine Man, Knock Knees, Little Wolf and Black Bear. A treaty was concluded, though nothing of importance was included in it. What the Arapahoes really desired was a treaty with the government similar to the one made by Washakie on July 3, 1868, granting them a part of his reservation. To this demand Washakie entered a vigorous protest, declining absolutely to permit the Arapahoes to settle permanently within his reservation, although he was willing to grant temporary permission to travel through it. He accused the Arapahoes of having committed the murders in the Wind river valley, as well as those at the Sweetwater mines, South pass, Atlantic City and Miners' Delight, the previous summer. To these and other accusations the Arapahoes pleaded guilty, but at the same time declared that they now desired peace. In the face of all the many manifestations of peaceful and friendly relations Washakie retained his savage stoicism, scornfully declaring that only three "moons" before this council the Arapahoes were storing in their camps arms and ammunition obtained from traders. "I have no confidence in you," said Washakie, "because you offer such large amounts in trade for ammunition." [67]

Confident that the Sioux and Arapahoes had formed an alliance to make raids on his tribe, Washakie determined to leave the reservation. He said, on his departure:

I cannot go for a buffalo hunt, as my people will be left unprotected. I cannot farm, for my crops will be destroyed. I am afraid of the hostile bands, one of which you wish to place on my reservation. Next year, if the government will make me buildings and give me farm implements, I will be glad to farm and have my men put to work. I am anxious now to have the Bannocks located on my reservation; they have not yet come to live in the valley.

He then crossed the mountains to the west, placing

---

[67] Fleming, Agent G. W. Fort Bridger, *Report*, July 11, 1870.

his camp on the headwaters of Green river. All the Shoshones and Bannocks living in Bridger valley — even the indian women, wives of white men who had lived in that vicinity for a quarter of a century — left and joined him. After many weeks he appeared at Carter station, twelve miles from Fort Bridger, on the Union Pacific railroad, where he was joined by Chief Tab-en-shen and Bazil with about sixty-four lodges. His followers were without provisions and without any chance of finding game, and the Bridger agent was obliged to issue flour and beef to them. Much sickness and many deaths from smallpox induced a few of them to submit to vaccination, though the larger number wished "to think about it" first. The band seemed willing to settle on the reservation and begin farming just as soon as the government gave them protection. Washakie was insistent that his agency was at Fort Bridger until the promised buildings were erected and the farming implements furnished. From the new agent he received another substantial tribute to his character:

Washakie, their [the Eastern Shoshones'] chief, is in all respects a superior indian. He has great influence with his tribe, which I have endeavored to retain for him by always recognizing him as their chief and referring all others of his tribe to him as the only one through whom I can hold any communication with them. Washakie is very anxious that his tribe should go to farming and that his children should go to school, and will give the aid of his influence to the agent for this purpose next summer.[68]

On March 28, 1870, Camp Augur had been renamed Camp Brown, in honor of Captain Frederick Brown, a victim of the Fetterman fight of December 21, 1866. Established as a sub-post of Fort Bridger, it was made an independent post on August 20. The location, how-

[68] Wham, Agent J. W. Fort Bridger, *Report*, October 11, 1870.

ever, was regarded as a temporary one, and on June 26, 1871, Captain Robert T. Torrey, Thirteenth infantry, received orders to select a new site, nearer the heart of the reservation. About the same time, to give greater protection to the mining settlements, a new post, Camp Stambaugh, named for Lieutenant Charles B. Stambaugh, who was killed by indians on May 4, 1870, was established near Atlantic City and Miners' Delight.

Washakie, however, was not greatly impressed by this additional safeguard. He had taken his people to Utah, and there for a time he decided to keep them. In the spring of 1872 the new agent at the reservation, Doctor James Irwin, reported the deplorably unprotected condition of the agency. Company A, Thirteenth infantry, which had been assigned to Camp Brown, one and a half miles from the agency, was helpless without horses, and "the infantry cannot in any way or manner afford the least protection to the agency, or to the Shoshones and Bannocks, and aside from the daily and hourly danger of having our families murdered, it is difficult to get men who are willing to run the chance." He made an earnest plea for the addition of a company of cavalry which he believed would quiet the fears of Washakie and induce him and his followers to return to the reservation. Washakie also appealed to the authorities. "Tell the Great Father," he said, "that I am desirous to settle down to farming and stock raising and to have schools as the government promised, but it would place my people in a defenseless attitude and subject them perhaps to a massacre. Please talk protection all of the time." Protection was somewhat slow in coming, but he received from President Grant, as a testimonial of regard, a saddle, bridle, leather panier and a suit of clothing.[69]

The southern boundary of the reservation had been defined in the treaty of 1868 as "running along the crest of the divide between the Sweetwater and the Popo Agie rivers." None of the mining camps and none of the lands occupied by settlers were meant to be included within the tract. The early surveys, however, were faulty, and the discovery was soon made that the camp of Miners' Delight and the homes of eight white settlers were inside the boundary. Though these white inhabitants were not trespassers, for they had come there before the treaty was made, they were regarded by the Shoshones as intruders, and their presence resulted in occasional clashes. The government thereupon decided to treat with Washakie for a cession of the reservation south of a line crossing the mouth of the Little Popo Agie.

On September 9, after a courier had been sent to Bridger valley for Washakie, the chief and 1000 of his people came to Camp Stambaugh, which was just within the reservation. The council convened at Camp Brown. After prayer had been offered, all indians reverently standing, Commissioner Felix R. Brunot, chairman of the board, explained to the Shoshones the desire of the Great Father and the mutual benefit that would result from the proposed agreement. Washakie was then called upon to express his wishes. He said:

I would like to have houses here. I do not like to live in lodges. I am afraid of the Sioux. They come here to hunt for scalps in this valley. I would like to have houses. In that valley [the one to be relinquished] there is plenty of grass, berries, prairie squirrels and fish;

[69] Walker, F. A. *Report*, February 27, 1872.

plenty of everything. It is good land. I do not know what to do about it. I have two hearts about it. The land is good; that in the north is poor, and, I think it belongs to the Crows. When you were at the Crows, did the Crow chief tell you to trade this land off?

To this question, the agent replied, "'I did not say anything to the Crows about it; it is none of their business. The land does not belong to them."

"But," continued Washakie, "the Shoshones think it belongs to the Crows, the Sioux and everybody. If we went there the Sioux might come in and scalp us. I do not want that land. If the white man wants to buy this land, it is all right. But I do not want to trade it for land anywhere."

"Do any of the other chiefs," continued the agent, "wish to say anything?"

Quickly Washakie spoke, "Whatever I say they all say."

Picking up the argument again, Washakie expounded:

We do not want that land up north, but we will sell the land for cattle. We will trade our land for cattle. It would be good to milk the cows and drink the milk. I do not know how many cattle, but I think about a thousand. We would corral them and milk them. We would herd them like we do our horses. Whenever we move up Wind river we would have to take the cattle along. We would like to have cattle. The Utes and the other indians have cattle. We are poor and have none. We would take the same care of our cattle as we do our horses.

"How much land do you wish to sell for cattle?" asked the agent.

"We wish," cautiously replied the chief, "to sell all that you have read in the letter [treaty] to the dividing line you spoke of."

"Suppose you give the president the land and the

president gives you $5,000 worth of cattle every year for five years, what then?"

After consulting with his men Washakie said, "That is right, they all say the same."

The agreement was signed on September 26, 1872. The terms ceded to the government about 601,120 acres of land and granted to the Shoshones the sum of $25,000 the money to be expended by the government under the direction of the president in annual payments for each of five years of $5,000, and for the purchase of stock cattle, the cattle to be delivered to the Shoshones on their reservation. In addition, Washakie was to have a special appropriation of $500 annually for a period of five years. The government further provided that six months from the date of the ratification of the treaty a survey would be made of the southern line of the reservation, and that white men would be prohibited from entering any part of the district.

To this agreement appear the names of Felix R. Brunot, indian commissioner for the government; Washakie, his sub-chiefs Bazil and Norkuk, and other headmen and men of the Eastern band of Shoshone indians, a total of one hundred and nineteen, who constituted a majority of all the adult male indians of this band were duly authorized to act in this capacity. The signatures of the indians were attested by Norkuk, Mc-Adams and William Rees as interpreters. The witnesses were James Irwin, indian agent; Lieutenant J. B. Guthrie, Thirteenth infantry; Thomas K. Cree, secretary; James K. Moore, indian trader; Darius William, Frank Trumbull and James Irving Patten, teacher.

Camp Brown, Discovery of Gold, and Indian Warfare on the Shoshone Reservation

Originally Camp Brown was located on the south side of the Popo Agie river where the stream was intersected by the indian and military trail running north into the Shoshone reservation. The trail from South pass to Camp Brown (Lander) to Fort Washakie and further north out of the reservation to Meeteetse, was a natural indian and game trail, traveled also by the first prospectors and settlers, afterwards improved by the homesteaders and by the county of Fremont.[70]

Camp Brown was named for Captain Frederick H. Brown, who with others under-rated the fighting ability of Chief Red Cloud's warriors on the destructive day of December 21 in the year of 1866, when battle between red men and soldiers was waged near Fort Phil Kearney on the Bozeman trail. In this conflict under the leadership of Captain William Fetterman, against Red Cloud's forces, the entire command was annihilated, being one of the world's battles from which "there were no survivors." [71]

Prior to the naming of this camp for Captain Brown, there was a sub-post of Fort Bridger established on this site, bearing the name of Camp Augur, named for Colonel C. C. Augur, who had been identified with the Great Treaty at the Bridger valley council in 1868 at

[70] Nickerson, *Early History of Fremont County, Wyoming.*
[71] Hebard and Brininstool, vol. 2.

which time he was commander-general of the Mountain division with headquarters at Omaha, Nebraska. This camp which was established in 1869 by Lieutenant P. H. Breslin, United States army, subsequently, when it was reorganized as a separate post, received the name of Camp Brown. Camp Brown remained on the Popo Agie until 1873 when it was moved into the Wind river reservation, retaining only temporarily its name; in that year the name being changed to Fort Washakie in honor of the chief of the Shoshones. The abandoned Camp Brown, situated on the Popo Agie and diverging streams, ultimately became the site of the city of Lander, the present day county seat of Fremont county. This city, or town, originally known as "Push Root," was named Lander in honor of Colonel F. W. Lander, who had in 1857 been sent by our government to the West to survey along the Oregon trail with the purpose of obtaining information relative to the building of the "Fort Kearney, South pass and Honey lake wagon road." During this winter Colonel Lander had made his camp on the Popo Agie river at a point two miles northeast of where Lander now stands. The following summer the emigrant wagon road was commenced, Colonel Lander having negotiated a treaty with the Shoshone tribe for a right-of-way through the country owned by these indians, the road to extend westward from the Sweetwater to Fort Hall, Idaho. The indians were paid for this right-of-way in horses, firearms, ammunition, blankets and many other articles of value, all highly prized by Washakie.

Fort Stambaugh, placed midway between Miners' Delight and Atlantic City, served as a camp for military protection to both mining camps, was named for

Lieutenant Charles B. Stambaugh, who was shot from his horse by indians on May 4, 1870, while defending a freighting party. Lieutenant Stambaugh served in the Civil war as a private of Company H, Eleventh Ohio cavalry, ranking as first lieutenant, Second Cavalry, U. S. A. at the time of his death, having made for himself an enviable record for bravery and soldierly conduct. More exactly Camp Stambaugh was situated in the southeastern extremity of the Wind river range where it runs out to an elevation of 8000 feet above the level of the sea and is exactly on the divide.

Thus elevated in position, it lies between and commands two lines of approach and escape over which marauding parties, Sioux, Arapahoes and Cheyennes, from about Fort Laramie, and Fetterman, make their regular annual descent upon the Wind river and Sweetwater settlement and stage stations. These two lines are connected by different trails over the high foothills of the range, above and to the northwest of Camp Stambaugh, and the exposed mining settlement, so that either can be chosen as a line of escape after an outrage.[72]

In a short time after the indians had surrounded the freighting team, Major David Gordon, commanding Company D, Second United States cavalry, stationed at Atlantic City made his appearance, pursuing the indians and in a hot engagement with them, several hostiles were killed. Lieutenant Stambaugh falling dead from his horse was taken by the indians who robbed him of his possessions, watch, revolver and contents of his pockets, finally shooting several times into his body. The soldiers rallying regained the officer's body. The battle was fought on Stambaugh creek, a tributary of Twin creek. This camp after the establishment of Fort Washakie and the practical desertion of the mining camps was finally abandoned in 1877.

[72] Jones, p. 9.

Most reluctantly Chief Washakie gave his consent to the Arapahoes camping on his reservation, the final consent being given through the request of Governor Campbell, who urged this hospitality notwithstanding Washakie's protest when he said, "I mistrust the tribe." "The visitors," the old chief would not call them otherwise, settled on the Big Wind river about thirty miles below where Lander is now located. Captain Herman G. Nickerson, who was in the Sweetwater country at this time helping to establish peace not only between the white and red man but between the hostiles has said:

The Arapahoes promised friendly relations with the Shoshones and the white settler and the miners, always promising to notify both of the coming of any northern hostiles with whom they were not at peace. Neither of these promises were kept, for after their coming the stealing of stock and the killing of whites continued and were accredited to the Sioux and Cheyennes. But it was suspicioned that the Arapahoes were committing the depredations or at least a part of them, or, to say the very least, would inform on other indians who might be guilty of the crimes. Stolen stock was found in their camps, they claiming to have bought it from the indians.

To end these intolerable depredations, a force of two hundred and seventy-five white men, well-armed and equipped, was organized to go into the Popo Agie valley where the Arapahoes were located. Chief Black Bear and a small band of sixteen Arapahoes were killed on April 7, 1870, and the wife and squaw of Black Bear and seven children were captured. These indian children were placed in the families of the settlers who raised a part of them as their own family. Among the captured children was a full-blooded Arapahoe given to the soldiers at Fort Washakie, who took care of the boy, naming him William Tecumseh Sherman. In time General C. A. Coolidge of the Seventh United States infantry, and his wife, stationed at the fort, adopted the Arapahoe boy, giving him the name of Sherman Coolidge, who was educated in the public schools, a military academy, graduating from a divinity school in Minnesota in 1884. Reverend Sherman Coolidge at one time preached and worked among his tribe and for many years was rector of the Episcopal church at Fort Washakie, afterward becoming a Canon of a cathedral in Denver, Colorado, in which state he continues, 1928, in his chosen field of labor.

In place of making apologies for his indian origin, Reverend Coolidge takes pride and pleasure in his parentage. It is told of him that once when he was at a reception given in his honor in an eastern state, the conversation turned to the subject of ancestors and their services in the Revolutionary war. When the talk came to "Mayflower descendants," Mr. Coolidge quickly exclaimed, "Yes, indeed, wonderful! My ancestors were in the receiving line when the Pilgrims landed." [73]

Doctor James Irwin and his family for a long time resided in the Sweetwater district and on the Shoshone reservation. One child survives the immediate family, a daughter, Mrs. W. T. Chalmers of California. Mrs. James Irwin possessed unusual educational qualifications, having attended college in the state of New York, thus bringing to the Sweetwater valley and the Shoshone reservations an intellectual training much beyond the ordinary for that period of pioneer life. "She was an astronomer of unusual merit, as well as a botanist; she also wrote easily and interestingly."

Mrs. Irwin's home on the Shoshone reservation was near the cabin belonging to Sacajawea, the two women

[73] Talbot.

becoming well acquainted, Mrs. Irwin learning to use the Shoshone language under the tutelage of the indian woman who told the white woman of her journey with Lewis and Clark. Washakie also was a frequent visitor at the Irwin household, all the members of which were very fond of the old chief for "he was a good-hearted indian and was fond of children."

Many were the depredations committed by the enemies of Washakie in the valley of the Shoshone reservation – conflicts that the combined forces of the white men, soldiers, and the friendly Shoshones under the chieftainship of Washakie, could not prevent and could not control. These depredations continued in the Sweetwater country until the year of 1882, when northern Arapahoes raided and robbed camps of ranchers, in which fight two indians were killed, who just previously had murdered two white men. After this year there were no depredations, the country gradually acquiring many white settlers and so outnumbering the hostiles; consequently protection seemed adequate in that part of the territory and the hostiles carried on their depredations further to the north.

There are many versions – even expert opinions varying widely – as to the causes resulting in the battle of Crowheart buttes, and the naming of that geological formation located near the middle northern boundary of the Wind river reservation. Norkuk, the Shoshone scout, gives an interesting history regarding the naming of the butte, as does James Bridger, also Edmo LeClair, the Shoshone interpreter, to which may be added the testimony of one Wa-we-chee, an elderly indian, born in 1840, as well as other people who were, or are, familiar with the many traditions surrounding Crowheart. All narrate a story of a prolonged battle for the supremacy of this land which Washakie wished to have as a part of his reservation or hunting ground.

The different stories all agree in the fact that there was a battle waged between Washakie and hostile indians, Crows or Blackfeet, in order to establish the right of possession or title to hunt in a certain territory in which was located what is now Crowheart buttes.[74]

The battle was fought March, 1866, between the Shoshones and Bannocks against the Crows.[75] At the time indicated, the Bannocks were camped on the Big Popo Agie river where the town of Hudson is now located. A large party of Crows was camped on the Big Wind river near where is the Kinnear ranch. Washakie, as the chief of the Shoshones, sent a peace envoy to the Crows, an indian and his wife. The Crows killed the Shoshone indian. The squaw escaped and returned to Washakie's camp telling the chief of the murder. Washakie sent runners to Tigee of the Bannocks for help and reinforcements. As the result of this conference a war party was organized between the Bannocks and the Shoshones in which it was agreed to battle with the Crows, who taken by surprise, waged a running fight which lasted for four days.

The Crows at the end of four days of combat abandoned their lodges, which all fell into the possession of the Shoshones and their allies. This decisive battle was fought on Black mountain near the head of the Crow and Red rivers. Marks of this combat are at this day in evidence – flint arrowheads and other evidence of battle

[74] Located in township 40 north, range 102 west, about forty miles south of Washakie Needles.

[75] LeClair, Edmo. *Letter*, courtesy of Senator William G. Johnson, Crowheart, Wyoming.

having been found on the mountain. A few Crow scouts were captured on what is Crowheart buttes, but no battle was fought within two miles of them.

There were seventeen or eighteen young Crow braves captured. Washakie had their heads shaven and sent them back to their tribe with the information that they were too young to be killed, and also with the warning not to appear again under penalty of death. One of the young Crow girls captured at the time of the battle later became one of the wives of Washakie.

The story, often repeated, that Washakie ate a Crow's heart is not given credence by those who knew Washakie, although it is true that he, at the war dance after the battle, displayed a Crow's heart on his lance.

With a small group of frontiersmen working at Fort Washakie – all known and well-liked by the military community – was a typical Irishman, William Mc-Cabe. He was a United States government scout, a veteran of the Mexican war and chief of the scouts in the Bates battle. He came into the region of Fort Washakie in the early sixties, making his home there until his death in 1914. In the capacity of a scout, McCabe gave valuable and fearless service in the Bates battle in 1874. One of his important duties while working for the government was that of being a wagon boss over the indian freighters when they hauled goods overland from Rawlins to the Shoshone agency. "Scout McCabe was a fine man and every one had a kind word to say of him," is the frequent tribute paid to this man of the West.

Thomas Cook was the official shoemaker and cobbler for many years at the post and one of the worthy pioneers of the city of Lander, where he, for a long time,

THE THREE GRACES

A Group of Fort Washakie pioneers. *Left to right*, John Sheard, freighter; Thomas Cook, post shoemaker; William McCabe, U.S. scout, served in Bates Battle, July 4, 1874

WASHAKIE'S CROW WIFE – A TROPHY OF WAR

Left to right, Washakie's granddaughter, *standing*; his Crow wife, Ah-ah-why-per-sie, *seated*; and his daughter, *seated*. Ah-ah-why-per-sie was captured by Washakie at the Crowheart Buttes

lived and worked at his profession. McCabe, Cook and Sheard were about the same age, and were generally called, affectionately, "The Three Graces." All three were well advanced in years when old Fort Washakie was abandoned.

Of John Sheard there seems to be more available historical material than of his two partners and tested friends of pioneer days. Fortunately, from the Reverend John Roberts's pen there is preserved for history a statement of the outstanding characteristics of this frontiersman, who is reported to have been a graduate from Yale University and who, with the great tide of restless humanity immediately after the Civil war, drifted into the alluring West, which was calling for men of courage and ability. Mrs. Mary Carter, of the interesting William A. Carter family of Fort Bridger, writes of Mr. Sheard, "He used to boast that he could make the whitest biscuits, with the blackest hands, of any one in the country."

Quoting from Reverend Roberts, the following teems with the spirit that is peculiarly that of a pioneer.

The man with the watch-chain is my old friend, Thomas Cook, one of the worthy pioneers of Lander. The other with his hands folded is John Sheard of the indomitable wagon freighters between Rawlins and Fort Washakie in the pre-railway days. With a string-team of sixteen or eighteen horses, he would haul great loads of freight over all but impassable trails, steep and dangerous; through winter snows and spring mud – and he "kept to the road" until over eighty. I remember once driving past his outfit in a terrible snowstorm on the top of Beaver divide, his horses knotted up with the cold, were tied to the wagon wheels. In his little dilapidated tent, close by, a sage brush fire was roaring through the stove pipe. Some days after my return home I found the old man seated by the warm kitchen range, at the mission. He had pulled through with his freight – and with one of my little daughters on his knee, he was singing for her at

the top of his voice, Mrs. Heman's "Better Land." I asked him how
he had gotten along in the storm at the top of the divide. He replied,
"Well, sir, it snowed and blew one continuous blast for three days
and nights, but we had plenty of hay." Then dropping his chin, he
shook his head and muttered to himself, "The hay and grain played
out on the second day, but – " he said cheerily, looking up, "we made
it."

On another occasion being asked how he managed when his wagon
breaks broke on the mountain-side, he simply said, "We came down as
fast as the law of gravity would permit." Another time on delivering
some damaged freight he shook his finger at me saying, "Don't you say
a word! Don't you say a word! You would not say a word if you
knew what I came through on this trip." I asked him another time
how he got through a part of the road which that spring was too
muddy to drive through with a buggy. "Oh," he said, "We hooked
on two strings (thirty or forty horses) to a wagon and floated her
through."

Sheard's experiences on the road were sometimes as humorous as
they were thrilling, a record of them would be interesting to read, as
would be a biography of McCabe or Cook. The three have been
gathered to their fathers.[76]

---

[76] Roberts, Rev. John, *Letter* of 1927 to author.

A Buffalo Chase Down the Big Horn

When the indians engaged in a buffalo hunt, it was not designated as "a buffalo hunt," but was called "to buffalo." To hunt the buffalo was not a mere pastime but a necessary task with its thrills, in order to furnish the tribe with meat to eat, skins for the tepees, robes for winter wear, fat for cooking – and for greasing the human body – marrow for stews, sinews for cord and sewing material, and horns for ornamental purposes.[77]

Great economy was exercised by the indians in the killing of the bison, every portion of the animal being put to economic use. Indian legends relate that two centuries ago a terrible blizzard swept over the sides of the Rocky mountains until all signs of life were gone. "About three old men ago a great snow came in the early winter. It was as tall as the tallest man and killed all of the buffalo and most of the indians starved to death." "Three old men" is the term used to indicate three generations, or the life of the grandfather, the father and the son, each representing sixty years or more or a total of about two centuries. Gradually, in the course of many years, the indians annually came "to buffalo" in the "Warm basin" – "You-ah-die" – or the territory embraced in the reservation selected by Washakie.

A buffalo hunt amounted to a sacred pilgrimage – ceremonies being performed before the hunt, and invo-

---

[77] In the late years of the sixties in the Powder river country the indian would barter first class robes, well tanned, for three metallic cartridges.

cations made to the gods for many buffalo and a rich
and abundant harvest. When our government, through
its official representation, was at Fort Bridger in 1868
endeavoring to make acceptable terms with the Shoshones for a reservation, Washakie was asked, "What
lands do you wish set aside for your people?" Without
hesitation the chief answered, "In the warm valleys
where the game animals winter and my people will be
assured of food from one snow to the next snow." Washakie knew all of the streams, passes, mountains and
trails of these valleys – the Sweetwater and Wind – for
he had for many years made innumerable hunting trips
up and down and across all the streams and "warm"
parks and hunting grounds. In these haunts then, as
today, with the exception of the bison, were to be found
mountain lion, wolf, lynx, wildcat, black, and white-
tailed deer, antelope, elk, and moose – these foothills
and parks were indeed a hunter's paradise. Far up in
the majestically lofty mountains the horned sheep made
his home, while in the fastnesses of the peaks were to be
found the silver-tip grizzly bear – the big prize for an
ambitious man with a gun. The "Warm valleys" with
their wealth of brilliant flowers, kinnikinick – for their
tobacco – wild fruits, streams filled with fish, were the
happy hunting ground of Washakie's people – the land
he has selected to be set aside as a home for the Shoshones for all time to come.

There are evidences to show that the buffalo in Wyoming made his last stand in Fremont county in the
upper reaches of the valley in the Dubois district. Here
it is believed the bison in that region were finally exterminated by the indians who used the animals for food
and clothing and, to a larger degree, by the fur traders

who more for sport than for an utilitarian purpose
hunted and shot the buffalo.

Thus it will be seen from records and reports of early
explorers and members of expeditions, as well as from
written testimony of fur trappers, that the buffalo was
the most numerous of all wild game in the Wind river
country, for the hunting of which there was a perpetually open season. In this hunting paradise of the Shoshones, Washakie was known as a great hunter and
trapper, "bagging more game, taking more furs and
pelts, catching more fish than any other member of his
tribe."

During the days of October, 1874, Mr. James I.
Patten, for many years officially identified at the Shoshone agency as instructor to the indians, went with
Washakie and his people – including women and children – into the wilds, fastness and snows of the Big
Horn basin, lying north and east of the Shoshone reservation, which territory at that time extended as far
north as the crest of Owl Creek mountains.

After the Shoshones had settled on their reservation
it was their custom each year, when the harvesting and
housing of the crops had been accomplished, to make a
long and extended buffalo hunt – the duration of the
expedition continuing through the fall and all of the
following winter. Mr. Patten, as a teacher of the Shoshone children, had been advised that no salary could
be drawn from the government except during a period
of actual instruction.[78] To fulfill the regulations rela-

---

[78] The original manuscript of this buffalo chase was written for the
author in April, 1917, by Mr. James I. Patten, Shoshone Indian government
teacher in 1873. Generous quotations from this material have been used.
Mr. Patten held a position as "teacher and lay reader" from the bishop of
the jurisdiction of the Episcopal church of Wyoming territory for the Shoshone reservation indians, his term of office commencing in 1873.

tive to remuneration for indian instruction the United
States commissioner of indian affairs, who had rendered the decision that a teacher could draw no salary
during the absence of the tribe from the agency, suggested to Mr. Patten that he make an application to the
authorities at Washington asking them to grant a
special permission to an agency teacher to establish a
"roaming school" for the benefit of the indian children,
as long as the hunt lasted. Immediate acceptance of the
request made it possible for Mr. Patten to make all
preparations for carrying out the inauguration of this
new method of instruction. The proposed innovation
being very much akin to the present day "camp summer school" found in universities where all instruction
given by college instructors is carried on in the open.

Before the hunting party started, October 16, 1874,
one of Washakie's sub-chiefs, Bazil, and one of his
warriors, Baptiste, (Battez) appeared with a tent at
the agency, requesting that some provision be made for
the care of their mother while the sons were away buffalo hunting. "Wrapped in a bundle was the aged and
decrepit form of that famous Shoshone woman, Sacajawea, who had acted as a pathfinder for the Lewis and
Clark expedition of 1805-1806. Bazil spoke of her as
his mother and informed Doctor Irwin, the indian
agent, that she was too old to go on the hunt, and
wished to leave her in his care until they returned. A
tent was accordingly erected, close to the agent's house,
where she might receive all necessary care and attention." [79]

On October 19, when the camp was moved to Muddy

[79] It is agreed that Sacajawea was born "about" 1788, thus making "the
little woman" at the time of the hunt eighty-six years of age. *Journal of
American History*, vol. 1, no. 3.

creek there were 1800 indians – including women and children, some Bannocks who had come from the west side of the Wind river mountains for this hunt, a few mexicans, one portugese, one Penobscot indian and, as was general, several men with indian wives. "As we moved," said Mr. Patten, "over the wild waste of sagebrush hills and dry creeks I confess to feeling, surrounded as I was by such a motley cavalcade, like a sure nomad of the desert."

When the camp was made in Owl creek basin the tepees were stretched up and down its banks. Here was experienced something novel – several stray deer rushed through the camp. The indians, yelling and whooping, took up arms, firing "an indiscriminate fusillade after these invaders." No one, nor animal, was hit – the deer making their escape from the invaders of their domain.

At this camp Mr. Patten made another observation of the nature of the red man, where he observed them in a new light. To him the indians did not seem like the mild and pacific people he had known a few days before at the Shoshone agency. That they were entirely different is shown by the following description. "Huge fires were built through the camp; haranguers proclaimed in loud voices throughout the length of the village, calling the people to assemble. Medicine men exhorted in stentorian voices, drums were beaten and the rattles rattled." Washakie, like another being from his ordinary self, presided at the meeting, addressing his people with a face of smiles, a voice joyous and in an enthusiastic manner, reminding them of the former buffalo hunts and expressing his belief that the Great Spirit would lead them to capture much game at this time. At the conclusion of the speech great joy was made manifest, the drums continued to beat, the cheers resounding on the weird scene.

Again Washakie sent out runners to find the exact location of the buffalo, all returns reporting herds on the Gooseberry about forty miles above its mouth. As the tribe moved northward toward the creek, Washakie asked Mr. Patten to travel with him. Arriving at a high point where far and near one could see the face of the country, the chief took out his field glasses, which were his constant companion, and carefully looked over the landscape, then handed the glasses to the instructor, telling him to look. Discovery was made of what seemed to be a shadow on the plains but which upon closer observation proved to be a herd of buffalo, "more numerous than I had ever before witnessed."

In the exact words of the indian instructor, the following description is given. "Now as the herd was pretty well concentrated the old fighting general of the tribe rode quietly to the front and in a voice as if in common conversation ordered a charge. Then there was excitement! What a rush! Every man apparently wanted to get there first, but those of the swiftest horses were already there. Each man struck for the point of the herd he chose and selected his animal, did his killing, and then onto another until his ammunition was exhausted – this method being followed by all. Among the Shoshones, to him who kills, the game belongs – the meat to anyone who wants it, was the common custom." [80] While most of the killing was done with modern rifles there were those who used the bow and arrow,

---

[80] The site of this buffalo chase is in what is now Washakie county and Hot Springs county between Grass and Gooseberry creeks, a circular field in townships 45-47 north, range 95-97 west.

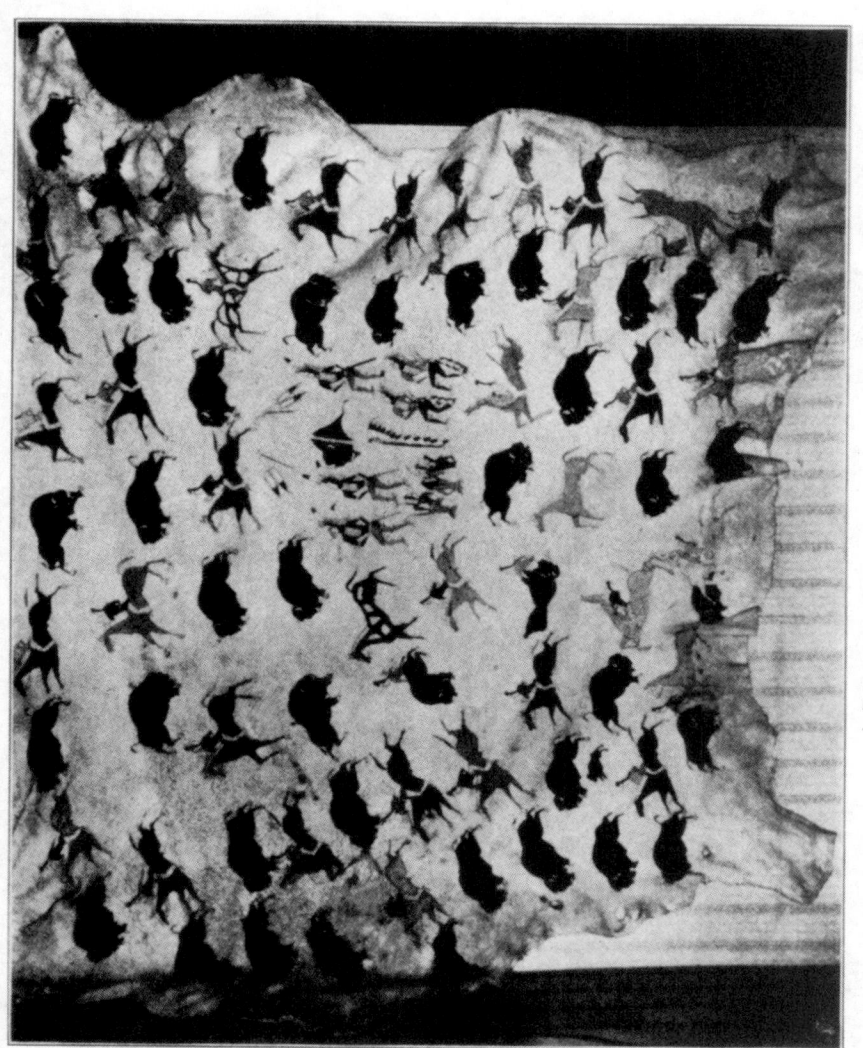

A Buffalo Dance after a Hunt

An elk-skin painting in red and black, made in 1906 by Cadzi Cody, a Shoshone

these being the elderly indians who were skilled arti-
sans with the native implement of war; they drove
their arrows home with great accuracy and shot them as
rapidly as they could be notched and pulled.

When the butchering was finished an accounting was
made of the slaughtered; the dead buffalo on the arena
of action numbered one hundred and five. In this camp,
Washakie remained until all of the meat was put into
proper condition for transportation. When the work
was finished, movements were made for moving camp
and preparing for another drive upon the inescapable
buffalo.

The next camp was made after trailing straight
across country over Greybull river, about where Otto
now is. Then the move was to the Shoshone river, which
then was called Stinking river, "tich-e-pah-gwann-
nert." The Big Horn river was the next camp. This site
was as far north as this buffalo chase extended, the turn
southward being near the present day cities of Lovell
and Kane.

At this period of the chase the indians were constantly on the move – camps changed almost daily – for
November was well on its way. The fact that this condition of constant travel might· continue indefinitely
made the indian teacher conclude that no definite results could possibly be obtained through conducting so
intense a roaming school, under such unfavorable conditions, and he thought the most reasonable thing to be
done was to return to the agency.

There seems to be no question but that the buffalo for
many years had made their home in the "warm valleys"
where Washakie had selected the territory for his reservation. Mention is made by the Astorian party of en-

countering herds of buffalo when it reached the Wind river mountain valley. The party on its way to the Pacific in the interests of John Jacob Astor, under the leadership of Wilson Price Hunt, had by the middle of September, in the year 1811, reached the territory of the Shoshone tribe, where the fur men indulged in the sport of "to buffalo." The hunters made great havoc among the buffalo and brought in quantities of meat; the voyageurs busied themselves about the fires, roasting and stewing for present purposes, or drying provisions for the journey; "the camp presented a picture of rude feasting and revelry, of mingled bustle and repose, characteristic of a halt in a fine hunting country." A party of Shoshones was encountered which had come over the mountains from the west on their autumnal hunting excursion to provide meat for the winter. They had been successful in their hunt, and their camp was full of jerked buffalo meat, all of the choicest kind, and extremely fat.[81]

The process of "jerking meat" when on these buffalo chases was by cutting the fresh meat into very thin slices, hanging them in the sun on poles – in modern day on the strands of barbed wire fences – there to hang until thoroughly dried. When on a hunt this meat was then placed in *par-fleches*, thus making it not difficult to pack the meat on the horses and in this manner of packing be free from dust and dirt. Par-fleches are envelopes made of some style of hide about three feet long and a foot and a half wide, the sides of the skin or hide being long enough to cover a foot of meat, when packed on the horses.

[81] Irving, *Astoria*, chap. xxx.

Reports were sent to Washington in 1877 [82] stating
that the annual hunt of the Shoshones did not take
place because the buffalo were ranging so near the
agency the indians refused to "be discouraged from
going to take them." Efforts were made with Washakie
to wait before killing these animals so near to the reservation camp but Washakie would not wait to hear from
Washington about obtaining ammunition declaring,
"By the time the Great Father receives the letter and
sends word to have more powder given us, the buffalo
would be far off, and further, I do not believe that the
authorities want the indians to have cartridges, so I will
take a short hunt now and kill what I can with my bow
and arrow." "The Shoshones," wrote Agent Patten,
"also understand that with the treaty of 1868 permission
was given to them to hunt upon the unoccupied lands
of the United States as long as game may be found
thereon and that the same does not interfere with white
settlers. The indians will remain out but a short time,
as there is but a small amount of game in the country.
There are now nearly one hundred indians at the
agency, and if desired, I shall bring them in immediately, as soon as I am fully informed as to the prospects
of opening a school among them, which latter I hope
to accomplish soon.

"After the buffalo were decimated and disappeared
from Washakie's territory, he gave up the pleasures of
the annual hunt, devoting himself to domestic and pas-
toral pursuits and in looking after the welfare of his
people. These changed conditions of life, in all of which
he seemed to take the deepest interest, visiting the

[82] Patten, James I., Shoshone and Bannock agency, indian agent, *Report*,
November 21, 1877.

schools and manifesting the greatest pleasure and satisfaction with the extreme kindness and treatment that the children received and the general progress being made on the reservation, all this being what he had hoped to see in his life-time, filled him with gratitude to all who had been interested and assisted in the work of the betterment of his people."

The Prelude to the Custer Tragedy

By a treaty concluded between our government and several tribes of indians, living on both sides of the Oregon trail who were committing depredations along the white-top wagon highway, there was reason to believe that many of the indian troubles, if not totally ended, were to be lessened, and peace might be partially established. The making and breaking of many of the indian treaties signed by government officials were the cause of many indian wars, not only on the trails to the west and the roads to the gold-fields of Montana, but in mining camps situated in the mountains and hills within the hunting ground areas set aside for the red man. These wars were somewhat constant until the culminating tragedy of June 25, 1876, when General George Custer and a portion of the Seventh United States cavalry were "rubbed out" on the Little Big Horn.

With the finding of gold in Montana at Virginia City, Bannock, and the towns of Helena and Nevada, and much rich sand along the streams of the upper branches of the Missouri river in southern Montana, the white man virtually took possession of the lands set aside by council agreement in 1851 as the indians' hunting grounds and for their lodges.

The Bozeman trail ran from Julesburg, Colorado, to the historic Fort Laramie then along the North Platte river, up into the Powder river country, across the Big Horn river, toward the Yellowstone river, then west parallel with the river through Bozeman pass into the land of gold and wealth; this road transcending the land of the Sioux, Cheyennes, Arapahoes – who made a stubborn and determined fight against the white man's invasion. A military road was established on this trail, forts were erected thereon – as Reno, Phil Kearney, C. F. Smith and Ellis; armed soldiers were marched over the trail, killing and driving to the mountains the indians' game – particularly the buffalo – each act of which was a direct violation of the treaty of 1851, which treaty only granted a road of "transit," through the indian territory not military occupation and fortified posts.

As the soldiers fiercely and bravely fought to gain partial possession of the indians lands, the red men as relentlessly and fearlessly battled for their cherished territory.

> Go round!
> I do not want you in my hunting ground!
> You scare my bison, and my folks must eat.
> For sweeter than your words are, home is sweet
> To us, as you; yonder land is home.
> In sheltered valleys elk and bison roam
> All winter there, and in the spring are fat.
> We gave the road you wanted up the Platte,
> Make dust upon it then! [83]

This coveted land originally belonged to the Crow tribe, though constantly claimed and roamed over by their ancient enemy, the Sioux. The contest for this land forced the Crows into an alliance with the Shoshones and the Bannocks, the three tribes fighting against the Sioux and their allies, the Cheyennes and Arapahoes. The result of these wars from 1866 to the fall of 1868

---

[83] Neihardt, *Ibid.*, chap. ii.

was a daily besiegement and disaster on the gold trail to the Virginia City country, with a constant loss of life of white and red men. These conflicts were the cause of the Fetterman (Wyoming) disaster of December 21, 1866, from which conflict no white man emerged – a battle commanded by Red Cloud's warriors; the Hay corral combat of August 1, 1867, near Fort C. F. Smith (Montana) ; and the Wagon Box fight of August 2, of this same year – the last two battles resulting in heavy losses to the indians.

The treaty at Fort Laramie, under the command of Colonel C. C. Augur, of April 29, 1868, gave this Crow country to the Sioux and the Cheyenne tribes. After this treaty was signed these lands were constantly under siege until, finally, for their safety, the Crows moved from the eastern side of the Big Horn mountains to the western side, where they were in nearer and more intimate contact with Washakie and his people, with whom they were now generally in alliance and friendliness.

When our government in the fall of 1868 ordered the troops to leave the Bozeman trail and abandon the forts established on this road, Chief Red Cloud of the Sioux visioned a day when, with other victories, the indians would control all of the lands from the North Platte to the Yellowstone river. The Custer battle of 1876 virtually ended strife and war with the Sioux; this was when Sitting Bull, the medicine man of the Sioux, with his chiefs, won his great victory over the armed forces of the whites.

When gold was found in the Black Hills, territory of the Sioux, the Arapahoes and the Cheyennes by virtue of the government treaty, our government made an

honest effort to keep the white men, with their shallow
mining pans and shovels, out of the indians' territory.
But the attempts to carry out the white man's treaty in
keeping the Sioux country free of forbidden whites,
owing to the vast wealth of the gold fields in the Black
Hills and the unlimited frenzied prospectors and eager
miners rushing to the "gold diggins," were absolutely
futile.

In vain the government issued its proclamations, in vain were our
veterans' regiments of cavalry and infantry, commanded by warriors
true and tried, drawn up across the path of the daring invaders; in
vain were arrests made, baggage seized, horses confiscated and wagons
burned; no earthly power could hinder that bewildering swarm of
human ants.[84]

In fact at this very time surveys were being pushed
through that territory for the different lines of rail-
roads, the principal one being the Northern Pacific.
Numerous people were eagerly seeking opportunties to
establish colonies, take up lands, open mines and establish other interests in that country.

As a matter of fact some military expeditions were sent into the
territory to explore and reconnoitre with a view of discovering its
natural resources. This was especially the case in 1874 and 1875. The
country was at that time practically overrun by prospectors and mine-
hunters through the region of what is now South Dakota, and particularly in that district known as the Black Hills.[85]

Defending the operations of the army in its attitude
toward the indians, Lieutenant-general P. H. Sheridan,
when commanding the Division of the Missouri, at one
time stated his policy in the following terse terms:

I have in my command at least five hundred miles of frontier
settlements, my chief and only duty being to give protection to the

[84] Finerty, *Ibid.*, p. 41.
[85] Miles, p. 193.

families residing on the long lines against the outrages of indians. The government had invited these settlers by opening the lands to them for pre-emption and improvement. The number of men, women and children on the extended frontier is very great, and there is not a day from one year's end to the other that these families are exempt from the fearful thought of being murdered in the most fiendish manner. . . I have no hesitation in making my choice. I am going to stand by the people over whom I am placed and give them what protection I can.[86]

As a consequence of the efforts to fulfill army policies the officers were accused of wishing to exterminate the indians. In summarizing the frontier situation relative to the settler, indian, and army, during the years of the greatest conflict upon the plains Doctor Welty has drawn the following conclusions:

The army was a servant, and its duty was to obey. It had been accused by well-meaning persons of being harsh and cruel, and an enemy to the indian. Much of this is true. The very basic principle of the use of an army is cruel and harsh for it is trained to kill. The army was sent to the frontier by the government of the United States to kill if certain conditions existed, namely, the war of the indians upon the whites. In a purely theoretical sense the army had no choice in the matter. If the indian war was caused by the whites, the army had to make war against the innocent indians. If the indian system bred dissatisfaction and war, the army had to shoot down the indians if they could be found. Therefore, it seemed to be the duty of the army, under its policy, to punish the indian when he murmured at the wrongs inflicted upon him.[87]

Finally, peaceful methods proving unsuccessful, the government, through the Interior Department to which the Bureau of Indian Affairs was transferred, adopted regulations demanding that all indians in the northwest must live on reservations. The last date on which to

---

[86] United States House Executive Document, no. 269, 41 Cong., 2 sess.
[87] Welty, p. 367.

meet these requirements was set finally for the first of January in the year 1876.

The plans to drive the indians onto the reservation were instituted by Lieutenant-general P. H. Sheridan, Commander of the Division of the Missouri, in which division were located all of the northern hostiles; the major operation was to be the mobilization of his fighting forces. To carry out this campaign there were three bases of operation: one at Fort Abraham Lincoln (Dakota), with General Alfred H. Terry of the Department of Dakota in charge; one at Fort Ellis (Montana) with General John Gibbon in command; and one at Fort Fetterman (Wyoming), directed by General George Crook of the Department of the Platte. With these three forts as starting stations it was the design to drive "converging columns wedge like" into the red man's country whereby a process of concentrating and crushing, the indian would be forced to surrender.

It is the Fort Fetterman base under General Crook, with whom Chief Washakie fought on the Rosebud river, that is of particular interest at this time.

Believing that the hostiles would be located somewhere on or in the neighborhood of the headwaters of the Powder, Tongue, or in the valley of the Rosebud rivers, General Crook concentrated his forces at Fort Fetterman near where the old Oregon trail running east and west was crossed by the Bozeman road, which extended into the northern country of the Powder. Storm, snow, zero days for the first two months in 1876 prevented an early start for the indians' country. It was not until the middle of March that Colonel J. J. Reynolds with five troops of the Second cavalry, five troops of the Third cavalry and four companies of the

Fourth infantry, marched from Fetterman toward the headwaters of the Powder river where under surprise, Crazy Horse and his village were captured. The soldiers destroyed one hundred and five lodges, a large quantity of supplies and carried off a large pony herd. Under rapid fire, Crazy Horse forced the troops to retire, with a loss of several hundred horses, which were recaptured from the soldiers by the indians.

The troops of General Crook returning with their wounded to Fort Fetterman did not start on a second expedition until May 28, Goose creek being the objective point, where was to be established a depot for supplies. From this point General Crook intended to operate against the Sioux and their allies "whom he expected to find somewhere about the headwaters of the Tongue, the Rosebud, the Powder, or the Big Horn rivers, but in what precise locality he would find them or whether they would meet him on the way there, he had no idea." [88]

Under the reorganization of the army of the Platte commanded by General Crook, there were sent into the indian country fifteen troops of cavalry. Of these ten were from the Third and five from the Second cavalry; added to these were two from the Fourth infantry and three of the Ninth infantry, representing an army of more than 1100 fighting men. It was with this army that General Crook expected to meet and fight the warriors of Chief Crazy Horse, whose forces were combined with the warriors under Sitting Bull. This indian mobilization represented fully ninety per cent of the indian fighting forces which, as latterly developed, were three times as many fighting braves against General

[88] Forsyth, *Ibid.*, p. 314.

Crook as he had trained soldiers. However, the troops of soldiers, it is said, represented the largest force in fighting men, with efficiency ranking very high, that had ever been sent against the indians in the Sioux country.

Over the scarred Bozeman trail, stained with the blood of both white and red men, General Crook's army marched north into the contested territory of the indians, passing the ruins of the headquarters of General Connor in 1865, old Fort Reno on the Powder; the burned remains of Fort Phil Kearney, then northwest to the Tongue river, where a warning message was received by Crook from Crazy Horse. The message warned the white men not to cross the Tongue river as any such move would be taken by the indians as an act of invasion and the soldiers would be killed. No attention was paid to this open challenge from the red man. The soldiers in column a mile long marched to the Tongue where Crook made camp. Here early in June was established the first camp on the Tongue, which had been reached under great difficulty, the troops marching at times against a zero blizzard and in a blinding snow storm – a storm that was superceded by warmer weather, testified to "by the singing of the meadowlarks, and the chirping of thousands of grasshoppers." [89]

Attacks made on Crook's camp by the Sioux and Cheyenne indians, when moving toward Goose creek, a tributary of the Tongue, coupled with the report received by General Crook that all able-bodied male indians had left the Red Cloud agency, caused great anxiety. Added to this was the fact that the Shoshone

[89] Bourke, *Ibid.*, p. 292, 296.

GENERAL GEORGE CROOK
Reproduced from a photograph taken at Fort Washakie

allies had not arrived from their reservation. Reports had been received that Washakie, in command, was sending one hundred and twenty of his warriors to help and that their arrival might be expected any day. However from the reservation in the Wind river mountains west of the Big Horn mountains, the indians were marching as fast as their ponies and an occasional buffalo chase would permit.

The grass having become scarce on the Tongue river, General Crook moved his army west to the junction of the Little and Big Goose creeks, a distance slightly over seventeen miles, toward the foothills of the Big Horn mountains.

While in camp on the Goose, three Crow chiefs — Old Crow, Medicine Crow and Good Heart — presented themselves as allies with the whites against the hated Sioux, who had stolen their hunting grounds by the treaty of 1868. One hundred and sixty-three warriors and three hundred and thirty-two ponies were added to General Crook's fighting force by this friendly band.

On the day of June 14, final instructions for an engagement were given by General Crook to his forces which, through an interpreter, were translated to the allied Crows. Information was given that at the large Goose creek camp all of the wagons would be parked and that four days' rations would be given to each officer and soldier, the food consisting of hard tack, coffee and bacon; in addition there would be given to each person a blanket and one hundred rounds of ammunition in belts. The men who were not to go into battle were to protect the wagons and other property. The cavalry were to use their horses, the men of the infantry to be mounted on mules taken from the pack trains.

Scarcely had this brief conference been ended when a long line of glittering lances and brightly polished weapons of fire announced the anxiously expected advent of our other allies, the Shoshones, or Snakes, who, to the number of eighty-six, galloped rapidly up to headquarters and came left front into line in splendid style. No trained warriors of civilized armies ever executed the movement more prettily. Exclamations of wonder and praise greeted the barbaric array of these fierce warriors, warmly welcomed by their fierce enemies, the Crows. General Crook moved out to review their line of battle, resplendent in all the fantastic adornment of feathers, beads, brass buttons, bells, scarlet cloth and flashy lances. The Shoshones were not slow to perceive the favorable impression made and when order came for them to file off by the right, they moved with the precision of clock work and the pride of veterans. In the long line of horsemen brilliantly attired coming down the mountains were two scouts, each carrying a beautiful American flag. Each warrior had a narrow flag or pennant: all were armed with government rifles and revolvers.[90]

When General Crook on May 29, left Fort Fetterman, pushing his way into the Powder river territory, he sent on June 3, three messengers over the Big Horn mountains to the Shoshone reservation asking for recruits from the friendly Crows and Shoshones. A messenger thus detailed reached Fort Washakie on June 4, and within four hours one hundred and twenty-five Shoshone warriors, under Chief Washakie, were enroute to participate in the campaign.

The immediate response of the Shoshones is indicative of the firm leadership and quick decision of their great chief. When the recruits came over the Big Horn mountains on June 14, joining the troops, it can be realized that there was much quick action among the allies on their long march from the Wind river reservation, the prompt arrival into camp being a welcome reinforcement. There was no military alliance between the general of the troops and the chief of

90 Bourke, *Ibid.*, p. 303.

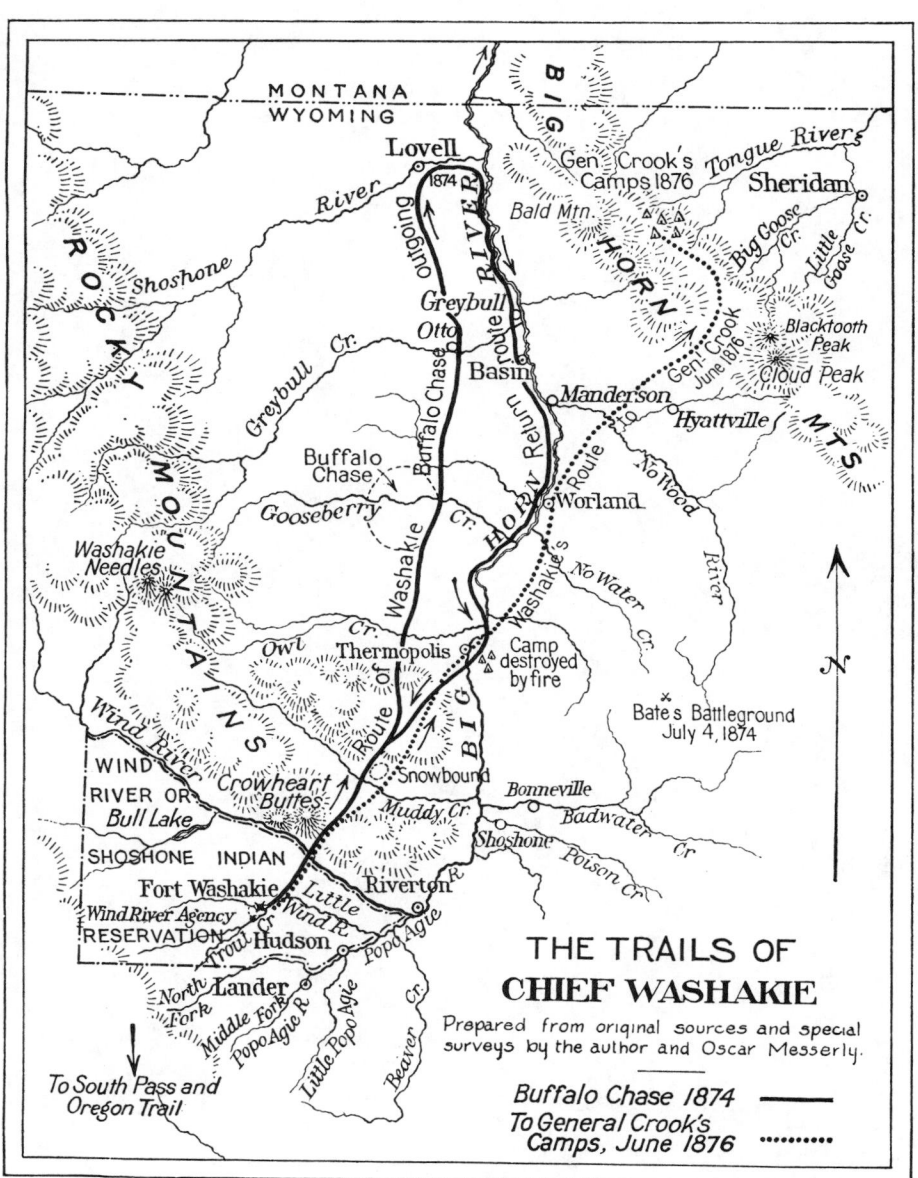

MONTANA
WYOMING

Lovell
1874

River

Shoshone

ROCKY

Greybull Cr.

Greybull
Otto

Basin

Buffalo Chase

Buffalo
Chase

Gooseberry

Washakie
Needles

MOUNTAINS

Owl Cr.

Thermopolis

Wind River

Crowheart
Buttes

WIND
RIVER OR
Bull Lake

SHOSHONE INDIAN

Fort Washakie
Wind River Agency
RESERVATION
Trout
Hudson

North Fork Lander

Middle Fork PopoAgie R.

To South Pass and
Oregon Trail

Outgoing Route
Return Route

BIG
HORN

Gen¹ Crook's
Camps 1876   *Tongue Rivers*

Bald Mtn.   Sheridan

Big Goose Cr.

Little Goose Cr.

HORN

Gen¹ Crook
June 1876

Blackfoot
Peak

Cloud Peak

MTS

Manderson

Hyattville

No Wood Route

Worland

Washakie's Route

No Water Cr.

River

Camp
destroyed
by fire

Bate's Battleground
July 4, 1874

Snowbound

Bonneville

Muddy Cr.

Badwater Cr.

Shoshone   *Poison Cr.*

Riverton

Little Wind R.

PopoAgie

Beaver Cr.

Little PopoAgie

N

THE TRAILS OF
CHIEF WASHAKIE

Prepared from original sources and special
surveys by the author and Oscar Messerly.

Buffalo Chase 1874 ———
To General Crook's
Camps, 1876 ··········

the indians. The Sioux were the age-long enemies of Washakie, their depredations and frequent invasions were not forgotten, no action could be too prompt for the old chief to respond to a chance to contribute to the common cause against their ancient enemy.[91]

Scout Grouard testifies to the arrival of Chief Washakie at this period at Goose creek:

Along about three o'clock the Crow indians arrived. About two hours afterward the sentinel gave the alarm signal. Going out to learn the cause I found it was the Snake (Shoshone) indians with Tom Cosgrove as their interpreter coming to join the command. I think he had one hundred and sixty-four or one hundred and eighty-two indians, I am not quite certain which. Their chief, Washakie, was with them.[92]

To the instructions given by General Crook to Washakie and his Shoshone warriors, there were but few signs of approval, though it was quite evident that nothing was lost from the address. After the council had ended the Shoshones asked to be allowed to scout in their own way when going to battle, which request, most fortunately, was granted.

With Chief Washakie, and Sub-chief Norkuk – who have been designated as "Washa and Nawkee" – had come from the Shoshone reservation, Tom Cosgrove, chief of scouts, and his assistants, Nelson Yarnell and Eckles – all three natives of Texas, the first two having been with Washakie in the Bates battle of 1874. With these scouts were two of Washakie's sons, Dick and Bishop.

Chief Washakie's grievance was that of the Crows. His people had been killed by these self same Sioux, Arapahoes and Cheyennes; he had frequently battled

[91] Faris, Chester E., United States district superintendent, indian field service, *Letter* of March 3, 1826 (formerly an instructor in the Shoshone agency schools).
[92] De Barthe, p. 221.

against them to protect the white man and his family going over the Oregon trail. The government had been generous to him; he would now show that the red man, though never forgiving, never forgot a kindness given. Now was the golden opportunity. He and his warriors were anxious to be off; to win scalps, to take them back to his tribe in the Wind river valley, which he wished to be kept peaceful as well as to be filled with buffalo. Yes, he and his men were ready, no time would be too soon.

It is not proposed to recount in detail the military maneuvers of General Crook's army in the fight on the Rosebud. Many authors and eye-witnesses have amply and graphically described that event which so perilously near annihilated this branch of the army and the loyal Shoshone and Crow allies.

Moving westward in the early morning of June 16, the Tongue river was crossed – the stream that Chief Crazy Horse had said, by his messenger, would mean the death of the white man if passed over. After effecting a crossing without opposition, the general direction of the march was north into Montana. Great care was exercised in the movement as the messengers in the extreme advance had returned to the main army and reported that a trail had been discovered of a very large village of the Sioux. The indian allies at first marched on the flanks, then soon moved into the lead, their medicine men much in advance. It was, as previously stated, upon the recommendation of the Shoshones that the indians were allowed to arrange their plan of march according to their own idea. Slowly, carefully and cautiously the soldiers trailed into the Rosebud country.

Reaching the extreme headwaters of the Rosebud,

the march on June 17, now was down the stream, when the fight was on. The Shoshones and Crows well in advance of the army returned shouting, "Sioux! Sioux! Heap Sioux! Heap Sioux!" The army had met a large force of Ogallala Sioux, under the command of the great strategic leader Crazy Horse. The Shoshones were perhaps five hundred yards from the main command, their position at the head of a large draw, or hollow, giving them a complete and commanding view of the enemies. "The Shoshones were collectively and individually effective in the action. Two of the scouts noticing the danger that General Crook had placed himself in on a small knoll, told him of his danger and protected him in his withdrawal to safe quarters."

The sagacious Crazy Horse moved his warriors under cover, when they made their bold dash to sweep the hollow in which some of the cavalry and a large portion of the main command we're concentrated. Then it was that the charge of the Shoshones, supported by the infantry of the left wing, turned the tide of the battle, repelled the enemy, forcing their withdrawal. In the action of Death Hollow, as the troops called the battleground, Captain Guy V. Henry, Third United States cavalry, was seriously wounded. He lay prostrate on the field. Tigee, a trusted lieutenant of Washakie, stood over the officer and held the hostiles at bay until both were rescued, and thus the life of a brave man was saved for future service to our country.[93]

General Crook at this period recalled the division that was in the canyon, the next order being for the advance of the whole line back to Goose creek camp, "the Sioux leaving the enemy forces in indisputable possession of the field." The total loss of the army was fifty-seven killed or wounded, the loss of the enemy is not known though the scouts "boasted of thirteen scalps."

[93] Faris, C. E. *Letter, Ibid.* [Various spellings of Tigee.]

Crazy Horse, after his ultimate surrender to General Crook at the agency, stated that he "had no less than 6500 fine trained men in the fight, and, that the first attack was made with 1500, the remainder of his warriors being concealed behind the bluffs and hills. His plan of battle was either to lead detachments in pursuit of his people, and turning quickly cut them to pieces in detail; or draw the whole of Crook's forces down into the canyon of the Rosebud, where escape would have been impossible, the vertical walls hemming in the sides, the front being closed by a dam and abatis of broken timber making a depth of ten feet of water and mud, the rear, of course, to be shut off by thousands of yelling murderous Sioux and Cheyennes." [94]

General Custer, although not marching in a position so dangerous, with a force nearly equal to ours, suffered annihilation at the hands of the same enemy, about eighteen miles further westward, only eight days afterward. [95]

It was Crook who was destined to strike the first blow of the new campaign, Crook was first to lead a heavy force against the most warlike indians of the world. Even as Sheridan had planned, Crook confidently marched on to the heart of "the indian story land," drove in confidently to the attack, and in an hour learned a lesson that revolutionized his idea of the prowess of the Sioux. At the end of that hour he was glad to be able to extricate his command, to fall back to his entrenched camp, there to double his defensive measures and send back to the states for reinforcements. [96]

That General Crook was not trapped with his army was due to his faith in Chief Washakie, who all day on

[94] Bourke, *Ibid.*, p. 311. George Bird Grinnell in his "The Fighting Cheyennes," p. 52, contends that there was no dangerous defile. "There was no effort by the indians to lead troops into a trap."

[95] Finerty, *Ibid.*, p. 132.

[96] Graham, p. xxii (King).

CHIEF WASHAKIE AND SHOSHONE WARRIORS

Seated, left to right, Dick Washakie (son of the chief); Chief Washakie; Tigee; *Standing, left to right.* Mat-ta-vish; So-pa-gaut; Pan-zook; Per-ra-go-sha

Thess six warriors were with Washakie during the expedition against the Sioux and Cheyenne indians, under command of General George Crook in the Rosebud Fight (Montana) June 17, 1876. Tigee and Per-ra-go-sha assisted Washakie in protecting Colonel Guy V. Henry, when seriously wounded, after the Rosebud fight

the seventeenth was a close riding companion of the officer, except when the ancient fantastically painted chief was at the front leading his warriors and the allied scouts. "The behavior of the Shoshones and the Crows was excellent. The chief of the Shoshones appeared to great advantage, he himself naked to the waist and wearing one of the gorgeous head-dresses of eagle feathers sweeping far along the ground behind the pony's tail. The Crow chief, Medicine Crow, looked like a devil in his war bonnet of feathers, fur and buffalo horns."

Crook had sallied forth and fought them on June 17, and found them altogether too strong and dexterous, so he retired to Goose creek once more and here he lay on June 25, when Custer was making his attack and meeting his fate only fifty miles away, and not a soul of our command had the slightest idea of what was going on.[97]

Before the Goose creek wagon camp was reached, the Crows took their departure, promising to return in a short time with others of their tribe and unite with the soldiers at the foot of the Big Horn mountains. On July 19, the Crows faithfully returned to the wagon camp, which during the absence of the command on the Rosebud had been turned into a fortress. Three days after the Rosebud battle as the command was returning to Goose creek, Washakie despatched three Shoshones to report the results of the war to the garrison at Fort Washakie. The Shoshones also had asked to be permitted to return to their reservation, leaving with Washakie and most of his warriors for Wind river. The return march was over the mountains directly west of the camp, not by the most direct route. The roughest and least traveled trails were carefully selected and the

[97] King, *Campaigning with Crook*, p. 54.

most inaccessible roads in order to avoid the hunting
parties of the Sioux who went frequently into the mountains to cut lodge poles for their villages and to hunt
game.

On the return journey to the Wind river reservation,
Washakie discovered some Sioux in the mountains. The
scouts avoided the hostiles by following the currents of
the streams, and by crossing and recrossing them by
means of fallen timber. Because of the limited provisions and forage of the army and the short grass range,
the Shoshones, save ten who remained with General
Crook as guides and scouts, returned to the fort, reaching there June 25, the date of the Custer battle. Thus
it seems on that fatal day Washakie and his warriors
were at home for provisions and new mounts, while
Crook's command was stationed at Goose creek, from
which place scouts were scouring the Yellowstone area
for communication with Terry and Gibbon.

An additional object for the return to their villages
of both the Crows and the Shoshones was to display
their enemies' scalps and to engage in a big scalp dance.
To look after the wounded Shoshones, Washakie left
five of his trusted warriors in the wagon camp where
the medicine men, into whose care the wounded had
been placed, won the deep admiration of the soldiers in
the skilled way they performed their medical duties.
The return to the Goose creek camp was made July 4,
when and where no word as yet had been received of
the command under Custer. No word having been received from Terry, Custer or Gibbon, waiting seemed
to be the only thing that could be done. They waited.
While waiting General Crook with a number of officers
climbed the Big Horn mountains "floundering along

in the trail not generally used by the hostile indians," made by the Shoshones on their way home to the reservation. It is asserted that Crook's party was the first of white men to have climbed to the top of this mountain at this place, where far to the west were seen the Wind river mountains, the home of Washakie and his Shoshones.

"We Did Not Drive the Sioux, They Drove Us."

The camp on Goose creek was never for long in one place. It was moved frequently for two reasons; for fresh grass, and to familiarize the soldiers with the art of taking down and putting up tents and the making of camps. This movable camp regulation is one of the reasons why the pioneers of that territory, where Crook's camp on Goose creek was situated, could never definitely locate the wagon camp by the finding of any large amount of discarded and buried relics of an army site. Mule shoes, mashed canteens, nails and parts of blacksmith forges are found over a wide territory – some many miles apart. No one camp remained for a long period at one place, thus leaving camp débris in no one exact site.

That the troops finally moved close to the Big Horn range on the Little Goose creek made it a matter of no difficulty to take daily trips into and upon the mountains where excellent hunting, fine fishing, and great pleasure from mountain climbing were to be had.

Growing tired of waiting for Ute allies from Fort Bridger, Washakie started from Fort Washakie with his own men and two Bannocks, wishing to fulfill his promise of a speedy return to the wagon camp to reinforce General Crook. Washakie brought with him from Fort Washakie two squaw wives of the Shoshones who were wounded on the Rosebud. During the fight of

June 17, Washakie had one of his wives with him, who followed him into battle.

The Shoshones on July 12, commanded by "their grand old chief, Washakie," returned to the wagon camp. Washakie at this time was described as "an indian who greatly resembled the Reverend Robert Collyer." With Washakie were his two sons, the ones who were with him on the Rosebud. "In the camp on Goose creek, July 14, 1876, we find two hundred and twenty Snake indians and half breeds who have joined the expedition, are here. Washakie, their principal, is with them. He is a fine-looking Indian, nearly, if not quite, equal in appearance to Spotted Tail." [98]

Desirous of finding the definite location of the Sioux, a reconnoitering party was dispatched with twenty enlisted men under the command of Lieutenant Sibley of the Second cavalry with Frank Grouard as guide, and John F. Finerty, a volunteer from whose pen comes *War-Path and Bivouac* – a faithful and fascinating narrative of the Crook campaign. To this scouting party Washakie, on July 12, united together with his two hundred and thirteen Shoshones. It is at this time that Captain John G. Bourke stated that Washakie bore a resemblance in face and bearing to "the eminent divine, Henry Ward Beecher."

"It should be understood that Washakie kept in close touch with his tribe on Wind river. There was hardly a day that messengers were not going to and from the scene of hostilities to his reservation. The limited supply of rations of the army, the scant range over which the hostile indians roamed, and the usual

---

[98] Lieutenant Thaddeus Capron, *Diary*. (Ninth United States infantry; served through the Sioux campaign).

drought, held sway, necessitating close communication with his people for supplies and change of horses for his warriors." [99] Chief Washakie also brought from his scant storehouse on the reservation supplies to General Crook for the soldiers and their horses and mules.

A message from General Terry to General Crook was brought into Camp on July 10 – it bore the news of the catastrope that had happened to General Custer and his two hundred and thirteen faithful men on that fateful day of June 25, on the Little Big Horn.

In order to always be at the most complete point of efficiency, Washakie with his scouts exercised every morning and evening as did the army. In order that new recruits might not mistake the Shoshones for hostiles, the chief asked General Crook for a detail to be with him; Captain Bourke being chosen for the position. Therefore, there is to be obtained from his *On the Border with Crook* many intimate touches of the events of this campaign, about Washakie and his warriors, not elsewhere to be obtained. Captain Bourke is most informing as to the devoted care that Washakie took of his warriors, making for efficiency and skill. "In all the glory of war bonnets, bright blankets, scarlet clothing, head-dresses of feathers, and gleaming lances and rifles, the Shoshones mounted on spirited ponies, moving slowly around camp, led by Washakie along side of whom rode a warrior who carried the oriflamme of the tribe, a standard of eagle feathers attached to a lance staff twelve feet in length. Each warrior wore in his head-dress a small piece of white drilling as a distinguishing mark to let our troops know who he was." The tragedy of the white drilling was that the Sioux hear-

[99] Faris, C. E. *Ibid.*

ing of this device craftily placed some white strips in their own headdress that they might be taken as allies. This deception worked very well and, as a result, a company of the Third cavalry was ambushed and a number of them killed and wounded before they could retreat.

"In October of 1876 about one hundred Shoshones again set off for service with Crook, under Washakie, who continued with the army under General Crook or General Mackenzie until the defeat of Dull Knife and the Cheyennes in the Big Horn mountains, in which battle Washakie and his Shoshones gave invaluable service. In the defeat of the Cheyennes, Crazy Horse lost his best support, and it seemed the hand of fate that gave Washakie the leading role in the two engagements which factored most in the defeat of that hostile chief of whom it was often said, 'He was the bravest of the hostile Sioux, had many of their vices and all their virtues too, and always displayed good military ability, which most indian leaders lacked.' "

The remainder of the experiences of Washakie in his association with General Crook in the campaign is briefly told. The old chief, now in his seventy-eighth year, accompanied by his Shoshones went with the command down to the mouth of the Powder and its junction with the Yellowstone river where he and his warriors and the Utes on August 20, commenced a return journey to the Wind river reservation. At this time the allied Crows also took their departure, believing that their young men were now needed in their own country to fight the Sioux and Cheyennes.

Before Washakie took his departure for the Wind river reservation he had several interviews with General Crook in which he plainly told him that his people would not remain longer with Terry's column because of the inefficiency of its transportation; "with such mules nothing could be done, the infantry was all right, and so was part of the cavalry, but the pack train was no good and was simply impeding progress."

On July 24, 1876, Indian Agent Irwin wrote the commissioner of indian affairs at Washington reporting that all of his fighting indians had departed for General Crook's camp on July 5; since that time no report had reached him, though the papers told of their arrival on July 11, on the Goose creek. "Washakie," writes the agent, "is with them and there is no more able man to manage an indian battle. He tells General Crook to hold on, make a connection with General Terry and get all the outside troops he can before he risks another battle or he will be badly whipped, and the old man knows what he is talking about. I am proud of the record my indians made at Goose creek, and promise a still better one in the next battle."

As a recognition of the prominent and efficient part Chief Washakie had taken in the Crook expedition on the Rosebud, President Grant had a wonderful saddle fashioned and sent to the warrior on the reservation. The saddle was mounted with bright silver ornaments, red, blue and yellow colors used in its decoration, such as appealed to an indian.

The presentation was made a public affair in honor of Washakie's services in war. His warriors; the white men; the soldiers, and, by special invitation Black Coal, chief of the Arapahoes with a few of his warriors, were all present. While holding the saddle before its presentation the indian agent explained to Washakie

how the Great Father at Washington appreciated the
many deeds that the chief had performed to help the
white man; how he had saved the lives of many innocent women and children in the early days of the
Oregon trail; that the government recognized what he
had done in trying to educate the Shoshones, and, in
recognition of all of these things and his fearless fighting, particularly in the Crook campaign, the saddle
was now to become his personal property "a gift from
President Grant, who is one of your admirers."

No word was spoken by the old chief who stood
straight and tall, arms folded, tears running down his
cheeks — he was speechless.

"What word shall I sent to the Great Father," asked
the indian agent.

"Nothing," said the war hero, "I cannot speak. My
heart is so full my tongue will not work."

"Do say a few words so that President Grant may
know how pleased you are," urged Agent Irwin.

"When a favor," slowly, and with great emotion,
replied Washakie, "is shown a Frenchman he feels it
in his head and his tongue speaks. When a kindness is
shown to an indian he feels it in his heart, and the heart
has no tongue. I have spoken." [100]

"That is just the reply I wish to have President Grant
to receive," responded Doctor Irwin, "something out
of the ordinary." [101]

On the Shoshone reservation in the early days of
September, 1926, in a personal interview, information
was obtained relative to Chief Washakie's services
given to General Crook during the summer of 1876,

[100] After Chief Washakie's death in 1900, Chief Dick Washakie presented
this saddle to the chief's great friend, James K. Moore, at Fort Washakie.

[101] Morris, *Ibid.*, p. 88, Olden, p. 61, Talbot, p. 37.

Chief Dick Washakie, son of Washakie, offered the following: "My indian name is 'Coo-coosh,' though I am called Chief Washakie, being one of the members of a large family of Chief Washakie, who was my father and chief of the Shoshone tribe for sixty years. I was born on a creek near the town of Meeteetse, Wyoming, in and around the year of 1859 – Shoshone indians do not remember exact dates. As did my father, Chief Washakie, I believed in always being kind to the white people and especially being always loyal to the United States government.

"With my father, at the Rosebud battle, I remember, was only one woman of the Shoshones, that was my step-mother, the wife of Chief Washakie. There is no doubt that she accompanied my father, for I saw her in Crook's command. At this time my father had only one wife.[102]

"Not only was my father glad to go to war to help the whites, but his people were very enthusiastic about giving their assistance, and to give their lives, if necessary, to the white people, as my father had always been loyal to the government, and had always tried to maintain peace among his people. Before my father finally returned home to stay, he went as far with Crook as the Yellowstone river, or the mouth of the Powder river. One reason why my father was so willing to help the white people was because the white people had always been kind and friendly to the Shoshones.

"When my father's warriors, with the Crows, in June, 1876, came over the crest of the Big Horn moun-

---

[102] The belief that Washakie and his warriors were *enlisted* allies to General Crook has occasioned considerable confusion relative to compensation for fighting in "indian wars." Inasmuch as no regular enlistment was perfected at this time the Shoshone warriors' names do not appear on the official records, thus causing misunderstanding among the indians.

tains just before descending to where General Crook's army was, the Shoshones were carrying two beautiful American flags; I was honored in carrying one of them. My brother Conna-yah was a sergeant of the scouts.

"On the morning following our coming to the camp, as it was very late in the evening that we came to the camp of the United States troops, my father and General Crook held council in regard to whether or not they should make immediate attack on the Sioux; thereupon my father dispatched a number of Shoshone scouts to investigate the location and the fighting strength of the Sioux. Upon arriving at the camp of the Sioux and judging their fighting strength, the scouts, on their return, reported this to my father, who on hearing this report advised General Crook that they had better wait for reinforcements to make the attack, as the Sioux and the Cheyennes were combined at that time. My brother, Conna-yah, or Bishop Washakie, was at the head of the scouts on this occasion.

"On June 17, 1876, my father led his warriors down into the Rosebud where they encountered the Sioux.

"You ask, 'Why were not General Crook and Chief Washakie successful on this expedition?' I will say one reason was that they were so overwhelmingly outnumbered by the Sioux and the Cheyenes. If it had not been for the Shoshone and Crow indians who had come to the assistance of Crook, General Crook and his troops would have been wiped out the same as Custer was eight days later, on June 25, 1876. The Shoshones and Crows used the same tactics and methods of warfare as did the Sioux and the Cheyennes, therefore, delaying them, and giving Crook and his troops a chance to retreat, or escape.

"General Crook expressed to my father his indebtedness for the services that the warriors rendered the United States troops. General Crook highly approved what Chief Washakie, my father, and his indians had done for him on this occasion, and it was through the recommendation of General Crook that my father received a pension from the government for the services rendered at this particular instance.

"We returned after this June 17, skirmish. One reason for our coming back to the headwaters of Goose creek was because we had left all of our provisions there. I do not remember exactly but it must have been a month or 'somewhat over' before we finally left Goose creek and returned to Fort Washakie.

"Upon our return to the reservation we had a general war dance. The returning warriors had a number of scalps with them which had formerly been taken in other battles by the Shoshones and were presented at this particular dance.

"The warriors we lost on the Rosebud were buried where they were killed.

"My father, it is true, was quite old at this time, but he was ambitious and foremost in the leading of his warriors in this campaign. He did not take active part in the battle, but he was right at the front, encouraging his men to bravery. General Crook and my father were together during all of the Rosebud fight, though neither one took 'an active part' in the battle, but both were at the front during the entire fight, leading their men or directing them.

"I was in several other skirmishes besides the one on the Powder river, against the Bannocks and the Nez Perces and the Utes. I fought with General Howard,

against Chief Joseph of the Nez Perces. General Howard had but one arm. That was a bad war, they killed
the women and little children and many innocent people. Not only in that war, but we did the same with the
Bannock indians. In one instance, I saw a small child
crawling around the ground on her hands and knees.
I also saw one young woman who was shot in the spine.
All of these wounded and helpless people were left on
the battlefield in that condition."

At the time of this interview, September, 1926, Chief
Dick Washakie wore on his left breast an Indian War
Service medal for service during 1876 and 1877, also
two Custer memorial medals given to him June 25,
1926, at the Crow reservation. Chief Dick Washakie
stated that General Crook had blond whiskers which
naturally parted at the chin. These two parts of his
whiskers were usually in braids and drawn to the right
and left. "My father always called General Crook,
'General Cook.'"

One of the United States army officers at the Custer
semi-centennial celebration, June, 1926, visiting the
locality of the Rosebud fight, asked Chief Dick Washakie, who was locating the battle site, "Where did
General Crook drive the Sioux from here (the Rosebud)?" The chief promptly and with much force replied, *We did not drive the Sioux, but they drove us
back to the Tongue river in Wyoming.* The chief further stated that after his father had seen the camp of the
Sioux he reported to Crook, "There are too many Sioux
for 'Cook' and Washakie to fight."

From Mr. Fin G. Burnett, associated with the Shoshone agency from its early beginning in 1871 as the
farmer teacher until 1924, – however, not continuously

but with few intervals of absence – comes the statement that he certifies to all of the testimony given by Chief Dick Washakie, having been at the reservation during the entire period of the Shoshones fighting of 1876 and 1877 and afterward. He was at the reservation when the scouts returned with Washakie from the Rosebud and witnessed the scalp dance at the reservation. Mr. Burnett, how living at Fort Washakie, almost daily saw and conversed with Chief Washakie, consulting with him and teaching him how to profitably farm and to utilize water by the process of irrigation, makes the following statements:

"If the Sioux had had a leader like Washakie, the soldiers would have been annihilated in detail, as they were scattered in small divisions, thinking that the Sioux were trying to get away from them. The soldiers flanked around to try to keep hidden while the Sioux were leaving a broad trail for the soldiers to follow, fearing that they would not find them. If the Sioux were trying to get away, they would have scattered or fanned out over the country, a meeting place having been appointed before. It would have been like throwing his men into the grave for General Crook to have followed up the Rosebud fight.

"Washakie always had a great admiration for General Crook's bravery and generalship, as he also had for Captain Guy V. Henry. Washakie and his Shoshones fought for the rescue of Henry, after he was wounded and had fallen from his horse, and thus saved the officer from being mutilated and massacred. After Captain Henry was wounded, Washakie and his Shoshones held the Sioux back until Crook could reorganize.

"After the Shoshones came back to Fort Washakie, they were filled with the war they had had to defend Crook. Before going, in early June, Washakie and his men met at the agency and paraded in all of their war paraphernalia. All was glorified. Each man displayed his war bonnet, shield, revolver, lance and rifle. The indians were always better equipped than the white soldiers. The Shoshones and Pawnees were the only indians who stood up and fought like white men.

"Washakie's first wife, an old woman, would frequently go with him into battle, although not fighting. She would follow him, and if in a rush he would leave any paraphernalia behind him, she would gather it up and hasten after him with it. When Washakie came back from the Rosebud fight, he and his Shoshones had scalps, horses and war trophies that they had taken from the Sioux, and they celebrated in war dances for weeks afterward, just above the agency on Trout creek.

"Nelson Yarnell was a fearless scout and a great friend of Washakie's and a particular friend of mine. I have listened to Washakie and Yarnell talk of the 'Cook' war, as Washakie called it. Washakie would never boast, as is characteristic of most indians, but Yarnell would tell of Washakie's brave deeds while Washakie would tell of some great or ridiculous thing that Yarnell had done. One day when we were all in the store at Fort Washakie, 'Old Bill,' a noted scout and a great friend of Washakie, rode up and fell off of his horse dead drunk. We carried him into the store and laid him on the floor. Washakie looked at him and shook his head and said, 'Bill is a Big Chief.' Then turning to Captain Mix said, 'You are a Big Chief and

I am a Big Chief, but whiskey is the biggest chief of all.'

"Officers and our government may give great credit to the allies in the Crook campaign, but no written record can ever give the credit due the noble Washakie for his personal and tribal risks, sacrifices and efforts, and for his superior military judgment and leadership against the hostile people of his race." [103]

[103] To the testimony of Finerty, Burnett, Grouard and Dick Washakie, recorded in the preceding chapter relative to Washakie's generalship in the Rosebud fight, might well be added that of Oliver Hanna, *Letter* of October 3, 1927. "About June 14 or 15, Washakie with other Shoshone indian scouts came to our camp on the Tongue river and on June 17 joined us in the battle of the Rosebud."

Letter of October, 1926, W. P. Miles, a member of the pack train – "Yes, old Chief Washakie was there and made his presence felt by wise counsel and strategic action."

Interviews, September, 1926, Captain H. G. Nickerson, of Fort Washakie, who perhaps knew Washakie and his people in an intelligent way better than any white man, recited information that had been received shortly after the Crook engagement; the methods of war employed by Washakie on the Rosebud is as told to him by the old chief.

Washakie and the Arapahoes

For one who continually advocated peace, Chief Washakie did an abundance of fighting; he enjoyed a peace that was determined to be obtained at the price of continual warfare. Had the Shoshone tribe been more numerous, Washakie would not have been obliged perpetually to fight – the mere size of this fighting army in itself was one of the potent causes for strife, in which the chief recognized valuable allies in the soldiers of the United States army.

The "Sand creek massacre" (Colorado)[104] of 1864, left the Arapahoe indians, as well as the Cheyennes of that district, without a home. Enraged with our government the two tribes sent a pipe of peace to the Sioux and Northern Arapahoes inviting them to enter into a joint war to exterminate the white man from the plains. Forming this proposed triple alliance the tribes joined forces in committing depredations along the Platte and over the Oregon trail for a distance of two hundred miles. The first point of attack was Julesburg (Colorado) on the Overland route. Before December had ended that year all of the roads along the trails to the west became infested with fighting indians to such an extent that passage became blocked; the wagon trains could not carry their freight; telegraph lines were down and the stations along the road were burned or had fallen into the possession of the red man.[105]

---

[104] Coutant, vol. I, p. 418: Perkins, chap. xii.

[105] Grinnell, *Ibid.*, chap. xvi: *Two Great Scouts*, chap. xi. Hebard and Brininstool, vol. I, p. 130; Perkins, chap. xi.

To terminate these outbreaks and depredations, particularly west of South pass, Chief Washakie and his warriors used every effort in their power to establish law and order, acting under the direction and advice of our government. The Arapahoes at this time and for years immediately following, joined with their allies, waging war in Washakie's hunting grounds in the Bridger valley and the Sweetwater country.

Following the Sand creek battle, the indians of the tribe of the Arapahoes under Chief Left Hand moved from Colorado into the north, making their homes wherever the allies would extend their hospitality and make a home for them. In 1872, the Arapahoes were assigned to the Shoshone reservation where they stayed but for a short time, returning east to the Pine ridge agency. Here they made their home for a few years until the winter of the years of 1877 and 1878 when they were again located by the government on the Wind river reservation, again as "guests" and where they have since been enjoying the hospitality of Washakie's band for a period of half a century.

During the month of October, 1877, the indian agent for the Shoshones, Doctor James Irwin, under direction of the United States Indian Department obtained the reluctant consent of Chief Washakie to have this northern band of Arapahoes placed on the Wind river reservation for the winter of 1877-1878. "The Arapahoes were conveyed to the Wind river reservation by a military escort in the fall of 1877 and have been there ever since and are today."

Washakie did not at that time in council assembled, nor at any other time consent to the Arapahoes being located permanently and perpetually upon his reservation. As a matter of record no portion of the reservation has ever been ceded to the Arapahoes by an indirect treaty or a direct agreement.

Old Chief Washakie is reported to have asked, "When are they going to move the Arapahoes? They asked consent to allow the Arapahoes to stay on the reservation until a place could be found for them. They were asked to be allowed to stay but a short time on the reservation. I never would have consented to the Arapahoes being permitted to settle on my reservation had I known that the government intended to keep them there. I did not understand that the treaty said that any other tribe of indians could be put on the reservation," referring to the Great Treaty of July 3, 1868. Continuing, the chief said, "The Arapahoes occupy the best agricultural part of the Shoshone reservation. The Shoshones, however, want to be near the mountains so as to better hunt game. The Shoshones were and are more of a hunting tribe than an agricultural tribe." The claims which the Shoshones made for their reservation are on file in the Department of Claims at Washington.

In 1926, in an interview, Mr. Farlow, pioneer of Lander which adjoins the Shoshone reservation, stated:

The Arapahoes had given up all of their rights of their home and independence and were placed on the Shoshone reservation, to live with the Shoshones who had always been their enemies. The Arapahoes did not want to be put there. The Shoshones did not want the Arapahoes. The whole thing was a most unfortunate affair and a poor settlement of the difficulty. The Arapahoes are still on the Shoshone reservation and still undesired by the Shoshone indians. The two tribes have nothing in common. There is no intermarrying of one member of one tribe with a member of another tribe. Just as hard existence for the Arapahoes as for the Shoshones.[106]

[106] Farlow, Mayor E. J., of Lander, Wyoming, *Personal interview*, September, 1926.

In April, 1878, Agent Patten again reported to the commissioner of indian affairs at Washington, stating:

I do not believe that much difficulty will be experienced in settling this tribe (Arapahoes) on this reservation. It is known to be the desire of the government to have this accomplished. The Shoshones although they are opposed to it, and look upon it as an encroachment of their rights, yet will make no great objections to the settlement of the former tribe upon their land, knowing that it is the wish of the Great Father to bring several small tribes of indians together upon the same reservation. Washakie and the head men, though they dislike bitterly to divide their property with other bands, have too great hearts to say *no*. But my sense of right and justice is that if other tribes are brought upon the Shoshone land, that it should be with the full consent of the tribe owning the land by right of their treaty, and that such indians should receive reasonable compensation for diminishment of their reservation. I would, therefore, earnestly ask that the Shoshones be allowed a just sum for the relinquishment of a certain tract of land within the limits of their reservation to the Northern Arapahoes.[107]

Exactly what Agent Patten earnestly recommended fifty years ago is what the Shoshones are contending for at this time, – a compensation for the use of their lands for "about" fifty years, without permission and without rent "or other valuable considerations." Messages of dissatisfaction in 1878 were carried to the governor of the territory of Wyoming, John W. Hoyt, asking him if there were no way by which the Arapahoes might be placed on a reservation of their own. The request seemed urgent enough for a personal interview with Chief Washakie and Black Coal, chief of the Arapahoes. Responding to the appeal, Governor Hoyt in a few days by train, stage, wagon and horse, arrived at the Wind river agency to visit Camp Brown on the

[107] Patten, James I. *Report*, April 8, 1878, to Commissioner of Indian Affairs, E. A. Hayt.

Little Wind river and some ten miles within the boundary of the reservation.

I gave notice to Washakie, chief of the Shoshones, that I would visit him at this time at his lodge, sending also word to Black Coal of the Arapahoes that I would visit his lodge on the same day that I counciled with Washakie. Going to Washakie's lodge I found him at work among his crops. The chief expressed great pleasure in this opportunity thus afforded him of speaking freely to me whose visit gave evidence of an interest in them, and assured me that he would be careful to make no complaint not fully warranted by the necessities of his people and the failure of the government, or its agents, to meet their just expectations.

Washakie presented his protest in a forcible and eloquent manner affirming that his people were without a sufficiency of meat, because he had to divide with the Arapahoes; they were without flour, and compelled to eat cornmeal which they did not like; they did not possess a proper supply of agricultural implements; they had no competent person to instruct them in the cultivation of the soil; they were at times compelled to work for the agent, as in hauling logs to the mill, without reward; and that they had been for some time without a school for their children; all contrary to the provisions of the treaty of 1868 made at Fort Bridger. Washakie also complained that the white man though forbidden to do so, trespassed upon his territory in search for game and for the grazing of his cattle.

One of the reports prepared by Governor Hoyt gives a graphic description of the gracious reception accorded him upon meeting the great chief of the Shoshones:

I was cordially received by Chief Washakie and thirty of his chief men, all rising, and with smiles and words of welcome in concert, which I could not quite, and yet did sufficiently, understand.

It was, of course, an instinctive politeness (for they had never been taught court etiquette) which prompted the chief, as he took my hand with a cordial grasp and with words of welcome, to waive me, in courtly fashion, an introduction to the full circle of sub-chiefs, still standing around the rim of the tepee, and then to lead me to my place of address, on an immense bear skin at the centre.

I would give anything for a picture of that scene — the majestic old Washakie, seated, after the reception and introduction, upon what would have passed for a modest throne, covered with the skins of the panther, bear and mountain-lion; his form as stately as that of Daniel Webster, and yet broader, his face wearing both the dignity and the benignity of Washington, his grey locks hanging in profusion far down his shoulders, and the thirty superior men of the tribe, with earnest faces, to the right and left, and in front of him. . .

The chief, rising slowly, then delivered himself of a speech as remarkable for its power and pathos as any ever heard.

"We are right glad, sir," he said, "that you have so bravely and kindly come among us. I shall, indeed, speak to you freely of the many wrongs we have suffered at the hands of the white man. They are things to be noted and remembered. But I cannot hope to express to you the half that is in our hearts. They are too full for words.

"Disappointment; then a deep sadness; then a grief inexpressible; then, at times, a bitterness that makes us think of the rifle, the knife and the tomahawk, and kindles in our hearts the fires of desperation — that, sir, is the story of our experience, of our wretched lives.

"The white man, who possesses this whole vast country from sea to sea, who roams over it at pleasure, and lives where he likes, cannot know the cramp we feel in this little spot, with the undying remembrance of the fact, which you know as well as we, that every foot of what you proudly call America, not very long ago belonged to the red man. The Great Spirit gave it to us. There was room enough for all his many tribes, and all were happy in their freedom. But the white man had, in ways we know not of, learned some things we had not learned; among them, how to make superior tools and terrible weapons, better for war than bows and arrows; and there seemed no end to the hordes of men that followed them from other lands beyond the sea.

"And so, at last, our fathers were steadily driven out, or killed, and we, their sons, but sorry remnants of tribes once mighty, are cornered in little spots of the earth all ours of right — cornered like guilty prisoners, and watched by men with guns, who are more than anxious to kill us off.

"Nor is this all. The white man's government promised that if we, the Shoshones, would be content with the little patch allowed us, it would keep us well supplied with everything necessary to comfortable living, and would see that no white man should cross our borders for our game, or for anything that is ours. *But it has not kept its word!* The white man kills our game, captures our furs, and sometimes feeds his herds upon our meadows. And your great and mighty government – Oh sir, I hesitate, for I cannot tell the half! It does not protect us in our rights. It leaves us without the promised seed, without tools for cultivating the land, without implements for harvesting our crops, without breeding animals better than ours, without the food we still lack, after all we can do, without the many comforts we cannot produce, without the schools we so much need for our children.

"I say again, *the government does not keep its word!* And so, after all we can get by cultivating the land, and by hunting and fishing, we are sometimes nearly starved, and go half naked, as you see us!

"Knowing all this, do you wonder, sir, that we have fits of desperation and think to be avenged?"

While I listened to this sad and eloquent recital, made doubly impressive by Washakie's expression of face, the quivering of his lip, and gestures most fitting and emphatic, I was so deeply moved that tears filled my eyes, and my response was for a moment tremulous. Suffice it to say that, when I had concluded, with expressions of earnest sympathy and of my purpose to report everything he said to the Great Father at Washington and myself to see that justice should be done them in the future, the noble chief came and took me warmly by the hand, and, with steady look into my eyes and soul said, "We believe you!" Whereupon the cry of "How!" "How!" rang in glad notes the whole circle 'round, as though a great victory had been won. . .

Arriving at the agency, I took a hasty lunch, mounted the horse by which I had gone to the reservation, and as soon as possible reached the railway, where I telegraphed to the Secretary of the Interior the state of the case – that peace had been made, and the hand of the red man very surely stayed, if the government would at once send assurances of good will and promptly follow them with actual supplies.

It is my pleasure to add that such assurances went by wire and mail to the agent, without delay, and that relief was granted as soon as possible – car-loads of the food supplies, clothing, implements, and all else that was needed; also the desired provision for the instruction of the children, and that a new happiness was by these same means conferred upon two to three thousand of the most deserving of the nation's wards.[108]

In concluding one of his reports Governor Hoyt stated, "It is important to Wyoming that these tribes should be kept upon their reservation, as the white people are detained from settling up the country so long as indian bands are known to be roving over the best of it. But it is very certain that they cannot be kept there unless reasonably supplied with the necessities of life." [109]

The Arapahoes look down on the Shoshones as do the Shoshones on the Arapahoes, each with tribal pride and prejudice. The two tribes very seldom intermarry, though it is true that one of Washakie's sons married an Arapahoe – each nation, thereby, feeling disgraced by the union.

With the coming of the year of 1880 are to be found a number of discontented Shoshones leaving the reservation on account of their Arapahoe "guests" and going to Salt Lake City – slipping away from the authority of Washakie. The chief explained that this departure was due to the fact that his warriors had gone to Utah to become Mormons, that they "have gone to Salt Lake to get washed" – baptized.

[108] Published through the courtesy of Kepler Hoyt, son of Wyoming's third Territorial Governor, John W. Hoyt, who became, in 1887, the first president of the University of Wyoming.

[109] Hoyt, Governor John W., *Letter* written at Cheyenne, Wyoming, July 17, 1878, to Carl Schurz, Secretary of the Interior.

The Old Chief Signs His Last Treaty

When the first white man placed his foot upon the shores of this continent, it was predestined that he should come into the inheritance of the indian.[110]

With the closing of the nineteenth century every evidence indicated that Chief Washakie was nearing the end of a long, eventful, as well as useful, career. When the treaty of April 21, 1896, was signed by the venerable chief, there was found his last "his X mark." This treaty transferred to the government the Big Horn

---

[110] McLaughlin, *Ibid.*, p. 260.

[111] De Smet, *Ibid.*, vol. 2, p. 675; Kappler, *Ibid.*, vol. 2, p. 594: Lowe.

[112] Young, Brigham, *Report* Superintendent of Indian Affairs, September 28, 1852.

[113] *Laws and Treaties, Ibid.*, vol. 2, p. 848.

[114] *Laws and Treaties, Ibid.*, vol. 2, p. 1020.

[115] *Laws and Treaties, Ibid.*, vol. 1, p. 153.

[116] *Laws and Treaties, Ibid.*, vol. 1, p. 624.

[117] United States Statutes at Large, vol. 33, pp. 1016-1022.

hot springs, the medicinal properties of which were
beginning to attract very wide and favorable attention.
Washakie and his people had used these hot spring
baths to cure their numerous ills for a great number of
years.

The land thus relinquished embraced the Big Horn
hot springs, about 64,000 acres, being a portion of the
original reservation presided over by Chief Washakie.

A portion of this land, equal to one square mile was
subsequently conveyed to the state of Wyoming, being
known as the Big Horn hot springs state reserve, at
present controlled and managed by the state board of
charities and reform of Wyoming.[118] The subject of
free baths as requested by chief Washakie does not appear in the April 21, 1896 agreement, though a Wyoming law has since been made to meet Washakie's
wishes that "the indians should have free use of the
springs." The free baths intended particularly for indians reads: "It shall be the duty of said board to retain
one-fourth of the water in the main or principal spring
of said state land on the eastern bank of said river with
a sufficient quantity of said state land adjacent thereto,
upon which suitable bath houses may be constructed
which shall be open and free to the use of the public and
to set apart as a suitable location a portion of said lands
for free public camping purposes."

The last transfer treaty, which was finally concluded
in April, 1904, four years after the death of Washakie,
made between our government and the Shoshone and
Arapahoe tribes and negotiated through Indian In-
spector James McLaughlin, ceded to the United States

---

[118] Wyoming Compiled Statutes, sect. 593, 601, – 1910: Session Laws, 1921,
chap. 25. Session Laws of 1929 changed name to Hot Springs State Park.

that portion of the Wind river reservation lying north of the Big Wind river embracing an area of 1,346,320 acres.

When Washakie's last treaty agreement of 1896 was signed, there appeared upon the document but two of the names that were signed to the first governmental treaty in which Washakie was interested. These were Washakie, then ninety-eight years old, and Norkuk. Eleven Shoshones signed the documents in 1863. In the treaty of 1868, signed by fourteen Shoshones and Bannock indians, headed by Washakie, followed by his sub-chief "Norku," "Bazeel," "Taggee," and others, there were only eight who had signed the 1863 treaty. The treaty signed in 1872, on which appeared one hundred and nineteen names for the Shoshones included five names of those who had signed both of the treaties of 1863, and 1868 – Washakie, Norkuk, Bazeel, as head men; that of Ko-na-ya, one of Washakie's sons, and Wanny-pitz. With the treaty agreement of 1896 appear for the last time the names of Chief Washakie and Norkuk. On this document were the names of two hundred and seventy-eight Shoshones and Arapahoes. Bazil, being "about" the age of Washakie, had died on the reservation in 1886. The names of four of Washakie's sons, Dick, Charles, Bishop and George, appear on the document – the name Bishop doubtless being that of a grandson, the original Bishop who fought with Washakie in the Crook campaign of 1876 had died in 1880. The son of "Bazeel," Andrew Bazil, grandson of Sacajawea, and another of her grandsons, John Baptiste, are signers of this agreement. Doubtless there are others of her family and that of Washakie's who appear under other names.

The two outstanding and interesting features of the signing of the 1904 agreement are the facts that of the two hundred and seventy-three signers, each one possessed a double name, family and given. These names were obtained or given the indians through the inauguration of a system of giving to all indians two names for identification. This system was started by Indian Agent Herman G. Nickerson, who served in the capacity of agent from 1898 to 1902. The additional informing observation is made that forty-nine of the indians personally signed their double names in writing rather than with their "marks." The "His X Mark," system of signature has been abandoned on this reservation, being substituted by "His Thumb Mark;" all indians who cannot write, are required to use the thumb or finger marking even in signing checks.

With thirty-one direct descendants of Chief Washakie on the Shoshone reservation there seems to be reason to believe that for all time to come whenever there are to be relinquishments of their land or other agreements requiring the "signatures of a majority of male indians over eighteen years of age," that not only will there be found the name of "Washakie" with a given name, but that the entire list of signatures to the documents will be in the indians' own handwriting.

The last agreement to which the Shoshones have severally attached their names was on April 21, 1904, when all of the land north of the Wind river on the reservation was ceded back to the United States. To this 1904 agreement there is for the first time since the Shoshones established themselves in the Bridger valley no signature by Chief Washakie, no agreement by "His X Mark," the veteran chief having died in February, 1900, in his cabin on his beloved reservation.

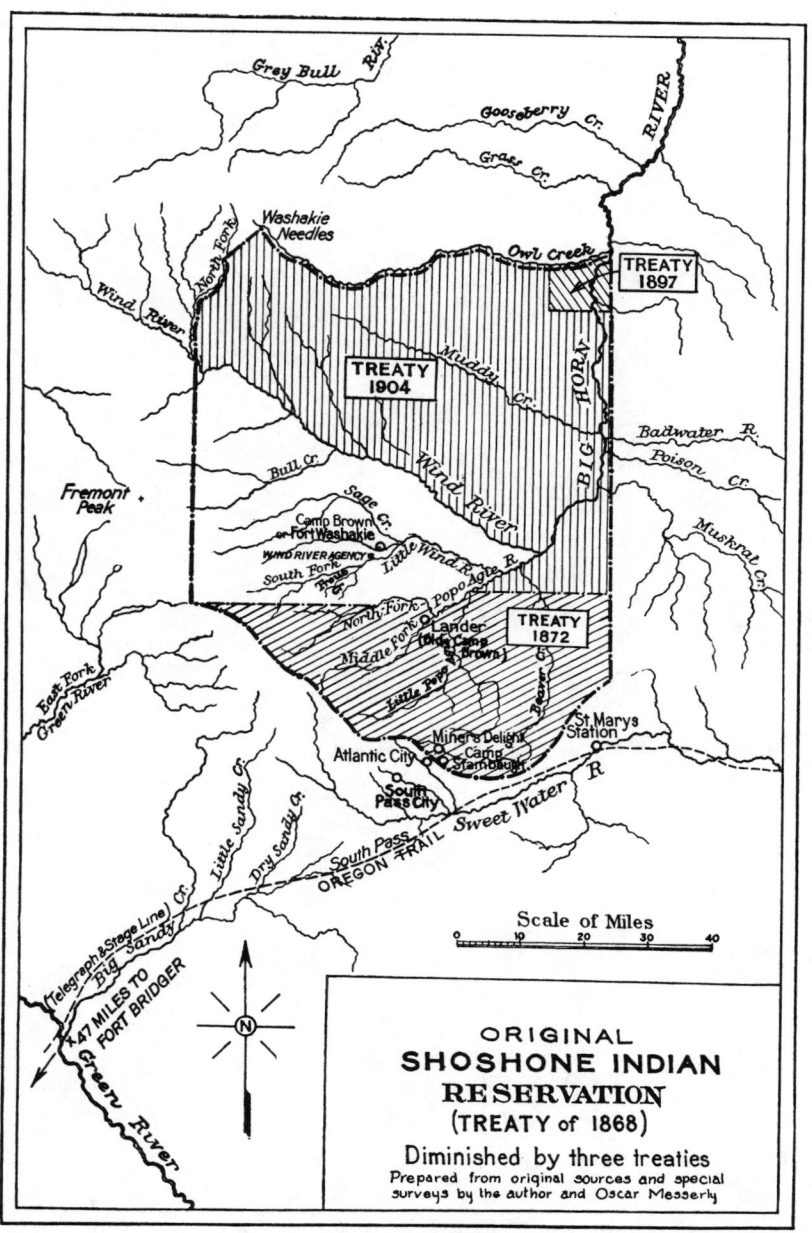

Scale of Miles

ORIGINAL
**SHOSHONE INDIAN
RESERVATION**
(TREATY of 1868)

Diminished by three treaties
Prepared from original sources and special
surveys by the author and Oscar Messerly

Copyright by The Arthur H. Clark Company, 1930

SUMMARY OF ACREAGE IN THE SHOSHONE RESERVATION AND
RELINQUISHMENTS

Original treaty, July 3, 1868, contained approximately	2,784,400 acres
Relinquished by agreement, Sept. 26, 1872	601,120 acres
Relinquished by agreement, April 21, 1896	64,000 acres
Relinquished by agreement, April 21, 1904	1,346,320 acres
Area alloted and reserved	248,000 acres
Diminished Reservation in 1929	524,960 acres
Total area	2,784,400 acres

The ceded land of 1904 was mainly given to the government for the purpose of opening unused lands of the reservation for homestead entry, and for sale under the general homestead and mineral land laws. In this ceded area of a million and a half acres, many of the buffalo chases and animal hunts were pursued by Chief Washakie and his braves.

Almost thirty-five miles directly northwest of the present day northern and western extremity of the Wind river reservation is a continental divide pass called "Two Gwo Tee" (Lance Striker) named by Captain William A. Jones, Corps of Engineers, U. S. A., when surveying "for a good route from the south, the Union Pacific railroad near South pass via the Wind river valley and Upper Yellowstone into Montana." [119]

Captain Jones had with him on this survey acting as scouts and guides a number of Shoshone indians obtained from Chief Washakie at Camp Augur and Fort Bridger; among the warriors was Chief Togwotee who was familiar with this opening into the mountains through which trails led to hunting grounds further to the west. Annually over these mountain trails the Shoshones made their journeys to the Snake and Teton

[119] Jones, *Ibid.*, 1873, the pass was named September 6, 1873, spelled "Togwotee," located in township 42 north, range 110 west.

valleys on their way to Fort Hall and the lodges of the
Bannock and Lemhi indians. In naming the Two Gwo
Tee gateway, Engineer Jones stated that he "preferred
to attach indian names, whenever possible, to the prominent features of the country." From Camp Augur
(Lander) to Two Gwo Tee pass, which the surveyor
also called "The pass to Wind river," the distance is one
hundred and fifteen miles.

The Yellowstone, Snake and Wind rivers have their
origins on the sides of the mountains of this pass. Their
beginnings are from the springs and small streams of
melting snow, the elevation of the pass being just short
of 10,000 feet – 9658 feet as given by Captain Jones.
The Snake river feeds the waters of the Pacific ocean;
the Yellowstone flows into the Missouri; and the Wind
river empties into the Big Horn, which mingles its
waters with the Yellowstone and it in turn empties into
the Missouri, the Missouri flows into the Mississippi,
which river mingles its waters with the Gulf of Mexico, which feeds the waters to the Atlantic. The continent is thus spanned with the melted snows of the continental divide in Two Gwo Tee pass. This Two Gwo
Tee pass was a favorite trail utilized by Washakie and
his Shoshones, being not only a very direct route across
the mountains, but one of unusually easy passage; the
wisdom of its selection by this sagacious chief being
well illustrated by our present day usage of it as a gateway to the Yellowstone park through which a main
automobile highway has its road. The pass is itself a
wonderful mountain park in view of the never melting
snow capping Teton mountains, and amidst the Brook
Lake mountains.

On Sunday, August 21, 1921, Two Gwo Tee pass

became a national highway when the road to the Yellowstone was formally dedicated and opened by Wyoming's officials and the indians, Chief Dick Washakie speaking for the Shoshones, and Chief Yellow Calf on behalf of the Arapahoes. In indian array and war bonnet, Chief Washakie related to the assembly his experiences at the time when he acted as a guide for General Sherman through this pass to the National Park, and again when he served in the same capacity for President Chester Arthur and his presidential party. Chief Dick Washakie "in very brief part" made through an interpreter the following remarks: "In my early manhood many years ago I escorted some of your people, the white people, through this very pass, and at that time I felt a great honor in doing it. Remember, my friends, prior to this time, my people hunted and roamed free from one hunting ground to another without even being molested by your people. But since I escorted the Great White Father and all his officials from Washington many years ago, through this very pass, my heart has grown sad. I have been told by your people that I must cease hunting. If I continue to hunt as I have in the past, I shall be put in jail. My people now at this time are hemmed in a small corral called a reservation and prohibited at almost every turn. My good heart feels sad if this may be the appreciation which my white brothers have bestowed upon my people. Upon the departure of the great government officials from Washington and my friends, they said, 'Mr. Washakie, we thank you for what you have done for us,' and I said, 'You are welcome.' "

The Intimate History of Washakie

The versatile Washakie did not confine his talents to the art of chieftainship and battling with the white man against renegades and hostile red men. From his gift as a musician he, early in his eventful career, earned the name "Rattle Box," or, "Gamblers Gourd." From his son, Chief Dick Washakie, is derived the information that, "My father, Chief Washakie, was a great singer. He had a very fine voice, singing tenor. When my father sang, he usually used a gourd with several small rattles inside of it as a musical instrument while singing." [120]

"My father," continued his son, "was an arrow-fashioner and bow-maker; he made his own bows and arrows, which he used when he was hunting in the earlier days of his chase and hunting – this being before firearms were generally available to the indians. These bows were made of elk's horn, covered on the back with sinew, and pitch gathered from the pine trees. Yet at times he used both firearms and the bow with arrows. Chief Washakie's first gun was a flint lock; in later years my father used a United States needle gun. After my father died I gave Chief Washakie's guns to J. K. Moore, a licensed indian trader at Fort Washakie. Mr. Moore was a great friend of my father who always called him "Jakie" – his name being James K. I also

---

[120] *Interview*, 1926. Dick Washakie generally spoke of his father as "Chief Washakie," or "My father, Chief Washakie," always in tones of great reverence.

gave to Mr. Moore the wonderful saddle that General
Grant, the President of the United States, gave to Chief
Washakie after he had served in the war of 1876."

Numerous elk skins have been artistically decorated
by Washakie to depict his hunts, buffalo chase and
battle – some of the painted history being in black paint,
many in bright red, yellow, greens and other colors;
these histories, when translated into words reveal interesting details of battles and hunts made by the sons'
illustrious father. This form of choice artistic ability
is also displayed by his two sons, Dick and Charlie.

During the world war the indians of the United
States generously and willingly gave of their services,
there being enlisted 10,000 in the army and 2,000 in the
navy. Some of these indians made a most commendable
record, receiving the Croix de Guerre for brilliant
achievements, as well as buying over $25,900,000 worth
of Liberty bonds; and in whatever they did, either in
service or bond buying, there was always exhibited a
spirit of great loyalty to our government.

From the Wind river reservation, fourteen Shoshone
indians served in the great war, one of whom, Chief
Washakie's grandson, John Washakie, enlisted at Camp
Lewis, Washington. While in training, he died on May
13, 1918. Five of these soldier Shoshones did overseas
service, one of whom saw service in Siberia and one in
the United States army in the Philippine islands. Added
loyalty is shown by the fact that the Shoshones over-
subscribed their quota on the reservation for the third
loan. Of any mention of their services they are extremely modest, though they are pardonably proud of
the fact that the service which the Shoshones rendered
to their country was of such high character as to war-

DICK AND CHARLIE WASHAKIE

Sons of Chief Washakie. Dick's mother was a Shoshone,
and Charlie a son of a Crow. Reproduced from original
photograph taken in 1925

CHIEF DICK WASHAKIE

"In the costume of my forefathers." In front of his
tepee. Reproduced from original photograph taken
in 1927 on the Shoshone indian reservation

rant commendatory recognition from the Chief of the United States army, the President. From the original certificate sent to these World war Shoshones, the following is copied:

THE UNITED STATES OF AMERICA

To all to whom these presents shall come, Greetings.

The thanks of the nation is extended through the president, Commander-in-chief of the army and navy of the United States, to the people of the Shoshone tribe for their unswerving loyalty and patriotism, the splendid service rendered, the willing sacrifices made and the bravery of their sons in the military and naval service of the United States when the nation was in peril during the World war of 1917 and 1918. Signed by the President,

CALVIN COOLIDGE

John, son of George Washakie, is buried in the Shoshone indian cemetery near Wind river, his grave marked by an American Legion marker and a marble headstone. His grave is near that of Chief Bazil, one of Chief Washakie's headmen for many years. Due to the efforts of Reverend John Roberts this indian cemetery presents a very modern appearance to what it did twenty years ago when there was but a single stone grave marker. The graves then were marked in the primitive indian manner with lances, decorated with bright pieces of cloth; with bedsteads, some wooden, some brass and some iron; with wagons, minus the boxes; and various property of the dead brave that were highly valued during his days of life on the reservation.

Chief Washakie, if living, would have taken exceptional pride in the war achievements of his direct family and the several offsprings of his Shoshones, they having done what he himself always endeavored to carry out — to give to his Great Father the first and foremost service.

At a War Mothers' convention held during the month of July, 1926, Chief Dick Washakie made with great composure a patriotic address, which carried a great message, a speech filled with affective earnestness, delivered in his native tongue with frequent injections of the sign language of his tribe. Mr. James E. Compton, official interpreter for the Shoshone indians, translates Chief Washakie's remarks as follows:

"Ladies and Gentlemen: It is with deep feeling of inspiration that I appear before you adorned in the costume of my forefathers of many years ago, which at this time is fast becoming extinct. I am highly elated to receive the honor and pleasure of being present here this evening to express my feelings in behalf of my people, the red men, the vanishing race.

"Through the mountains and forests the trails of my forefathers stretched in those earlier days gone by. They knew the songs of every bird and all of the woodland lore. The moccasins that they wore on their feet were silent and swift, and often times carried them for many miles away, for my people, the red men, once owned the whole of this land. But as time went by the white man came and a welcome was found from the chiefs, stately and proud, the pipe of peace was solemnly smoked and friendship solemnly vowed. To the memory of that vow of those gone by days I can proudly state that the loyalty and unswerving patriotism of my people, especially the Shoshones, have undoubtedly proven this.

"My friends and ladies of the War Mothers, as I understand this meeting tonight is held under the name of 'War Mothers Union,' whose sons and daughters served in the World War, my friends, I wish to impress upon the minds of your people and my people that there is nothing that we can do that is more loyal to our country in time of need than to give that which we cherish so sacredly as our sons and daughters.

"I am proud to state that my people, the red men, rallied to the call of our country during the World War in the form of contributions for Liberty bonds and willingly gave their young braves, the flower and pride of my people. I am proud to state that among this number there was a Washakie, a nephew of mine, the pride of all of his people, who gave his young life for the love of his country, your country and my country, that freedom and liberty might live.

"With the fervent hope that God our Father above shows no partiality as to color or race, for the difference lies only in the outward appearance, but sends his blessing down on all mankind equally alike, I have finished."

Born of a Crow mother, a trophy of the Crow Heart butte fight, Charles Washakie, "Wo-ba-ah" in 1873 first saw day near the mountain where Chief Washakie obtained his wife, the mother of this son.

Chief Dick Washakie, half brother of the Crow son, presents a short biography of his younger brother, who is more of a typical Crow in stature than is the present chief who inherits the shorter and more stocky physical frame from his mother, a full Shoshone woman. Chief Washakie says: "The disposition of Charlie has been since childhood of a quiet and even temperament. The mother of Wo-ba-ah is "Ah-ah-Why-per-sie," meaning "Crow Indian Woman," came to the Shoshone indians somewhat mysteriously. Back in the earlier years, a war party of Crow indians from Montana came down from the North into the Shoshone country on one of their migratory war expeditions, customary to the indians for many years past.

"It seems that several of the Crow warriors had their families along with them on this occasion. It was during this battle which took place, the Crows being overwhelmingly defeated, that many of the Crows were killed and several were taken as prisoners of war. "Ahah-Why-per-sie" was one of those Crows who was taken prisoner, being a beautiful young girl of perhaps ten or twelve years. Naturally she was kept as a trophy of war. From the time of her capture until her death at which time she was about seventy-three years of age, she lived with the Shoshones.

"My father, Chief Washakie, married this Crow girl about 1872, or six years after the death of his Shoshone wife, my mother. Charlie has had a fair education, attending the government boarding school until he was nineteen years of age. Mention has been made of Bishop Washakie, son of the chief, who was with General Crook in 1876 on the Rosebud. Shortly after the return of the Shoshone scouts, the chief and his two sons, to their beloved warm valley, this young warrior died, in 1880."

When the Bannocks were on one of their periodical outbreaks at one time in the Jackson Hole country, directly south of the Yellowstone National Park, Chief Washakie, being asked the cause of the uprising characteristically replied: "Heretofore indians break out. This time white man break out." This was true, the trouble being with the white man. The chief's son, George, was suspected of being a keen sympathizer with the indians against the whites, asserting to his aged father that the whites were treating the indians unjustly and that the white man was in the habit of misusing the indians who always had to submit and that he intended to join the indians on the war-path against the whites. To this pronouncement, Chief Washakie said, "My son, with twenty-five other chiefs, I signed the Great Treaty to keep the peace with the Great Father and his children. I, alone, of the whole number who signed it, have kept my word, and now, rather than see you take up arms against the white man, I will strike you dead at my feet." The son, well knowing that his father would do just that in an extreme necessity, remained on his father's side.

As a father, Chief Washakie was very devoted to his children, who were twelve; he was careful in their training, exacting of them absolute loyalty, and was ever insistent upon their keeping faith with the white people and the government.

Many of the pictures taken of Chief Washakie were photographs taken in Evanston by the pioneer and skilled photographer, Charles Baker, particular mention being made of the one where the chief is in war bonnet, checkered calico shirt and jeans, holding a pipe of peace in his left hand, and a rifle across his knees.[121] Washakie was often the center of attraction in Evanston for the unusual and startling hat band which he wore on his high hat of the cowboy pattern. This ornament was a silver coffin plate on which appeared in wide letters the words OUR BABY. From a son of a

[121] The indian sign to indicate Washakie was a stroke with the forefinger of the left hand running from the middle of the nose down his cheek. This was the sign of the double scar received by the chief in a fight with the ever hostile Blackfeet. The chief, by his enemies, was called "Snake-with-Scar-on-his-Face."

furniture dealer the plate had been purchased by Washakie for a bow and arrow.[122]

Not only at Fort Bridger and Evanston, but at Fort Washakie, the citizens often took delight in entertaining the chief at their tables, surprised that he had so correctly achieved the white man's manners of entertainment. A former officer of Fort Washakie speaks of having invited Washakie to a dinner. Upon arriving at the home of his hosts, Washakie left his wife outside. After eating, which he did in a masterly way – even making no mistakes in the proper forks, knives and spoons, often a tangling problem for the average white man, all properly operated by the chief because of his keen power of unnoticeable observation and imitation, – he gathered together, at the end of the dinner, some of the remaining food, putting it in his ulster pocket for his children, who had carefully and unseen been looking through the window while the feast was in process of consumption. One good housewife invited the chief and his wives, he having three at this time, and his children to a chicken dinner. Washakie accurately negotiating the maze of forks, spoons and knives, rebuked his family for eating with their fingers. At the end of the meal the hostess was aghast to observe Washakie and his family pack into sacks, brought for the purpose, every morsel, "scrap and crumb" that had not been eaten and left on the table. "The failure to do this would have been, in their estimation, a slight on the hospitality of the host."

Washakie was always particularly cordial in his handshake with his white friends but when he could not avoid shaking the hand of an Arapahoe he indiffer-

---

[122] Stone.

ently extended the two fingers of his right hand, keeping the others shut into the palm of his hand. This was the Shoshone way of showing extreme distrust.

Additional testimony as to Washakie's control over his people is told by Albert D. Lane of Lander, Wyoming, who personally knew and highly respected the chief for over a quarter of a century, the period of their acquaintance.[123] "My impression of Chief Washakie is that he was a very bright man, a very intelligent man and a very fine man. He was chief of the Shoshones not in name but in reality, his word was law with all his people, anything he said, they knew they had to obey and that he meant it. I remember that Washakie told me that when the treaty for the land where Thermopolis now is [124] was drawn up, 1896, there was an interpreter there from Washington looking over the property, and that both tribes, Shoshone and Arapahoe, were also there. There they had their pow-wows and talked for days." Washakie in telling Mr. Lane of the circumstance said: "The Arapahoes, all sitting around in a circle and talking for several days, talked – all of them, but the Shoshones had just one man to talk," holding up one finger of his right hand, "and that man was Washakie." This was true. This showed to everyone that Washakie's entire people had complete confidence in his judgment, and "I found that was the way with everything connected with the Shoshones and Washakie," continued Mr. Lane.

"He was a very intelligent man, and if he had had the opportunities of a white man for an education and for leadership, he would have had the ability to fill the

123 *Interview*, 1926.
124 The Big Horn hot springs locality, now known as Hot Springs State Park.

chair of the presidency of the United States. Washakie
would come into our house and be as nice and polite
as any white man, and in fact, would act like a white
man. He was gentlemanly at the table and just as fine
and mannerly with his knife and fork as were the white
people we entertained. The officers at Fort Washakie
entertained Washakie at the time that President Arthur
and his distinguished party visited the Fort. Chief
Washakie was invited to meet the President of the
United States but he did not seek the presence of the
President; he waited, dressed in state, to first have
President Arthur call upon him as the Chief of the
Shoshones.

"Washakie always carried his hat with him, laying
it down by his side when not on his head; he was always
in regulation indian dress, wearing a blue blanket, but
he did not affect the high bright colors which the indians wore in later days, though his shirt was always
of color. He did not wear boots or shoes – always the
moccasins. I remember seeing him at North Fork, tall
and stately, with such a nice bearing.

"When the chief was sick at one time he said to me,
'They call Reverend Roberts, "White Robe," who has
talked to me of another world. He put the sign of a
cross on my head. What did he mean?' I told Washakie, continued Mr. Lane, 'that all who believed in a
life hereafter, a life after death, went into another
world happier than in this world, when they had the
cross made on their forehead.'

" 'Well,' responded Washakie, 'this world suits me
pretty well. I like it here. I come over to your engonnie
(or house or store). I talk with you as I did with
friends. I like to visit here. I go to Jakie's (J. K.

Moore) and I visit with him and his friends. I like that. I want to stay here with my friends, and I do not want to go to another world.' He knew he had to die, and he said, 'I may die tonight, I have to go sometime.'

"Washakie was always kind to children, a universal indian trait. There are those who have lived a quarter of a century with the Shoshones and never saw an indian child punished. If they did not keep their word with their mothers, when they were walking, she went right on without them, going to her wagon without speaking to the child. The child left behind would get up and run to its mother.

"Washakie's house or home was the largest one on the reservation, the government keeping it in repair. Washakie, however, spent much time in the tepee because the house 'was heap cold,' and at such times he kept his favorite horse in the house while he lived in the tepee.

"Washakie," concluded the narrator, "was a joker and enjoyed a good joke. He once came to my store and asked for 'O-ko-sho-yope' – 'O-ko-sho' meaning pig or hog, 'Yope' meaning 'grease.' I could not understand what he meant when he asked for 'O-ko-sho-yope' – but finally Washakie, freely laughing, said, 'Hog meat! – I want bacon.' "

"The Shoshones are the only indians that the Sioux were really afraid of, that was because Washakie was a good leader and, of course, the Shoshones were very brave."

In speaking of Washakie's ability to use the English language, Mr. Burnett, the Shoshone agricultural teacher on the reservation for thirty years or more, interestingly tells the manner in which Washakie made his wants known through a self appointed interpreter, declaring that "Washakie could speak our language so as to be able to be understood, but it was easier to have Billy McCabe come to the post as the chief's interpreter.[125] It was quite laughable to know that McCabe could not speak the Shoshone language at all, but did all of his interpreting and directing with the indians by Shoshone signs. Washakie could talk better English than McCabe could talk the Shoshone tongue. Both of them talked quite freely and lengthily by signs. Washakie was one of the best hearted friends I ever knew. He was particularly careful of me, for I was 'a pilgrim,' or a tenderfoot and new to the territory and unfamiliar with the kind of life I was undertaking and I had a poor outfit. Washakie always saw that I had plenty of meat and was very solicitous of my welfare. He was a happy chief, an affectionate leader, very fond of children, and if it were possible for any man to be absolutely devoid of fear, he was that man. My, what a splendid fellow he was!"

From a prominent woman who frequently came into contact with Washakie before he made his permanent home on the Warm Valley reservation, the following human touch has its interest.[126] "You ask, 'How did Washakie dress?' I laugh when I think how I once saw him. Pants, woolen shirt, big blanket wound tight about him (Roman senator he certainly was), big hobnailed shoes, and to top it all, a wide brimmed hat, rather tall in the crown. I suppose some soldier had given this costume to him – he certainly was an odd figure. But to see Washakie in his full majesty, was to view him in

---

[125] Scout William McCabe.
[126] Jeannette Young Easton.

indian regalia – feather headdress, long stemmed pipe
in hand, moccasins, buckskin leggings with fringe at
the side, always the blanket, sometimes the plaid shirt;
firm tread, head held high, eyes looking into a friend's
face, straight and piercing. I have shaken hands with
him, as we children always did when meeting indian
chiefs; though indians as a rule do not shake hands.
Washakie, like 'Kanash,' and other big noble indians,
recognized the white man's greeting and showed their
appreciation by following the custom. You will at once
be struck by his resemblance to our great Washington
in feature and personality. Washakie, like many of the
tribes, spoke a little English, never fluent in it, but he
could and did master many phrases and could be understood by shop-keepers and people when meeting them.
You know the indian mind is slow, rather heavy, stolid
in mental grasp, but alert when at their native heath and
among their kind. How superbly they have responded
to education and improvement in every walk of life."

Washakie's friend, James K. Moore, had a son who
succeeded to his father's position on the reservation as
Licensed Indian Trader. The friendship of the chief
and the father was handed down to the son, James K.
Moore, jr.

At an interview, the younger Mr. Moore displayed
in his recital of each incident of his relations with
Washakie a feeling that was akin to real affection and
frequently made manifest his deep respect for the aged
chief. Illustrative of the ability possessed by Washakie
of making himself known to his white friends through
other media than indian signs is illustrative of the
avenues of speech possessed by "Two Scar Chief," a
name given to him by his enemies due to the double

cheek arrow-scar, which is observable in many of his
photographs.

"Washakie spoke very little English but understood
more than he spoke and really understood more than he
pretended. He also spoke French. It was not unusual
for him to use short French phrases, particularly when
something had been given him to eat. At such a time the
chief would exclaim 'Heap good.' Then with a bow
continue *Je vous remercie*.

"After being away to school, where I had been taught
French, he would greet me with a *bon jour*; to me he
always called his pony *cheval*; his hat *chapeau*, and he
would whittle with his *couteau*. In this way he knew
and realized with fatherly delight that he was trying to
teach me French. The chief had long associated with
the early trappers and traders in Idaho, Utah and Fort
Bridger, as well as on his reservation. French thus became by him to be used more easily than English."

Agent Patten in an interview gave the following,
relative to the appearance of Washakie: "When I first
arrived at the Wind river agency in 1870, Washakie
and his warriors were visiting in Utah with 'Bigham'
and the Mormons. While they were away the reservation buildings were erected in part, as agreed in the
Great Treaty of 1868 – such as a blockhouse, school
building, corrals, flour mill, and blacksmith shop, as
well as dwellings for the agent and his working force.
During the absence of Washakie, which lasted until the
spring of 1872, much of this work was completed by the
time of the arrival of the chief. When the indians came
to the agency building I, for the first time, saw Washakie – a tall and straight indian of six feet; a man with
grey hair, good features, a most gentle and intelligent

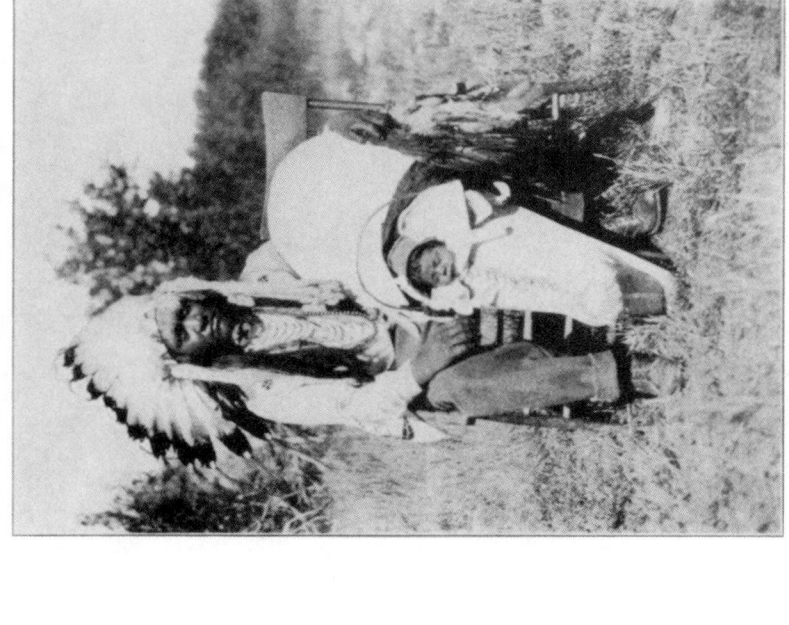

CHIEF WASHAKIE'S GREAT-GRANDSON AND
GREAT-GREAT-GRANDDAUGHTER

Reproduced from original photograph taken in 1926
near the tepee of Enga Peahrora

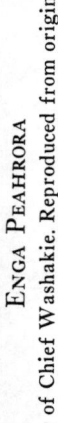

ENGA PEAHRORA

Daughter of Chief Washakie. Reproduced from original photograph taken in 1926 on the Shoshone indian reservation

face, kindly eyes, firm mouth; his dress being without a hat, his hair flowing freely down over his broad shoulders, around his collar was a cloth scarf, the ends of which were passed through slits pierced in a sea shell and tied in a knot to hold close to the throat; a three point mackinaw blanket, leggings reaching to the waist, and beaded moccasins completed his attire. During the winter the blanket was exchanged for a well dressed buffalo robe with the hair outside. His weight was about one hundred and seventy-five pounds, and not a pound more. His six-foot, well proportioned body and graceful carriage pointed out his importance. He had a haughty, dignified, even kingly, bearing, which with his usual thoughtful, kindly, benevolent face pointed him out as one who would attract attention anywhere. To me his profile had a close resemblance to that of Washington, even strikingly so."

General O. O. Howard, with whom Chief Dick Washakie fought in the Nez Percés war, was a personal friend of Washakie, bearing pleasing testimony of the friendship and the valor in battle of the chief. "I often met this good chief and we were fast friends. Once when I was riding through Yellowstone National Park he told me of his last battle. The Sioux indians had determined to break the power of the Shoshones, to defeat them in battle, and carry them off captives. Led by young Red Cloud, the son of the famous war chief, a band of Sioux came upon Washakie. He had so drilled his men that they held every pass through the mountains, and fought so hard that the Sioux were obliged to give up, particularly as their young chief, Red Cloud, fell in the last attack. Washakie received praise from the United States Indian department for the ability

with which he kept his indians together, and the help
he gave officers and soldiers. He was always glad to see
me, and in the Yellowstone he sent Shoshone Jack with
a band of indians to ride just out of sight on all sides
of us for guards. We were safe in that wild country
with them around us as we would have been anywhere
in America." [127]

Washakie was a skilled horseman and an intense
lover of a beautiful pony. Into battle he rode his finest
horses and took the most attentive care of them. In the
early history of most tribes, it was the custom to destroy
the right eye of all the horses, in the belief that they
could be more easily caught when wanted by slipping
up on the blind side. For Washakie there was no such
regulation; he loved his horses too well to thus mutilate
them, and prohibited his braves from performing such
a pitiless atrocity.

During the years of 1884 and 1885, a young man left
his home, located in a region of culture and education,
going to the Wind river reservation, giving his ability
and training toward the education of the Shoshones. Of
this teacher, Reverend John Roberts has said, "I can
never forget Mr. Jones's work for the reservation in the
early eighties. He came here and went right down in
the midst of the pit in time of snow and laid the foun-
dation of the mission, deep, true and enduring." Mr.
Arthur C. Jones gives many human touches of Washakie's life and his own personal experiences while on
the reservation in his school duties and during his
period of spiritual training to the Shoshones. "When I
knew Washakie he seemed to be full of life and vigor
though he was at that time eighty-six years of age. He

[127] Howard, General O. O., *Letter*, 1927.

was always serious when in repose, but when he smiled, his face would break into a charming expression, delightful to look upon, making him to appear almost like another being. The reason why Washakie did not converse in English, a thing that he could do, was because he was very sensitive and feared criticism and ridicule from the white people for the mistakes he might make. Washakie always spoke of the ministers of his church as 'White Robes,' having been confirmed by Bishop J. F. Spalding and received communion in the Protestant Episcopal Church, though there might be a question of a complete understanding by the chief as to the significance of the ceremony."

Into the life of the Shoshone indians at the Wind river reservation came a missionary, born in Wales and ordained into the Episcopal church in his native country, Reverend John Roberts. He came from Colorado into Wyoming where in the winter of 1883 he was sent by the Right Reverend J. F. Spalding in order to establish a mission for the Shoshones and Arapahoes. With a thermometer hugging the mercury around sixty degrees below zero, Reverend Roberts had his introduction to his field of work. The brave and determined heart to breast a storm of this severity was illustrative of the life work of Reverend Roberts on the reservation among the indians. For many a month he had charge of all of the churches within a radius of one hundred and fifty miles in the Wind river valley, not only administering spiritual help to the red men but to the settlers in this same territory. Two years after his arrival on the reservation, he had returned to the railroad to meet and marry the young woman of his choice, returning to the mission in the last days of December with

the mercury reading thirty-six degrees below. Here on
the remote reservation Mr. and Mrs. Roberts have continuously remained during their work in the spirit of
Christ and the hope of pioneers, their family of interesting children taking up different lines of the work
which their parents have for so continued a time performed with patience, ability and helpfulness, the children all having been sent from the reservation for their
college education.

At the end of active service of thirty-eight years,
Reverend John Roberts resigned his position as head
of the mission, but the resignation was more in words
than in deeds for the faithful servant of Christ continues in his spiritual duties with his wife and children,
for his heart is in his work; he continues earnestly concerned in the welfare of the Shoshones.

Into Reverend Roberts's home Chief Washakie was
a welcome and frequent visitor, receiving and giving
advice relative to the development of his people and
their adoption of the standards of the white people. In
one of his reports, speaking of Washakie and his attendance at church, Reverend Roberts states, "Into this
house for many years on each Sunday evening he gathered his neighbors and friends where words of encour-
agement and instructions in spiritual things were given.
He was a noble man and nothing but the spirit of God
could build up such a character as his was in his latter
days."

Influenced by the spiritual teachings of Reverend
Roberts, Washakie became very anxious that the Shoshones should be baptized, and accept the christian
faith. In one of his last messages to his people he said,
"One thing more I want to see and my heart will be at

peace. I want to see the school and church built for my tribe by the 'White Robes'." Toward having his great desires realized the chief donated one hundred and sixty acres of desirable land to the Episcopal church on which the school and church he longed to see have been erected.

At one time when Washakie was seriously ill, he sent for his spiritual adviser who performed, by request, the sacred rites of baptism for the chief. From that hour the old chief steadily and rapidly became better and better. The recovery was attributed, by Washakie, to the effects of baptism. When these results became known in the tribe countless indians came to the minister begging for the "good medicine" such as was given to Washakie and that had made him a well man again. "It was difficult to make them understand that the real virtue of baptism was spiritual and not physical." [128]

After a prolonged period of hospital experience when in a state of convalescence, Reverend Roberts presented Chief Washakie with what in modern times might be called a bath-robe. The chief frequently would use this not only in his cabin or tepee but when he rode on his beautiful horse. The garment, being light blue outside and lined with pink silk, made the picture almost ridiculous. "It was," tells Reverend Roberts, "really an old fashioned, invalid's reading robe, very light in weight and very warm. After the chief's recovery from his first stroke of paralysis I asked him to try it on. He was delighted with it. I had it re-covered with stronger material for him. It was of blue silk, heavily padded within with eider-down. He treasured it greatly. He hated any kind of a coat. The

---

[128] Roberts, Reverend John, *Interview*.

United States Indian Agent remonstrated with him for attending an important council in such an unsuitable garment. The old man was very positive in his reply, though respectful, as he always was to the government representatives. 'This,' he said, 'may not look well on me, but it is very comfortable, very warm and very light. It does not make my old shoulders ache as a heavy coat would. I shall wear it.' This he did."

Often Chief Washakie would go to the indian school house and talk with Reverend Roberts about the school and the problems which the two leaders of men had with the indians and their progress.

At one time when the chief was in the hospital, he asked to have Reverend Roberts come and see him, saying to the minister when he arrived, "White Robe, I am going to die if something is not done for me while I am here. My bed is so soft that I cannot sleep, nor can I rest, I ache all over."

"What do you wish me to do?" solicitously asked Reverend Roberts.

"Take that door off of its hinges," quickly replied the chief, "then remove the mattress from this bed, put the door where the mattress now is and help me to lie down on the hard door, without any blankets or coverings over it. Then I shall get well."

All of this was carefully and with great patience performed by Mr. Roberts. The chief affirmed that he was more comfortable than he had been since he came to the "soft" hospital. The remedy effected a swift sure cure, for in a few days Washakie was on his feet again and out of the too luxuriant hospital.

In the *Parish Register* of the Wind river mission is recorded:

Washakie, baptized January 25 A. D. 1897; date of his birth, A. D. 1798. Signature of clergyman, John Roberts. Burial, Friday, February 23, A. D., 1900. Date of death, Tuesday, February 20, A. D., 1900, Cause of death, Old age. Place of burial. Fort Washakie cemetery, Signature of clergyman, John Roberts.

The final tribute to Chief Washakie should come from his most beloved and trusted friend, his minister of the gospel. "Yes, Chief Washakie was one of my best friends. He was a man for whom I had the greatest respect and sincere regard."

Fort Washakie

The creation and establishment of Fort Washakie had its inception in the old Camp Augur, a sub-post of Fort Bridger, occupation commencing June 28, 1869, when Washakie had been assigned a reservation in the Wind river valley where he was to move his people from Fort Bridger and the Bridger valley to new headquarters at which place officers and representatives of our government were counciling with the chief relative to his occupancy of the "Warm valley." The next year on March 28, 1870, the name of the recently organized camp was changed to that of Camp Brown, which military site on August 21, 1870, was made an independent post, freeing itself from Fort Bridger. Finally, Camp Brown on December 30, 1878, legally became designated and known as Fort Washakie in honor of the chief of the Shoshones, abandonment of the fort taking place on March 30, 1909, when the area known as Fort Washakie reservation was given back to the United States Department of the Interior.

The establishment of military protection to the Shoshones after their migration to the Wind river reservation, was given to the indians at the earnest request of Chief Washakie who feared the hostile bands of Sioux, Arapahoes, Cheyennes and Crows, as well as other hostile bands. Hence, Camp Augur was a treaty post to protect the Shoshones not only from the red man but from renegade whites. The buildings at Camp Augur were, necessarily, somewhat of a temporary nature, though substantially built and susceptible of serving as a strong defense in time of attack from hostiles. These buildings were surrounded by a stockade of blockhouses protective from chance migratory bands that might invade the Wind river valley. Camp Augur was named in honor of Brigadier-general Christopher Colon Augur, who had held council with Washakie on this site after the Great Treaty of 1868 signed at Fort Bridger. At this council promises were made for the erection of buildings which were soon built and occupied by Company B, of the Fourth United States infantry, consisting of one hundred men ordered there by the request and directions of Governor Campbell, who was superintendent of Wyoming Indian Affairs, being the first company of United States troops to occupy the barricade which was under the command of Colonel Bartlett of the same regiment as were the soldiers.

The changing of the name of Camp Augur, established by Lieutenant P. H. Breslin, to Camp Brown, on August 20, 1870, was made in honor of Captain Frederick Brown, Fifteenth infantry, who was killed by indians on December 21, 1866, near Fort Phil Kearney, on the Bozeman trail. The location of the two camps was one and the same, the city of Lander being built around the center of this fortification September 26, after the camp was removed to the Little Wind river. Camp Brown was moved in 1873 onto Washakie's reduced reservation, reduced by Treaty of 1872. The locating of the new site commenced in the spring of 1871 when Captain Robert T. Torrey, Thirteenth infantry, then commanding Camp Brown, received orders to select a new site on June 26, 1871, although the

removal of the camp from the south side of the Popo
Agie river did not take place until 1873.[129]

The new location for Camp Brown was between the
Little Wind river and North Fork about one hundred
and fifty yards from where the two streams united. The
old post was gradually abandoned, the new post being
built as the old one was torn down – all available material being transplanted to and used in the construction
of the new post, Brown, adobe being the main material
for the construction of the buildings. By the summer of
1873 officers and troops were comfortably housed, the
construction of buildings being made almost entirely
by the troops' own labors.

For five years, Camp, Post, or Fort Brown retained
its name, though the locality was frequently called Fort
Washakie, when on December 30, 1878, the post was
officially designated as Fort Washakie.[130] On May 21,
1887, by an executive order of President Grover Cleveland, there was created a military reservation of 1405
acres surrounding Fort Washakie, known as the "Fort
Washakie Military Reservation," the concluding para-
graph of the order reading, "The use and occupancy
of the land in question be subject to such right, title and
interest as the indians have in and to the same, and that
it be vacated whenever the interests of the indians shall
require it." [131]

On March 30, 1909, the Secretary of War relinquished the military reservation surrounding Fort
Washakie, including the fort, to the United States Department of the Interior, and on that same day an order

[129] Nickerson, *Early History of Fremont County, Ibid.*

[130] General order no. 9, United States War Department, Division of the
Missouri, December 30, 1878.

[131] General order, no. 37, United States War Department, May 26, 1887.

of the commanding general of the Department of the Missouri directing an immediate abandonment of the post by soldiers. However, several officers remained at the Fort until April 7, 1909, closing accounts; Troop M, Eighth cavalry, leaving shortly before the absolute abandonment of Fort Washakie.

Fort Brown was situated on the right bank of the Little Wind river opposite its confluence with the North Fork, both streams rising in the Wind river mountains and the tributaries of the Big Horn river. The altitude was 5498 feet above sea level. The military reservation in which Fort Brown was situated was originally to be a one mile square tract of land to be taken from the lands owned by the Shoshone indians.

The exact dates of the construction of the first main buildings on the military reservation and at Fort Washakie (Brown) are not definitely known though with certainty a large part of them were constructed and completed before the troops in their entirety were moved from the original site of Fort Brown to the new site of the fort, from Popo Agie to Little Wind river. From the time of the selection of the new Fort Brown site in 1871 by Captain Torrey to the final moving of the troops and buildings in 1873 from old Camp Brown, there elapsed practically two years. When the troops were finally transferred there had been constructed not only many new buildings for the military force on the new site, but there were a number of new substantial buildings not far from the fort constructed at the Shoshone and Bannock agency for use of the Shoshone indians.

The long stretch of country from the fort to the agency overlooking the Wind river valley has been

GENERAL VIEW OF FORT WASHAKIE

Shoshone Agency in distance. Wind river mountains in extreme background. Reproduced from photograph taken from Sentinel Hill

described as "a broad mile of level plain stretches, gray
with sage, buff with intervening grass, hay-cocked with
smoky, mellow-stained, meerschaum-like canvas tepees
of the indians, quiet as a painting." [132]

The buildings on the fort reservation in its earliest
history were fifteen adobe structures, officers quarters,
commissioned and non-commissioned, barracks, married soldiers quarters, hospital, adjutant's office, telegraph office; buildings built of logs, the store houses
and stables; buildings of stone, the guard house and a
store house. Later in the history of the fort, a saw mill
was constructed, a hotel and the post trader's buildings,
the other buildings on the fort reservation being built
between the years of 1884 and 1897.

By general order number 95, of May 18, 1899, Fort
Washakie was directed to be discontinued with its reservation and both to be restored to the Interior Department. This order was speedily revoked by general order
number 101, June 2, 1899; again ordered abandoned by
general order number 191, when the order was executed
December 2, 1908, and all property relinquished to the
Interior Department, March 30, 1909. [133]

Thus, when Washakie was nearing the end of his
long and eventful career, the order came for the abandonment of the fort bearing his name. The chief became
much excited over this military order, maintaining that
the government had promised to give him military protection afforded from an established fort as long as he
might live. He earnestly asserted that this protection
was one of the provisions of the Great Treaty of 1868.
There seems to be no official records to bear out this

[132] Wister.
[133] United States War Department, *Records.*

statement, though easily there might have been some verbal agreement made by the government officials at the time of the treaty. Revocation speedily followed the order for abandonment after Washakie's protest. No doubt the services which the chief had rendered amply justified the government in revoking the order. The fact that Washakie was now over a hundred years of age and his span of life would not longer continue may have had its influence. General W. C. Brown in command of the fort in 1899 received the order for the abandoning of the fort, though "no previous order by wire having been sent." A petition from those living in the territory near the fort, based on Washakie's supplication, was hurried to Washington, resulting in the revocation of the abandonment order. Nine months after the order for abandonment, Washakie was dead, though formal and absolute abandonment of the post did not take place until December 2, 1908, when the old historic land-mark, the one protection afforded Washakie with his small band of braves against the hostiles, became the property of the United States Department of the Interior, March 10, 1909, four months after abandonment. Thus ending the activities of a frontier post that had seen constant service for over a third of a century.

Following the abandonment of the fort the Shoshone agency was moved from its former quarters into the buildings originally occupied by the military forces, at which place the agency has since had its headquarters. Many of the buildings erected in the seventies and eighties remain in excellent condition, due to their substantial construction of adobe, logs and stone, all material being locally obtained, built not only with a view for protection from hostile indians but from mountain winter weather. At the old agency there remains an interesting blockhouse built of stone, used in time of danger from indian invasion. There are a number of small narrow windows protected by iron bars placed high up under the roof; inside the building under the floor was a cistern kept filled with drinking water during those hostile days. Many times the women and children of the agency were hurried into this "isle of safety" upon the first alarm of indian danger. In one corner of the large room, the blockhouse being of one room only, is a cell with iron bars in which indians were placed when arrested. The buildings remaining at the agency are now utilized by the United States Irrigation Project officers.

During the years intervening between 1878 and 1890, Colonel Homer W. Wheeler was located at Fort Washakie, "filling the office of quartermaster, commissary officer, post treasury officer and in command of the troops part of the time." While in command of the fort, Colonel Wheeler partially rebuilt the post, erecting, or causing to be erected, a large storehouse, guardhouse, stables and an administration building which included an officers' club room, which the enlisted men could also enjoy, bowling alley, and a chapel which was provided with a stage for amusement. Most of the construction work was performed by soldier labor, the men going into the mountains, felling the trees and hauling the logs to the sawmill, which was provided with a planing and shingle mill. Only a citizen sawyer, carpenter, blacksmith and a few teamsters were employed, all the work being performed by the soldiers.[134]

[134] Wheeler, Colonel Homer W., U. S. A., Retired, *"Reminiscences of old Fort Washakie." Quarterly Bulletin,* vol. 1, no. 4, Historical Department of State of Wyoming; also *Letter* of February, 1926.

To add to the beauty of the fort, Colonel Wheeler purchased and had set out one hundred trees around the parade ground. Scenically, the grounds are most fortunately located near the banks of mountain streams; in sight of never-melting snow on the peaks of the Wind river mountains; with long stretches of prairie and seas of purple-tinged sagebrush, intervening between reservation and continental divide. "This tree transaction," Colonel Wheeler states, "was not looked upon by the government in a kindly spirit and I was directed 'not to do it again.' Today they have grown to be immense fine trees."

To the character of Chief Washakie, Colonel Wheeler adds his generous estimate. "Washakie was a real leader and always had complete control of his people. Red Cloud, and Crazy Horse both admitted that Washakie was the greatest general of them all. The latter years of his life were spent in the quiet enjoyment of his people and surroundings. He was an indian of most excellent character and always endeavoring to exercise a good influence over his people. He was extremely fond of his family and enjoyed the peaceful life. His disposition was most kindly. He was dignified and commanded the respect of all. Washakie was well known to the early pioneers and pathfinders, whose friendship they all sought. Kit Carson, the great hunter, trapper, and guide, appears to have been his favorite. No indian of mountain or plain was more extensively and favorably known."

Chief Washakie's son, Dick, taking part in the Nez Percés war, under Colonel O. O. Howard, expressed himself somewhat freely as to the methods of warfare in the campaign and final capture of Chief Joseph, in

PARADE GROUND AT FORT WASHAKIE
The trees were set out by General Wheeler

1877. His disapproval of the tactics used in battle has been given in no uncertain terms. After Dick Washakie had departed for the campaign against Chief Joseph and was taking part in the battles in Montana and elsewhere, troops belonging to our army were on their way to join in the campaign against these Nez Percés. The forces marched from Cheyenne across the greater part of Wyoming and into the Wind river valley to Fort Brown where Chief Washakie was at that time assembling another band of his indians to act as scouts in the war against the Nez Percé chief.

Lieutenant Charles King of the Fifth cavalry was among the officers who had arrived at Washakie's reservation at the time that Washakie was preparing his Shoshones for the war service. General King relates a personal experience with Washakie occurring at this time when he met and heard the chief address his braves just preceding their departure for Montana, stating, "Washakie was giving his parting address to the Shoshone scouts that went with us on the Nez Percés campaign. It was, in my opinion, entirely spontaneous. The speech seemed to be an exhortation to his warriors to faithfully serve General Merritt.

Of this worthy chief I heard much in the old days but only once did I meet and have conversation with him, and this was in 1877, when a greater than he – a chief cruelly wronged, was leading his bewildered people, like Moses of old, from the beautiful land that had been their home in the far northeastern part of Idaho, beating off each day the few horsemen of Colonel Howard, none too eager pursuers, for some of them had been with General George Crook when first they learned the little they knew of the Nez Percés, once forced to fight and compelled to flee or face additional wrong. Joseph and his warriors, burdened with their wounded, their women and children, made their way to passes of the Rockies far to the south end, beating off General Gibbon and his hard fighting little battalion at Big Hole, brushing aside another — even smaller force in the Yellowstone — tricking and turning the Seventh cavalry over toward Cedar mountain and had actually made their way to Bear Paw and sight of safety, the Canadian line, when they were blocked by General Miles and the Fifth infantry (with, of course, two or three troops of cavalry) which were just enough to send in to charge and die, as did the officers at their head. All this was taking place while we of the Fifth cavalry, sent all the way from Cheyenne were marching up the Wind river and on and over Owl Creek mountains, with Shoshones for scouts — old Washakie's parting injunctions holding them to faithful performance of their duties.

I heard the old chief's splendid speech to his silent braves — could almost understand it, though I did not know ten words of their tongue — and when the agent later presented me to him, I felt honored by the cordial handclasp. We all held him in respect, we knew he had been the white man's friend for several years and would keep his word to the end. Too old to take the field, he had sent his kinsman, Owatah, and he was a shadow in comparison with the chief.[135]

Further testimony illustrative of the respect which army officers and chiefs with high ranking fighting power and ability had for Chief Washakie is given by Captain James H. Cook, a warm and intimate friend of Chief Red Cloud. "I have often heard Red Cloud speak of Washakie. They were friends. Red Cloud regarded Washakie as a leader among his people. To be a leader among indians a man must be both brave and fair, in all of his dealings with other people. Red Cloud had great respect for any man, white or red, who was possessed of unusual ability and intellect and was considered *honest*." [136]

"Washakie," stated Lieutenant Colonel Hardin, "was the finest indian I ever knew, and we came to be

[135] King, Brigadier-general Charles, United States army, *Letter*, March 3, 1926.
[136] Cook, Captain James H., *Letter*, 1926.

very fond of him. He looked like George Washington in bronze, was very dignified and always most friendly. Many times he was a guest at our table, and he had excellent table manners and was always scrupulously clean." [137]

Once a case had been reviewed by the commanding officer of the fort in which a law had been violated that prohibited indians from patronizing the soldiers' bar. After this edict, Washakie made it his business to go to the bar once every day. Here he was told by the barkeeper that indians were not allowed there. He acknowledged that rule and told the bartender not to allow them to come there, saying, "It is a bad place for indians." But he himself kept visiting the bar until he made it perfectly plain that he considered himself as chief, entitled to go where he wished and that he intended to so do.

Additional tribute to Washakie is given by Colonel George H. Morgan, who was stationed at Fort Washakie from October, 1880 to May, 1882, thus having excellent opportunity to know and judge of Washakie's sterling character. He states, "When I knew Washakie he was an elderly, very dignified and efficient head of the Shoshone tribe. He was always a friend of the soldiers and when called upon, always furnished scouts for them.

"He seemed to be a real leader of his chosen people; keeping them from trouble when possible, had a fine although small tribe under good control, and the best behaved morally of any indians I ever knew. They were far superior to the Arapahoes, another tribe on the same reservation at that time.

---

[137] Hardin, Lieutenant-colonel E. E., U. S. A., *Letter*, March 22, 1926.

"Chief Washakie, with all his greatness, was a very human man, and without civilized education had a working knowledge of his people, their prejudices and beliefs.

"I remember a descriptive remark applied to the old chief, which was interesting to me. He was said to be "White Brave." This was intended to convey the idea that he would venture where he was perhaps likely to be injured. For this virtue, as we consider it in a soldier, the indian had some contempt, and perhaps more astonishment. In the case of Chief Washakie it enabled him to have a perfect control over his sometime turbulent people.

"His appearance was fine. He had a straight figure of, as I remember him, about six feet in height, and with his grand looking face he was the picture of a chief." [188]

Chief Washakie was deeply interested in the progress of the Spanish-American war. He was eager to know the progress that the Great Father's fighting men were making across the great body of water to the west. When Bishop Talbot, at one time one of the spiritual advisors of Washakie, had left his western diocese and had journeyed to the east to make his home, Chief Washakie, through Reverend Roberts, missionary to the Shoshones, sent word to his former friend and spiritual guide telling of his grief in growing so old and feeble, and "that he prayed day by day to the Saviour." Then pausing and looking earnestly, with face beaming with delight and satisfaction, said, "Tell the bishop my heart is dancing with joy because Uncle Sam's troops have whipped the Spanish!"

---

[188] Morgan, Colonel George H., U. S. A., *Letter*, 1927.

Chief Washakie served for many years in the United States army, years that were filled with helpful service, and years when he was totally inactive due to his advanced years. "There was an old law which authorized the enlistment in the army of a certain number of indian scouts who received the pay, rations, clothing of cavalry soldiers, with an addition of forty cents a day for the use of horse or horse equipments. It is probable that Washakie, who when enlisting in 1889, was about ninety-one years of age, was thus taken on the government payrolls as a merited reward for his exceptionally meritorious services to the government." [139]

Due to the fact that between the period from February 22, 1876, to September 10, 1877, when the campaign of our government was against the northern Cheyennes and Sioux indians, involving parts of Montana, Wyoming, Dakota and Nebraska, Washakie offered his services as a soldier to aid the United States forces. A company or detachment of indian scouts, most of them Shoshones with a few Crows, was mustered into the services of the United States, October 14, 1876, at Camp Brown (Washakie) to serve for a period of three weeks. In this "detachment of Shoshones and Bannock indians" as they at first were called, later to be known as "a company of Shoshone scouts," Chief Washakie was in command with the rank of first sergeant. In addition there were five sergeants, four corporals and eighty-five privates, there being mustered in a total of ninety-six indians.

About October 31, 1876, Thomas Cosgrove, United States indian scout, hired and employed by the United States Quartermaster's Department, took command of

---

[139] Brown, Brigadier-general William Carey, U. S. A., *Letters.*

the company, where he ranked as a captain, Chief Washakie retaining his non-commissioned office. After serving at Cantonment Reno on the Bozeman trail, where was established in 1866 Fort Reno in the Powder river country, the company took part in an expedition to the Powder river until December 4, 1876, at which time the company marched back to Camp Brown, Chief Washakie and the other indians being mustered out and honorably discharged, January 14, 1877, the discharge occurring by reason of the expiration of the term of the enlistment.[140]

The War Department further records services to the United States army by Washakie when he individually enlisted in the army as an indian scout, February 14, 1889, at Fort Washakie, with the rank of private, to serve for the term of six years. He afterward reënlisted as a private eleven times for periods of six months each, the last enlistment for six months being on August 15, 1894, when he had reached the age of ninety-six years; an additional enlistment was made on February 15, 1895 for a period of three years, which was a final service to the army though he again enlisted as a private in the scout detachment February 15, 1898, for an additional three years. It was during this period that Chief Washakie died, 1900, having continuously given his services from year to year, always honorably discharged from 1889 to the time of his death.

"There is nothing to show," states the War Department, "that after his enlistment of 1889 he performed any active military service. It is apparent that his enlistments from that time forward were for the purpose of enabling the government to extend to him a small

---

[140] United States War Department, Adjutant-general's Office, *Letter*.

gratuity in recognition of his past loyalty and material services to the government, at the time (January, 1898) of the approaching expiration of his three-years term of enlistment of February 15, 1895, the post commander asking the Commissioner of the Department of the Platte, for permission to enlist him again, stating that he was physically infirm and would be unable to pass an examination."

Finally the time arrived when abandonment of Fort Washakie became an actuality, those who were the last to take their departure from the old post site, being Lieutenant-colonel William A. McCain and Captain Frederick H. Sparrenberger, post surgeon, each of whom makes a historical contribution of immeasurable value to the old garrison bearing the name of the chief of the Shoshone indians.

"I went to Fort Washakie for duty in 1907 as Second Lieutenant Troop M, Eighth cavalry, Captain W. F. Flynn, Commanding. Chief Washakie had died so I never knew him. I heard him spoken of by everybody as having been a leader of integrity and wisdom. A most interesting character and one whom I liked immensely was Scout William McCabe.

"In December, 1908, Troop M, Eighth cavalry, was ordered to Fort Russell, leaving me with a small detachment to care for post and public property pending orders for the transfer of the former to the Department of the Interior. The only other commissioned officer left behind was the surgeon, Lieutenant Frederick H. Sparrenberger. Although our routine reports went forward regularly the powers that be appeared to have forgotten us, so we wintered at Washakie in peace, quiet, and snow. But about the time the bears began to come out and look around, so did the War Department; for along in March I began to receive orders to get things in shape for the final disposal of the military reservation and everything on it, including myself. The result was a public auction sale of most of the movables. Within a few days thereafter the detachment departed, leaving Post Quartermaster-sergeant (and an excellent one, he was), A. F. Cordes and me. We two had to remain over a little beyond the formalities in order to draw a red line, and render unto Caesar the final accounting. The last act was to turn over to the indian agent (Mr. H. E. Wadsworth) the lands, buildings and permanent fixtures, taking formal receipt therefor. Sergeant Cordes and I rode out of the post horseback on my polo ponies, and so far as I know, we two were the last men in the uniform of the United States army on official duty in an old time fort where, for example, one could catch a mess of trout while sitting on the back fence of an officer's quarters.

"I have no unpleasant recollections in connection with my service at Washakie. To the contrary I have many pleasant ones. To be sure there were some inconveniences, since I was married and my only child was born during my tour of duty there.

"When I left Washakie I was younger than I am now and did not realize what I was leaving. I did not appreciate the fact that service of that kind in the army would never come again. Since then I have been knocking about the world considerably – the jungles of the tropics, the bad lands 'somewhere in France,' the Towers of Babel standing just west of East river, etc., and I say positively that, with the possible exception of a mapping tour in the Black Hills, my service under the flag at old Washakie was the most pleasant of all.

"There is one truth which above all others impresses me most in connection with my service there and of which at the time I had only a sort of subconscious realization. It is this: 'Judge Henry' and 'The Virginian' and for that matter, 'Trampas,' too, and in general the folks out there – fact as well as in fiction – are of the same race as those who had the faith and the fortitude to set sail on uncharted seas, to endure Plymouth Rock and Jamestown and then work west over three thousand miles of wilderness. And just look – Our Country!" [141]

A methodical and painstaking diarist must have been Doctor Sparrenberger who furnishes detailed steps of the abandonment of the frontier post on the Little Wind river.

"January 21, 1907, Company M, Eleventh infantry, Lieutenant C. A. Delaplane in command marched into Fort Washakie, Wyoming, from D. A. Russell to relieve Troops E and F, Tenth cavalry, which were under orders to proceed to Philippine Islands.

"February 10, 1907, Troops E and F, Tenth cavalry, Major George H. Sands in command, marched out of Fort Washakie en route to the Philippine Islands.

"April 30, 1907, Troop M, Eighth cavalry, Captain William T. Flynn in command, marched into Fort Washakie, Wyoming, to relieve Company M, Eleventh infantry.

"June 7, 1907, Company M, Eleventh infantry, Lieutenant Delaplane in command, marched out of Fort Washakie, en route to Fort D. A. Russell, Wyoming,

---

[141] McCain, Lieutenant-colonel William A., U. S. A., *Letter*, May 3, 1926.

Captain William F. Flynn, commanding post and Troop M, Eighth cavalry puts his troop in summer camp one mile above post retaining the hospital building for his sick and the hospital stewards quarters for an office and quarters for the post surgeon, Doctor F. H. Sparrenberger and allowed the superintendent of the Shoshone indians to use other post buildings.

"October 17, 1907, Captain Flynn and Troop M, Eighth cavalry breaks summer camp and moves back into post, Fort Washakie.

"December 22, 1908, Captain Flynn and Troop M, Eighth cavalry marched out of Fort Washakie for Fort D. A. Russell, leaving behind a medical detachment with Doctor Sparrenberger and a detachment of M troop, Eighth cavalry under Lieutenant William A. McCain, to close and ship out government property and abandon Fort Washakie.

"March 30, 1909, Fort Washakie permanently abandoned. On this day the post colors were hauled down in person by Lieutenant William A. McCain and Doctor Frederick H. Sparrenberger and we marched out of Fort Washakie, Doctor Sparrenberger going to Fort Warren, Massachusetts, and Lieutenant McCain going to Fort D. A. Russell, Wyoming. Doctor Sparrenberger was last surgeon at Fort Washakie. Lieutenant McCain was last commanding officer at Fort Washakie." [142]

These colors were the last to float over the military post of Fort Washakie, Wyoming, and were presented to Doctor Sparrenberger by Lieutenant McCain.[143]

[142] Sparrenberger, Captain Frederick H., Medical Corps, United States Army, *Letter* and *Interview* with, 1926.

[143] Temporarily in the possession of Grace Raymond Hebard, a gift from Doctor Sparrenberger, 1926.

The Departure to «Where There is no Longitude nor Latitude»

Near the dawn of the twentieth century when the shadow of life lengthened, Washakie departed for "the land of the stars;" dying as he had lived, without ostentation, without royal homage; leaving his cherished reservation and his devoted subjects with no more pomp or vain glory than was the event of his humble birth in some obscure, unrecorded place in the twilight of the eighteenth century.

During the nineteenth century in which this fatherly chief reigned for three scores of years, Washakie not only attained but held unbreakable sway as a leader, winning for himself a power over his chosen people greater in authority than that of a king with a parliament having the power to make and repeal laws; greater than a president with a congress empowered to enact statutes. The laws governing his tribe were those made by Washakie; these mandates he enforced; he punished the violators of the rules promulgated by a one-man lawmaker; he was, hence, not only a combination of king, parliament and court of justice, but the actual and active head of his government; a czar in determination though a kindly ruler, combining and concentrating all avenues of authority and power in one person – Washakie, *L'etat, c'est moi.*

No century in the world's history has had crowded into its one hundred years as many achievements in science, government, and material gain as did the century during the years between the birth of this Shoshone chief in 1798 and his death in 1900.

Washakie was born at the time when George Washington had just finished his second term as president of the United States; he died during the first administration of William McKinley, the twenty-fifth president of our nation, thus, having lived during the years of presidential service of twenty-five out of thirty-one of our presidents, living through the period of our naval war with Great Britain in 1812; the Mexican war of 1846; the Civil war of 1861 and the Spanish-American war of 1898; born into a nation with 5,308,483 people, leaving a nation with 75,994,545 souls; born into a union with sixteen sovereign states created before his birth; leaving the nation with forty-five states to which, since his departure, only three have been added.

Washakie became familiar with that form of transportation and communication which he called "the white-top wagons" about 1832. This was the time when Captain Benjamin Bonneville conducted the first wagons through South pass when he came into the wilderness as a fur-trader. It was into the region of the "Warm valley" he journeyed by the route of the Oregon trail and its detours, exploring the Wind river valley, as well as the territory in the headwaters of the Snake and Green rivers. At this period of western exploration Washakie's only means of transportation were by the moccasin route, a horse, or, the use of the travois – the forerunner of the family wagon which the Shoshones called "wobbie pung" – wooden horse.

When the first locomotive of the Union Pacific railroad came into the Shoshones' lands near Fort Bridger,

Washakie, with his people gazing with unexplainable astonishment at the fire-spitting horse, called the vehicle of locomotion a "fire horse" about which he exclaimed and explained that "the fire horse has now about approached our lands. There is nothing that we can do to prevent its coming on, this fire horse, 'koona-woy-pung' of the white man. We cannot stop it. We are compelled to stand back and watch it come into our lands."

After the coming of the "rubber wagon," about which Washakie had no knowledge, the Shoshones spoke of this vehicle of transportation in terms of wonderment, and generally somewhat in contempt. "There are many white people coming into our land with automobiles (rubber wagons) that run swifter than any horse we have, our horses are nothing compared with this white man's wonder. It runs without horses, runs without anything drawing it. It is a wonder; all it leaves behind it is that awful smell as it passes."

About the time of Washakie's death he sent for his old time friend, Mr. J. D. Woodruff, pioneer of Lander and the Wind river valley, who was with Washakie at the time of the buffalo chase in 1874. Upon his arrival at the chief's cabin, Washakie told the visitor that he always had tried to lead a good life and since meeting "Father Roberts," applying that name to the Reverend John Roberts of the Episcopal church, he had been going to his church and worshipping the white man's God in the way that the good Father had told him to do, but now he was very much concerned for fear that he had in espousing the white man's God offended the Great Spirit of the indian; Washakie further declared that he did not want to go to the white man's heaven, but that he desired to enter the new world of the indians where all of his people had gone.[144]

Mr. Woodruff declared to the aged chief that the Great Spirit of the indian and the God of the white man were the one and the same, and that he was assured of a desirable place "among the stars" as a reward for the good life which he, as a chief of the Shoshones, had led. Washakie thanking the white man said, "I feel much better now and am glad to die, for this matter before our interview has caused me a great deal of worry and trouble and was heavy upon my heart."

The venerable chief had a deep reverence for the Divine Power he had learned to worship. "Washakie invariably bowed his head," stated Reverend Roberts, "when he mentioned the name of God, 'Our Father,' he called him 'Dâm Apuā' or 'Dâm Aputsee,' – our dear father. I never heard him make mention of 'the Happy Hunting Ground.' In speaking of the future life he always spoke of it as being in 'Our Father's abode' – 'Dâm Apuā ungan.' "

When realizing that death was near, Washakie sent a message to his former White Robe friend, Bishop Talbot, stating that "Washakie had found the right trail." At one time when Washakie's lands were to be partitioned off he was told it must be done by surveying, or by longitude and latitude which were quite bewildering terms to the chief, but were made more comprehensible by the use of a familiar term that "the lines of the boundary were to be marked by the stars." At this Washakie replied, "You say that the stars mark the boundary? I hope," pointing heavenward, "the time

---

[144] Farlow, Mayor E. J., Lander, Wyoming, *Interview*, 1926.

will come when, by and by, we all will be together in the stars, but for the present give me a home bounded only by mountains and rivers."

It is related by James K. Moore, Jr., son of Washakie's favorite Jakie, that in the fall of 1899 Washakie visited him in his store at Fort Washakie. The day was cold and very windy, the sand blowing in every direction. It seemed necessary to assist the chief into the saddle on his horse, a great feebleness having overcome the veteran indian. He tottered on his feet as he walked out of the store. In returning to his log cabin, a mile and a half from the store, Washakie had to face a blinding storm of dust and gravel on the long horseback ride, long for the chief at this time, due to his enfeebled condition. This dust and gravel ultimately caused his blindness.

"I used," continued Washakie's boy friend, "to visit Washakie very often after this, taking him a few delicacies to tease his appetite or little things to amuse him during his illness. His home was a cabin on the north side of the South Fork of the Wind river, his wife living with him in this personally constructed one room log home. At this time the reservation indians, who were more closely connected into one group under Chief Washakie than they are now, listened intently to Washakie's council, respecting him and his judgment very highly, making his reign one of supreme authority.

"During the winter of Washakie's death, Reverend Roberts was not only on the reservation a great deal but very frequently was with Washakie who now had grown totally blind from the effects of an eye trouble caused by the storm of wind, sand and snow during the previous fall. He could not see and when anyone came into the cabin he would always ask 'Who come in?' If it were Reverend Roberts, or if it were I, the chief was always happy, exclaiming, 'I am glad to have you with me!' During this winter day not long before his 'departure to the stars' he told me, 'when the sun goes down my spirit will go. I feel that my time has come.' Then he asked, 'Where is your father – Moore my good friend?' When I explained that father was in Washington seeing the Great Chief, Washakie replied, 'Sorry not going to see father again because he has been my very good friend for so long.' " [145]

The last photograph of Chief Washakie was taken in front of his cabin at the time Mr. Albert D. Lane visited the mortally ill chief. Desiring to have his friend, Mr. Curtis, take a snapshot, the chief asked Mr. Lane to put him into his stirrups and afterwards to lift him bodily from his mount, though "Washakie at this time was a marvelous looking chief." This was the last time that Washakie, who was always when mounted as if a part of his horse, sat astride his favorite indian pony.

During the last year of his illness, Washakie suffered from partial paralysis of his lower limbs, but insisted upon being helped into his saddle when he would call upon his friends, going from house to house, cabin or tepee. Inasmuch as he was not able to dismount without assistance he would sit in his saddle as if on a throne, carrying on his conversations with those upon whom he visited or whom he chanced to meet. Thus in his old

[145] Moore, James K., Jr., *Interview*, 1926. Washakie did not die at this exact time, as he had prophesied, though the end came not long after this interview. During these last days, the chief frequently spoke of the fact that he wished his son, Dick, to follow in his footsteps in regard to the leadership and chieftainship of the Shoshones.

age, "sitting erect in his saddle on his chosen horse, he presented a softened and gentle expression, looking sublime, but to his old time friends it was mournful and pathetic in the extreme." [146]

"On his death bed in his log cabin he gave me this message to deliver; being too weak to speak he used the indian sign language, 'I am dying. I pray our Father on high to have mercy on me. I pray our Father's Son to have mercy on me. Tell my white friends – those who are near and those who are far off – that I, dying, shake hands with them.'" [147]

In his much-loved log cabin at his bedside during the evening of February 20, 1900, Washakie had gathered his immediate family, his wife, his two sons and his daughter, where and when the chief delivered his last admonition to the family group, not to any one individual, but to the "family of Washakie" – a name he had ever held in high esteem and one which he had never dishonored.[148] Dick Washakie contributes the following "death-bed oration" from his father, the one that the dying chief left to posterity.

Chief Washakie's last statement to his family on the

[146] Nickerson, Captain H. G., *Interview*, September, 1926, Shoshone indian agent at the time of Washakie's death. "He died in his own cabin, having every care that two military doctors could administer to a chief. At his funeral were all the men of the two tribes, Shoshones and Arapahoes, as well as military people and civilians, probably two thousand in all. Washakie did not die in his tent; I saw him in his cabin the night before he departed, and I helped place him in a coffin which had been purchased by the government of the United States as was the stone now resting at the head of his grave."

[147] Reverend John Roberts who had baptized Chief Washakie in 1897.

[148] *Letter* of 1926. Chief Dick Washakie writes, "My father and mother brought forth a very large family, perhaps ten to twelve children, several dying in their infancy. My father had a number of wives, though there are of his large family only three now living, myself, my sister, Enga Peahrora, and my half-brother, Charlie, who is a son of my father's Crow wife.

night of his death as told by his son Dick: – "In believing that it might be some good for you, I want to say a few words which I have had on my mind, to my children and family who are present here tonight. I want you to open your ears and heart so that you will know what I am saying to you. It has always been my fervent hope and policy through these long years to maintain peace and harmony with the white people and especially the government. I have never permitted a disgraceful depredation by my people, the Shoshones, as long as I have lived, when it was possible for me to prevent it, and it was to my knowledge. I am today receiving a pension from the government for loyalty and service rendered. It is my earnest prayer that you, my children, who are here tonight, will follow the footsteps which I have made for you, and you will always be highly respected both by our people and the white people. I am not telling this to one of you, but to all who are present here with me tonight, and I hope that what I have said will enter your ears and your hearts." [149]

After delivering this eulogy, the chief requested his family to take their night's rest. The members thereof obeyed. Before the coming of a new day, Washakie went to sleep from which there was no awakening.

Early the next morning the authorities at the agency and Fort Washakie were informed by the members of his family of Washakie's death, no one having been present at the hour of his departure to the stars. Following this notice a telegram was sent to the Adjutant-general of the United States army.[150]

[149] Washakie, Chief Dick, *Interviews* with, September, 1926.

[150] Nickerson, Captain H. G., *Interview* with, *Ibid*. "After Washakie's death, Dick came to see me to ask me to write to Washington to have him

The Burial of Chief Washakie

The only military funeral ever granted an indian by the U. S. government. The burial honors for the old chief conformed to those acorded an army officer with the rank of captain. Washakie was buried in the soldier's cemetery at Fort Washakie

"Indian Scout Washakie, Chief of the Shoshones, died at eight-thirty last night. Overton, *commanding*."

Following the announcement of the death of Washakie a General Order was issued as follows:

GENERAL ORDER, NUMBER 2: OFFICIAL

Fort Washakie, Wyo., February 22, 1900

1. With sorrow is announced the death of Washakie. For fifty years as chief of the Shoshones, he has held the confidence and love of his tribe. His friendship for the whites began with their earliest settlements in this section almost that long ago. Washakie was born in the early years of 1800, so his life covered almost a century with its changes. His great influence preserved his tribe not only a friend but an ally of our people in their struggles here. It was his pride that he had never allowed a white man's blood to be shed when he could prevent it.

Washakie was of commanding presence and his resemblance in face to Washington often remarked. His countenance was one of rugged strength mingled with kindness. His military service is an unbroken record for gallantry, and officers now wearing a star fought with him in their subaltern days. The respect and friendship of these former commanders was prized to the day of his death. Washakie was a great man, for he was a brave man and a good man. The spirit of his loyalty and courage will speak to soldiers; the memory of his love for his own people will linger to assist them in their troubles, and he will never be forgotten so long as the mountains and streams of Wyoming which were his home, bear his name.

His last request was a christian burial in the Post Cemetery with the soldiers who were his friends.

---

made head of the indian affairs of the Shoshone reservation. My reply was, 'Your father was a great and good chief, one of the best, but now the indian wars are all over, and there is no more need of indian chiefs.' I suggested that the indians be assembled and that they select six of their best men as a council with which to transact business. Dick Washakie made no serious objection to this movement and never assumed real chieftainship, though he is called Chief Washakie. For a time the indians used a council of six men, both Shoshones and Arapahoes, for their chief councilors to represent two councils, continuing this for many years. Lately, this has been changed, and the white man acts as chief of police, the others are called indian police. They transact their affairs through the council, the indian agent and the government."

The Post Commander directs that Washakie be buried with military honors in the Post Cemetery at 2:00 P.M. tomorrow and that a copy of this order announcing his death be mailed to officers under whom he served the government. By order of

CLOUGH OVERTON, *1st. Lieutenant 1st Cavalry, Commanding Post*
AUBREY LIPPINCOTT, *2nd. Lieutenant 1st Cavalry Adjutant*

To the dead chief was accorded a burial in the military cemetery of Fort Washakie with full military honor such as would have been given to a United States officer with the rank of captain. This military burial is the only one that history records as having been accorded to an indian. All burial formality was arranged by Lieutenant Aubrey Lippincott, Commander at Fort Washakie, his Troop E, First cavalry, furnishing the escort at the procession and the burial. Previous to the procession to the cemetery, Troop E marched to Washakie's cabin, forming in line presented sabers as the body of the departed chief was placed on the carriage. From Washakie's log cabin the cavalry acted as an escort to the fort cemetery, there dismounting and forming in line facing the grave. The usual rifle salute was fired; the troop trumpeter sounded taps; the ceremony thus conforming in every way to the military requirements. Finally all that was mortal of Washakie, the Shoshone chief, was placed in the ground over which the scarred warrior had hunted and for which he had battled against numerous hostiles, his own "Warm valley" giving rest and embrace to his time-worn and tired body.

"A great number of Shoshone and Arapahoe indians followed the procession to the cemetery, in fact every grown indian paid homage to the dead chief; Washakie's family were all at the grave, their mourning being in the manner of the indian.[151]

---

[151] Washakie, Chief Dick, *Letter* of April 4, 1928. "Only the immediate

"At the time of the burial of Washakie, the ground was covered with snow, the country about being naturally picturesque was on this particular day unusually wonderful.

"It was believed that ordinarily the indians would not have looked with favor on the burial of one of their number in a white man's cemetery, but in the case of their chief they not only acquiesced, but seemed to look on it as the appropriate thing." [152]

Washakie's funeral procession has been described as the largest in the state of Wyoming, a mile and a half long, his coffin strapped on a cannon caisson, draped with a large American flag. Following the casket were his wife, sons and one daughter, the mounted indian police, all on horseback, the indian agent, with an indian escort, the agency employees, the officers and the soldiers of the United States army, and the Shoshone and Arapahoe indians. Long before the last of the procession was in line, the beginning of the funeral procession had reached the little military cemetery, where it had to wait a long time before all of the people who were paying tribute to Washakie had arrived.

The Episcopal service at the grave was conducted by Washakie's white friend, Reverend John Roberts, assisted by his indian friend, an Arapahoe, Reverend Sherman Coolidge.[153] After the formal ceremony the casket was lowered into the grave, Troop E fired three

family and the closest relatives showed their sorrow by bobbing off their hair, although the whole Shoshone people or tribe mourned the death of their great chief and showed their respect by attending the chief's funeral."

[152] Lippincott, Lieutenant-colonel Aubrey, U. S. A., Executive Officer, The Cavalry School, Fort Riley, *Letter*, February 12, 1926.

[153] "Washakie was a personal friend of mine, a friend of the Arapahoes, as well as a strong and loyal friend of the white people during the stirring days of our frontier struggle in the far West."

volleys over the aged chief's mortal remains, Bugler
Veribloom sounded taps and the burial was at an end.[154]

Reverend Roberts in his official announcement of
Washakie's death writes, "I am greatly grieved to report the death of an indian churchman, Washakie.
With Washakie the chieftainship of the Shoshones has
passed away. No successor will be appointed to his
office. The present policy of the government in dealing
with indians is to break up the tribal relations and to
deal with indians as individuals and to prepare them
for citizenship. He was buried with military honors in
the post cemetery. Besides the soldiers of the garrison, a
great concourse of indians attended the funeral and
many whites from the settlements outside the reservation."

In the year of 1905 the War Department erected over
Washakie's grave a noble granite monument, on the east
side of which in deep, sunken letters are chiseled the
words: WASHAKIE 1804-1900; on the north side appears,
A WISE LEADER; toward the setting sun, CHIEF OF THE SHO-
SHONES; the remaining side bearing the final tribute:

ALWAYS LOYAL

TO THE GOVERNMENT

AND TO HIS

WHITE BROTHERS

---

[154] Roberts, Reverend John, Letter of January 7, 1928. "In the picture I
appear with surplice and stole back of the mules. The gray haired man,
bareheaded, to my left, is William McCabe, famous post scout. Lieutenant
Overton, commanding Fort Washakie at the time, is seen on horseback between the heads of the two leading mules. The Reverend Sherman Coolidge
is the clergyman whose back is shown in surplice and hood. The man standing bareheaded beside him (gray haired) is Captain Herman G. Nickerson,
United States indian agent. No women appear in the photo. The indian
raising the coffin in front of Captain Nickerson is 'Tigee,' Sergeant of Indian
Scouts – Washakie's chief henchman. The indian at his side is Iagwar; the
one facing Tigee is Mat-ta-vish, all three Lemhi, or Salmon-eating Shoshones, kinsmen of Washakie, whose father, I was told, was half Lemhi and

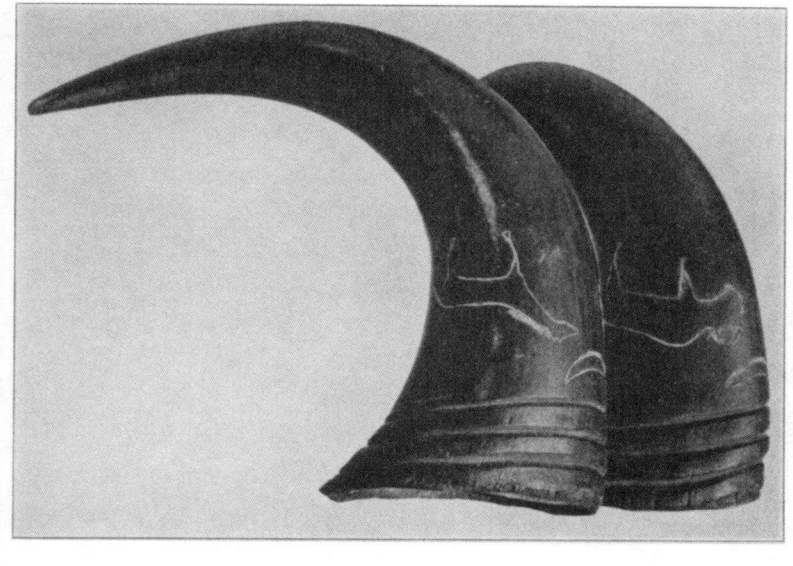

A SHOSHONE PRAYER HORN

THE EMPTY TEPEE

When a Shoshone leaves his tepee for a short
time he places a little brush before the flap
to give notice that he will soon return. If
away for some time the brush is higher — the
more sagebrush the longer the departure.
The pile rises toward the lodge poles when
owner is never to return

"No more truthful or deserving epitaph was ever inscribed upon a tombstone."

All of the bodies of the soldiers buried in Fort Washakie cemetery were removed in 1907 and interred in the national cemetery at Fort Leavenworth, Kansas. No steps, however, for the removal of the bones of Chief Washakie and the monument erected over his grave were made. When the land embraced in the Fort Washakie reservation was returned to the Indian Department from the War Department, the cemetery where rested Washakie became a part of the Shoshone indian reservation and "should be held as other lands therefore for the use and benefit of the indians." Thus the custody and care of Washakie's grave was placed in charge of the Shoshone agency and the agent thereof became the custodian of the monument erected to his memory as a great chief, "a man of unusual ability, sterling character, eloquent at the council fire, sagacious in planning campaigns and fearless in warfare." [155]

When Indian Agent Nickerson made his report for the year ending June 30, 1901, there was included the following statement:

SHOSHONE AGENCY, WYOMING, August 15, 1901.

On June 12, Sharp Nose, chief of the Arapahoes, died and was buried in the rocks by his people before they could be prevented from so doing. Chief Washakie, of the Shoshones, died last year and was given christian burial in the post cemetery. These are the last chiefs of these tribes. Each tribe now has a council of six to speak and act for them.

Today on Washakie's reservation there are, of the

half Flathead. Washakie was always partial to the Lemhis here, which seems to indicate that the information concerning the old chief's relationship to the Lemhis is correct. There is no doubt of his relationship to the Flatheads."

[155] Curtis, William E. August, 1909.

family of Washakie, two sons, Dick and Charles, a daughter, Enga Peahorra, eight grandchildren, nineteen great grandchildren and one great, great grandchild.[156]

When the Shoshone indian leaves his home for a short journey, in front of the closed flap of his tepee are piled numerous sage-brush, bushes, or boughts from trees, the height of the pile being indicative of the period of the absence of the owner from his tepee home. Just a bit of sage – to be gone but for a short time, a few weeks or months of absence. The barricade rises higher for a departure for a long time. The pile mounts toward the top of the vacant tepee for Washakie; his tepee door is blocked with sagebrush that climbs toward where the smoke used to rise between the meeting poles of his tepee. He is to be gone for a long, long time.

[156] Nickerson, Herman G., 1927.

APPENDIX I: Ceremonial Dances, Beliefs, and Customs of the Shoshone Tribe

All of the ceremonial dances of indians grow from very simple beginnings, but once inaugurated, tend to become more complex and are imitated by different tribes; the sun dance being no exception to this statement, for nineteen different tribes have elements of this semi-religious dance of which number are the Arapahoe, Wind river, Shoshone, Crow, Blackfoot, Gros Ventre and northern Cheyenne tribes, the other thirteen being generally scattered in different places of North America.[157]

The sun dance is one of the most striking of indian ceremonies, combining the spectacular and the sacred in almost equal measure. It is also a tribal ceremony and is everywhere the culmination of religious and even social activities. The name, sun dance, was given it because in one aspect of the ceremony a ritualistic dance was held in which the participants gazed at the sun, in reality a kind of torture.[158]

Bazil (also Basil, Brazil, Bresil, Bazille, Bazeel, Breezill) son of Sacajawea officiated at the first sun dance given by the Shoshone indians of the Bridger valley where Washakie was chief. Andrew Bazil, son of Bazil and grandson of Sacajawea, in time, became chief of this religious ceremony, being looked upon today (1930) by his people on the Shoshone reservation

---

[157] Wissler.
[158] Lowie, *Sun Dance of the Shoshone.*

as their chief of the sun dance. Being advanced in years he now does not take as active a part in the dance as in former years.

"Andy Bresil," interprets the sun dance somewhat as follows: "All of those who take part in this ceremonial dance expect to obtain good by the ceremony. Some have merely this general object, others go in it for the specific purpose of being cured of sickness. I generally have a dream that I should give the sun dance. I dream of it frequently and when I do so, about the proper time, then I give it. I tell my friends and they announce it to the whole tribe, then I set some time before July 4 and between June 20 and 27."

From Chief Dick Washakie has been obtained an account of the origin and practice of the sun dance.[159] "From old tradition that has been handed down about two centuries to the present time I have learned that the sun dance was first introduced to the tribe of Shoshone indians about two hundred years ago, or about the year 1726.

"The sun dance, which perhaps some of the white people have witnessed or heard tell of, has always been considered one of the most heathenish and most barbarous and unchristian ceremonies ever participated in by the savages, as we red men have been termed by many of our white brothers, who, I must say, have failed to make themselves thoroughly acquainted with the sacred and religious beliefs of our so-called sun dance. We indians call it the 'fasting dance.' Our sun dance in reality, according to our indian beliefs, is in religious beliefs, the same as that of our white brothers. The indians pray to God, our Father above, or the Great

[159] Description given to author on the Shoshone reservation, September, 1926.

Spirit, as some of our white brothers have termed it. Some white people have even accused the indian of worshipping the center sun dance pole, which is a great mistake. When the indian prays, he looks upward into the blue sky and says, '*Tomah-upah tomah-vond*, Our Father, who is above.' He does not pray to the sun, or to the center sun dance pole as some white people would have it.

"The reason the indian seems to worship the sun to some people is because the indian believes that the sun is a gift from God, our Father above, to enlighten the world and as the sun appears over the horizon they offer up a prayer in acceptance of our Father's gift. Then the medicine man, or the chief of the sun dance who acts similar to that of the priest or clergyman in a white man's church, offers up prayer beginning thus *Tomah-upah, tomah-vond undiddahaidt soonda-hie*, 'Our Father who is above, have mercy upon your children.'

"The sun dance hall (an out-of-doors structure) is constructed in a large circular corral perhaps some hundred feet in diameter, the circumference of which is lined on the outside with branches of trees to give shade to the dancers. Each dancer has a certain place in the dance hall which he must keep throughout the duration of the dance when he enters it. Two small poles or young saplings of pine or cottonwood are placed on each side of the dancer. The bark of these saplings may be peeled off or not, whichever the dancer may wish. If the dancer is a medicine man or has been wounded in battle sometime he should show this on the poles or saplings by painting them red, which signified his blood was lost in battle. The center pole which should always be a cottonwood was chosen by the originators of the dance because of its superiority over all other trees as a dry land tree growing with little or no water. This tree represents God. The twelve long poles that are placed from the top of the center pole down to the circumference of the dance hall represent, according to our indian beliefs, the twelve apostles of God, our Father.

"The eagle feathers at the top of the poles above the center pole also represent the twelve apostles of our Father, or God, and also being a sacred bird of our race, we indians naturally regard the eagle with the highest esteem. The buffalo head in the crotch in the center pole represents a gift from God, our Father above, to his indian children for food and clothing.

"The sun dance has been handed down to my people for generations as a sacred dance in which we may pray to God, our Father, for those who may be sick, that they may be healed. In many cases, I can truthfully state, many have been cured of long standing illnesses through their faith in prayer and fasting from food and water for the duration of the dance, which generally lasts three or four days. Many of our white brothers have condemned my people's sacred dance, and their form of worship. This form is, in the belief of my people, identical with that used by our white brothers in their christian church and in the form which they consider just and proper.

"My people, the indians, worship this same Being as that worshipped by our white brothers, but only in our own way and in our beliefs, which I know is very strange to the white people. But this is the only form of worship the red man, my people, have known for generations past and is known throughout the indian race as the indians' church. Every indian tribe has its own form of worship which is somewhat different, but I wish to explain that they all worship the same Being, God, our Father above. I am told that many years ago some tribes of indians used drastic forms of worship in which they signified their bravery and fearlessness, but these forms of worship have long since vanished. We hear of them only through indian tradition.

"Many years ago the sun dance among the Shoshone people was very plain. The worshippers were dressed in skins of animals. Today sun dance worshippers, though believing in the same form of worship as that of their forefathers of many years ago, wear gorgeous apparel, which is more for exhibition than true religion; with this exception, our form of worship is carried on identically in the same form as that of our forefathers.

"The sun dance, according to the custom of my people in the past, is generally held once a year, about June or July. This is the season when grass and the trees are in their splendor and the weather is favorable. Before entering the sun dance hall the worshippers, or dancers, twice circle the hall. The chief of the sun dance or the medicine man is always in the lead. This is done merely according to our old indian customs, which according to our indian beliefs signifies that the dancers are all ready and willing to begin their dance or ceremony.[160]

[160] Colonel William Henry Corbusier, United States Army, Retired, through whose courtesy the Shoshone prayer horn is produced in photograph, states that this horn was used at many sun dances, and was given to him at the Shoshone and Bannock indian agency, near Fort Washakie, Wyoming territory, after a sun dance in October, 1880. The buffalo horn is fifteen and three-fourth inches on its outer curvature, and a small hole at the top of the inner curve through which has a string by which to suspend it. The

"I shall state, though I know that it will sound very strange to some of our white brothers that of course they could not understand what was said in our prayers or otherwise they would have understood the meaning of our sacred dance. The indians believe in a Supreme Being, or God, our Father, as generally termed by many people, the creator of all things, and we worship and pray to God in our crude but comprehensive form as do our white brothers. It has been the custom of my people for generations past as well as at the present time to show our friendly relations, especially at the closing of our ceremonies of the sun dance, to give presents of some kind to some of our own people or visiting indians from other tribes which signifies that we have given these presents with a free and willing heart and all of our sins committed during the year past have been forgiven by our Father above.

"I shall state here that the term 'our Father' is used in place of God, as there is no Shoshone word which signifies the word 'God.' This word is an English word. Therefore, if an indian or interpreter must use this word he repeats the word 'God' in English and not indian. Never once have I heard the indian tradition where there was any religious controversy as to the true form of worship of God or our Father. All indians, so far as I have ever heard, believe and worship in this one form.

"I have tried to explain our so called sun dance to the reader in the best form possible and hope that the reader may be able to gather in a few facts from this."

The scalps captured on the Rosebud on June 17, 1876, were used in the scalp dance on the Shoshone

three rings around the top are for the three days dance, and the etching of the crescent of the sun and the buffalo and the horse are a prayer to the sun.

reservation on the night of the return home of Chief Washakie and his scouts; the war trophies were taken into their camp where the scalps were raised on a pole in the center of the lodge around which the indians danced. After this ceremony, the scalps were distributed to the women and boys who paraded up and down the camp, occasionally insulting them with taunts.[161]

In the wolf dance of the Shoshones, only the men take part, decked out in war attire. In this round dance the indian appeals to the great wolf mystery for great success in his undertakings and prays that he might overcome his enemies. The most gifted of the dancers were believed to be able to attack an enemy in the dark, for they were able on account of their special gifts to see the footprints of the wolf illuminated.[162] The wolf dance is the most finished of the Shoshone dances, used only on state occasions and considered as the highest social function held among the Shoshone indians. The dancers are in the most brilliant colored feathers, they are highly painted, wear bustles and even powder their hair. The dancing is to the accompaniment of drums and loud chanting. "There were no words; it was all soul." [163]

The thanksgiving dance is given for ceremonial purposes, taking place about the end of September or the beginning of October each year, the tribe being brought together in some appointed locality near where is planted a hemlock or cedar tree. The tribe – men, women and children, in close order, form a circle about the tree and move around it, keeping time with a low, monotonous chant, thanking the Great Spirit for his bounty and

---

[161] Lowie, *The Northern Shoshone*, in "American Museum of Natural History," vol. 2, pt. 2.
[162] Morris.
[163] Olden, *Ibid.*, p. 38.

begging a continuance of His mercy. Entreaties are made for the sending of rain; that it shall come upon the mountains and the rivers and the trees, the chant ending with a petition that the earth cease "swallowing" their fathers, mothers and children.

The Shoshones had a tradition relative to an illness. They would pick up a stone as they traveled along moccasin footed, finally depositing it along the trail where other stones had been deposited by other indians; that is, deposited it along the road at different intervals, creating what they called "medicine piles" – "believing that by leaving a rock behind them as they journeyed on the trail, their ills, sicknesses and bad feelings towards other indians would be forgotten." One today sees many of these monuments erected to forgotten ills.[164]

The Shoshones at Wind river reservation have a tribal cemetery about two miles west of Fort Washakie, in which is buried Bazil, by the side of his mother, Sacajawea. This is the sub-chief who introduced the sun dance into the Shoshone tribe of the Bridger valley. Formerly the indian deposited his dead in caves and in crevices of rocks. Three caves have especially been used for these burial purposes; the larger cave is used when the indians have killed the horses and dogs which might be wanted by the dead warriors. Then there are two small caves, not far apart. In these is the sepulchre, a deep shaft into which the indian bodies, wrapped in tanned robes of the larger game – buffalo, elk and bear, are dropped. In more modern time, due to the scarcity of these animals, the bodies are placed in bright colored indian blankets. When these bodies are

164 Burnett, F. G., *Ibid.*

A GRAVE MARKER
A new glass washboard, the choice possession of the departed indian woman

A SHOSHONE TRAVOIS
A "prairie buggy" constructed by Andrew Bazil for his wife, 1927

to be thus buried the remains are placed on an incline at the edge of the deep shaft and pushed down by one of the chief mourners, who holds to a robe for safety. The dead body is dropped to a great depth with a splash that can be distinctly heard, deep down into the hidden river flowing under the mountains.

In more recent years the Shoshones bury their dead as do the white men. Their caskets are often elaborate and expensive, but generally the coffin is plain and furnished by the government. One of the white head-stones to a child in this cemetery carries the inscription, "Coffin same as white man."

On the grave of one woman the marker is a wash-board of the most modern make, with corrugated glass front, evidently too much cherished even to have been put into practical use. In the Arapahoe cemetery were counted nineteen frying pans on as many graves.

In preparing the body for burial, it is dressed in the very best fashion the family can afford. The face is painted, the body adorned with indian regalia – furs, feathers, beaded moccasins and headdress, these tokens of affection and regard being supplied by the several mourners.

The friends assemble on the day of the funeral, at the camp of the deceased, where they spend several hours bewailing the dead, extolling his virtues and eating the dinner provided by his relatives. This latter function is one of great expectation. At the proper time, a procession is formed which sometimes consists of many wagons, and in the present day, automobiles, and proceeds to the burial ground, the wailing still contin-uing. Where there is true grief there is less weeping, but at most funerals there are paid mourners, who shed no tears, but mourn to such a degree that they can be heard for a mile or two. At the grave the coffin is opened and the friends and neighbors bid farewell to the dead, usually shaking hands with him. The burial service of the church is read and the belongings of the deceased placed in or on the grave.[165]

The Shoshones' native belief is very different from that of any other tribe. The creator they do not know as the Great Spirit but worship him as "our Father." While the Arapahoes have always believed in the resurrection of the body, the Shoshones, like the Hindus, believe in the transmigration of the soul, and that after death they are made over again in the "abode of our Father, in the land beyond the setting sun." This was their ancient belief which today under the instruction of Reverend Roberts is their hope in "our Father's Son," and they look for the resurrection of the body and the life of the world to come.

The Shoshones are an exception to the common rule amongst the indians, in that they never eat dog flesh. They do not eat magpies, crows or eagles, for the reason that they regard them as friends to whom they are indebted for the feathers of their headdress. Howls of the coyote at the time of the full moon presage good luck; when a child rejoices at the first thunder in the spring it is an omen that it will live to an old age and enjoy distinction.[166]

The Shoshones also believe that the chickadee discovered the world. To kill one would be a very bad sign, bringing hard luck; when the little bird is seen it is always a harbinger of severe snow storms. These in-

---

[165] Marion Roberts Tyndall, daughter of Reverend John Roberts, an instructor in the Shoshone mission school.

[166] Lowie, *Ibid.*, p. 232.

dians believe also that God pulled out the upper teeth of the elk because the elk were meant to be eaten by the indians, and not the indians by the elk.

President Grant during his administration parcelled out to the several churches the various tribes of indians, thus making a distribution of spiritual advisers to the indians living on the reservations; the Shoshones were allotted ecclesiastically to the care of the Episcopal church, the spiritual duties extending to the Arapahoe tribe. To this position Reverend John Roberts was assigned in 1883. At the commencement of his missionary work in the Wind river reservation, Reverend Roberts had the care of both Shoshones and Arapahoes, members of both tribes attending his mission school which was supported by the Board of Missions. After the government assumed the financial charge of this mission and school, Reverend Roberts became superintendent of the schools. In 1887 Bishop Ethelbert Talbot, being made Bishop of Wyoming and Idaho, built a church for the Shoshones and also a girls' school on the tract of one hundred and sixty acres of land which Washakie donated for religious and educational purposes for his tribe. In this school many of the Washakie descendants have been educated and taken into the church of the white man.

In a recent report made by Reverend Roberts he has written: "One can hardly say that the Shoshones are naturally religious though they have a strong faith in the power of prayer, and at the approach of death their confidence in God, "our Father," as they call Him, and in "our Father's Son" is remarkable. They appreciate and value church membership. Hundreds of them have been baptized and many confirmed. From an irrespon-

sible and untrustworthy tribe of nomads they have become a good people – honest, industrious, self-support-
ing and self-respecting." On the Shoshone reservation
there are a number of churches. There is a chapel at the
Shoshone Episcopal mission where Reverend Roberts
preaches to both Shoshones and whites; "The Chapel
of the Redeemer," for Shoshones at Wind river; a Pres-
byterian mission for the Arapahoes at Arapahoe; the
Roman Catholic mission for Arapahoes near Riverton;
the Episcopal mission, and St. Michels chapel at Ethete
for Arapahoes.

The indian children attending the Shoshone indian
school have all of their clothing furnished to them by
the government, also are given their board and room
while they are at this government school located about
half a mile east of Fort Washakie, or, the agency headquarters. In this school, taught by trained white men
and women, the boys and girls go as far as the eighth
grade, provision being made for attendance at non-
resident school for paying their expenses as in the residence school, the instruction continuing through high
school. The Shoshone school is allowed a sum to defray
expenses.If attendance is less than one hundred pupils,
the rate of money is three hundred dollars per capita; if
there are more than one hundred the per capita dona-
tion from the government is two hundred and fifty
dollars. In the mission school the allowance is one hundred and twenty-five dollars per person a year. The
entire education expense for the Shoshones' education
in Wyoming is annually about $25,000.

The census of 1926 of the Wind river reservation
gave the Shoshone population as nine hundred and fif-
ty-two, the Arapahoe population being slightly less,

nine hundred and forty-seven, these figures remaining somewhat constant from year to year and indicating the relative strength of the two tribes for many years.

All of the indians used to wear their hair long, keeping it long until the young people went to school or they were sent away to be educated, when their hair was cut, as it was when they entered the World War, thus acquiring the habit of putting a handkerchief over their heads while their hair was in process of growing long again. The process of handkerchief wearing is kept up even today. Shoshones wear, usually, bright colored handkerchiefs and on top of their handkerchief the men wear a high black felt hat.

Captain Nickerson has stated that the indians have improved in his fifty years of knowledge of them, improved to a marked degree. "When I first knew them," explained Captain Nickerson, "whenever they moved from place to place, it was on ponies; if they had enough to carry the men and women they both rode, but if there were just enough ponies for one sex, the men rode and the women walked. Their saddles were made of elk skin and buffalo skin over that. They had poles or tent poles tied to each side of their horses with rawhide ropes running from these poles to the rear of the horses. Something like ponies dragging a ladder. On this construction called a 'travois' they put their sick and the papooses and the supplies. When I first knew the indians, their mode of travel was by ponies without saddles; then saddles came next; then travois; then wagons; then buggies; then carriages; now they have any amount of automobiles with the entire family in the car.

"As to dress," continued Captain Nickerson, "they

attempt to adopt all of the white man's manner of dress
and fashion, though not all of the worst fashions;
women also have grown to dress as white women dress
but very few of them wear paint on their face. They
let the white women do that. They do not color their
faces as much today as the white woman colors her
face with red paint." [167]

In 1926 while a guest at the Shoshone indian school
the observation was made that there was not a girl pupil
with long hair, every head being bobbed, though un-
marcelled – their hair as straight as the arrow of their
ancestors.

Each indian on the reservation now has a separate
name for himself, one original family name. The old
regulation of naming an offspring made the tracing of
family relations not only very difficult but impossible.
Captain Nickerson further reports: "I had family
names given to everyone on the reservation and thus
brought families together, but no one can trace far
back their heirs by family names among the reservation
indians. Now every family has a name. Every father,
mother; every husband and wife and children bears
the last names of these people; now property goes to
descendants as the property of the white man goes to
his descendant. Spoon Hunter and his wife had a large
family and they were simply known as, for instance,
Tom, Dick and Harry, Mary, Jane and Alice, but no
one knew who these children belonged to and that their
father's and mother's name was Spoon Hunter except
the father and mother.

"This irregularity of naming offspring made difficulties of inheritance and posterity. 'Who's Who' became

---

[167] Nickerson, Captain Herman G., *Interview, Ibid.*, 1926.

a very complicated matter, and hence I took steps to perfect an arrangement whereby to put all Spoon Hunter's family in a group so that they might be in order to properly inherit and acquire property. What I did for Spoon Hunter I did for others.

"The family and its name had to change often. I changed for instance, the family name 'Wahwanabiddie,' an indian name, to Waugh, the father became William Waugh and the children were known as Tom, Dick, Harry and Mary Waugh, in place of Wahwanabiddie. An Arapahoe's name was 'Runs-across-the-river.' I changed that name to 'Rivers,' thus anglicizing a very unpronounceable indian name. During my administration I took a census of over two thousand names and had them all changed, though it took over two years to accomplish the task."

The Shoshones, as did all other tribes who knew of the mysterious nature of the Yellowstone National Park, believed that the geysers, paint pots and weird rumblings were a real conflict of the evil spirits as they fought within the recesses of the earth; for this reason, the wonder of the park were shunned and feared by the red man.

When acting as escorts or scouts for military or exploration forces marching into the Yellowstone country, the Shoshones always offered up a sacrifice before entering the land where were "the rumbles within the earth that heralded the geyser eruptions, which the red man regarded as the forging of warlike weapons by the spirits; each eruption bespoke a victory or defeat of one band of spirits."

Pictography is not an art exclusively belonging to the North American indians, their works of rock writing by brush or maul being found in various stages of development, not only in North, South and Central America, but Australia, Europe, Africa and Asia. The pictorial tribal designators display four styles of writings represented by records of expeditions, battle, migration and notable or sociological events.

The last of these styles of recording events would include a recording of a great prairie fire destroying lodges and the burning off of grass, the food for the necessary pony; the advent of deep snows; the abundance of good water; of personal exploits by chiefs or headmen, or, when there was a record made by paint or carving giving a series of continuous events, the story might represent an autobiography.[168]

When Captain William A. Jones, United States army, was on the United States government expedition into northwestern Wyoming during the summer of 1873, having with him many of Washakie's warriors serving as guides, there were discovered many hieroglyphic rocks in the Wind river valley, particularly when the expedition reached the Popo Agie river. A number of crude, "mere daubs of black paint," figures were found. Near this pictograph were also discovered some petroglyphs upon many vertical walls, "rude figures chiseled." Further to the north in the upper valley of the Wind river were other "instances of rock sculpture."[169]

Many other petroglyphs discovered by white man and indian are found through the canyons of the Wind river country. One of special interest, inasmuch as rock history confirms word of mouth traditional history, is

[168] Tenth Annual *Report* of the United States Bureau of Ethnology, p. 770.

[169] Jones, *Ibid.*, p. 269.

ROCK WRITINGS ON THE SHOSHONE RESERVATION

The carvings in part, as appear in the Dinwoody canyon, representing starvation.

at this place of unusual significance. These Wind river rock writings are declared to be the work of "Pawkees," or Blackfeet (Satsika) indians, a tribe which formerly occupied that region. The markings according to Doctor Corbusier, United States army, located at Fort Brown in its earlier days, were made by indians, neither the Shoshones or Arapahoes knowing the authors, the work in many ways showing great similarity to the Algonquin type, that tribe ranging from Virginia to Labrador and thence west to the Rocky mountains.

In the Dinwoody canyon near the most northwestern boundary line of the Shoshone reservation on the western side of Wind river are found well defined petroglyphs carved on the sheer sides of the colossal rocks of this great canyon. A partial interpretation of these hieroglyphic rock-inscriptions tells the tragic story of famine and hunger, the pictorial designation indicating an act of supplication. At the right of the vertical crevice women are "encircled," meaning cut-off, or dead. In the record there is no sign of war, thus indicating that death did not come about in that manner. Near this crevice to the right is a small shaman, or priest, or mediator between the world of spirits and the world of men, in the act of supplication before a meat drying rack, two vertical sticks with a bar across the tops which designated plenty. Thus the supplication is for plenty of meat, in this case asking for buffalo meat shown by the large figure of a shaman with buffalo horns. Everything in the rock picture, which is carved, not painted, is in a suppliant attitude, even the warriors are depicted in that condition. The thunder-bird is present, which is the go-between for God and the indian. A medicine man with buffalo horns is making a zig-zag mystery symbol that is ascending to the sun-god.

"This writing, it may be, represents that these people have had or are having a famine or pestilence and they want relief or a supply of sustenance and are asking for it. The chief who has had this writing executed is shown at the right of the crevice, he and his medicine man or shaman are in a suppliant attitude and are asking for buffalo. The tribe, or people, making this rock history is not ascertained though whatever is figured out of this picture centers around the one idea – supplication.[170]

In this record of notable events translated from the chiseled sides of Dinwoody canyon, there seems to be a substantiation of the indian legend told by word of mouth to the white people, "that two centuries ago the indians along the Rocky mountains experienced a killing blizzard, raging in its fury until not only were indians killed but all signs of life destroyed, the time of the devastating storm being about three old men ago. About three old men ago a great snow storm came in the early winter. It was as tall as the tallest man and killed all of the buffalo." The phrase "three old men" designates three generations of seventy, more or less, years each.

Another legend of more recent date is told by indians of the Shoshone tribe about a great snow storm that came in the Yellowstone valley that was "three squaws deep," this second legend having no reference to the "supplication" story, though it illustrates the event of a great snow which covered and killed much of the game, somewhat similar to the buffalo killing storm. The snow must have been at least fifteen feet on the level. The Shoshone women are short, averaging but little over five feet in height.

---

[170] John E. Rees, historian, interpreter of indian language and indian petroglyphs.

APPENDIX II: Official and Unofficial ways of spelling Washakie and Norkuk

Wah-she-kig   Narkok
Was i kuk   Nawkee
Wahaakee   Norkok
Washikeek   Norkuk
Wesha   Narkawk
Wash-Ah-Wee-Ha   Nawkee
Wash-a-kie   Narkuk
Waushakie   Norku
Wash-o-keg
Wash-A-Kee
Washekuk
Washikee
Waushakie
Washakii
Wash-a-kii
Wah-she-kig
Wash-o-kig
Wassh-i-kee
Washekuk
Wus-sik-he
Wash-akee
Wash-ake
Washhekuk
Wash-i-kee
Who-sha-kik
Washiki
Washukie

Bibliography of References Cited

ALTER, J. Cecil, see *Bridger.*

ARTHUR, William H., (U.S.A.) Original letters, in possession of the author.

ASHLEY, William Henry, see *Dale.*

AUGUR, C. C. (U.S.A.) Original letter to president of Indian Peace Commission.

BANCROFT, Herbert H., History of Utah. San Francisco, 1889.

BECKWOURTH, James P., Life and Adventures, ed. T. D. Bonner. New York, 1856.

BONNER, T. D., see *Beckwourth.*

BONNEVILLE, Captain [Benj. L. E.], Adventures, Washington Irving.

BOURKE, John C., On the Border with Crook. New York, 1891.

BRIDGER, James, J. Cecil Alter. Salt Lake City, 1925.

———, Biographical sketch. Grenville M. Dodge. New York, 1905.

BRININSTOOL, E. A., see *Hebard.*

BROWN, James S., Life of a Pioneer. Salt Lake City, 1900.

BROWN, William Carey, (U.S.A.) Original letters, in possession of the author.

BURNETT, F. G., Shoshone Indian Agent, Original letters, in possession of the author.

BURTON, Richard F., City of the Saints. New York, 1862.

BYRNE, P. E., Soldiers of the Plains. New York, 1926.

CAMP, Charles, see *Clyman.*

CAPRON, Thaddeus, (U.S.A.) Diary.

CAREY, Joseph Maul, Province and the State, vol. 1. Madison, 1904.

CARTER, William, Original letters in possession of the author.

CHITTENDEN, Hiram M., American Fur Trade of the Far West. 3 vols. New York, 1902.

———, see *DeSmet.*

CLYMAN, James, His Diaries and Reminiscences, ed. Charles Camp. San Francisco, 1925.

COMPTON, James E., Government Shoshone Interpreter, Original letters and manuscript, in possession of the author.

CORBUSIER, William Henry, (U.S.A.) Original letters, in possession of the author.

COUTANT, C. G., History of Wyoming, vol. 1. Laramie, 1899.

DALE, Harrison C., Ashley-Smith Explorations and Discovery of Central Route to Pacific. Cleveland, The Arthur H. Clark Co., 1918.

DEBARTHE, Joe, see *Grouard.*

DESMET, Father Pierre-Jean, Life, Letters and Travels, 4 vols., ed. Hiram M. Chittenden and Alfred T. Richardson. New York, 1905.

DODGE, Grenville M., see *Bridger.*

DORSEY, George A., Arapahoe Sun Dance. Chicago, 1903.

DOUGLAS, Walter B., see *James.*

DRIGGS, H. R., see *Russell; Wilson.*

EASTON, Jeannette Young, Letters to author, 1926.

ELLIOTT, T. C., see *Ogden.*

FARIS, Chester E., Indian Field Service, Original letters, in possession of the author.

FARLOW, Edward J., Original letters in possession of the author.

FINERTY, John F., War-Path and Bivouac. Chicago, 1890.

FLEMING, G. W., Shoshone Indian Agent, *Report,* 1870.

FORNEY, Jacob, Report of as Superintendent, Sept. 6, 1858.

FORSYTH, George A., Story of the Soldier. New York, 1900.

FREMONT, John Charles, Memoirs of my Life. New York, 1887.

GEBOW, Joseph A., Vocabulary of the Snake or Shoshonay Dialect. Green River, 1867.

GHENT, W. J., Road to Oregon. New York, 1929.

GRAHAM, William A., Story of the Little Big Horn; introduction by Charles King. New York, 1926.

GRINNELL, George Bird, Fighting Cheyennes. New York, 1915.

———, Two Great Scouts and their Pawnee Battalion. Cleveland, The Arthur H. Clark Co., 1928.

GROUARD, Frank, Life and Adventure, Joe deBarthe. St. Joseph, 1894.

HAAS, R. P., Shoshone Indian Agent, Original letters, in possession of the author.

HAFEN, LeRoy R., The Overland Mail. Cleveland, The Arthur H. Clark Co., 1926.

HANSON, Joseph Mills, Conquest of the Missouri. Chicago, 1909.

HARDIN, E. E., (U.S.A.) Original letters, in possession of the author.

HEBARD, Grace Raymond, Pathbreakers from River to Ocean. Chicago, 1911.

——, and E. A. Brininstool, The Bozeman Trail, 2 vols. Cleveland, The Arthur H. Clark Co., 1922.

HODGE, F. W., ed. Handbook of American Indians, 2 vols. Washington, 1907.

HOWARD, O. O., My Life and Experience among Hostile Indians. Hartford, 1907.

HOYT, John W., Governor of Wyoming, Original letters and manuscript, in possession of the author.

HUNTINGTON, D. B., Vocabulary of the Ute, and Shoshone or Snake Tribe. Salt Lake City, 1872.

IRVING, Washington, Astoria.

——, see Bonneville.

IRWIN, James, U. S. Commissioner of Indian Affairs, Original letters, in possession of the autor.

JAMES, Thomas, Three Years Among the Indians and Mexicans, ed. Walter B. Douglas. St. Louis, 1916.

JENSEN, Andrew, Fort Supply in Utah Genealogical Magazine, vol. 4, no. 1. Salt Lake City, 1913.

JOHNSON, William G., Original letters in possession of the author.

JONES, William A., Reconnaissance of Northwestern Wyoming, 1873. Washington, 1875.

KAPPLER, Charles J., Indian Affairs, Laws and Treaties, vols. 1, 2. 58 Cong., 2 sess., Washington, 1904.

KING, Charles, Campaigning with Crook. New York, 1890.

——, Original letters in possession of the author.

——, see Graham.

LANDER, F. W., see U. S. Senate.

LANE, A. D., Original letters in possession of the author.

LEWIS AND CLARK, History of expedition. Philadelphia, 1814. 2 vols., reprinted in various editions.

LIPPINCOTT, Audrey, (U.S.A.) Original letters, in possession of the author.

LOWE, Percival G., Five Years a Dragoon. Kansas City, 1906.

LOWIE, Robert H., Notes on Shoshone Ethnology, in *Anthropological Papers*, American Museum of Natural History, vol. 20, part iii.

———, Sundance of the Shoshoni, in *Anthropological Papers*, American Museum of Natural History, vol. 16, part v.

McCAIN, William A., (U.S.A.) Original letters, in possession of the author.

McLAUGHLIN, James, My Friend the Indian. Boston, 1926.

MANN, Luther, Indian Agent, *Report*, 1862.

MILES, Nelson A., Personal Recollections. Chicago, 1897.

MOKLER, Alfred James, Transition of the West. Chicago, 1927.

MOORE, J. K. jr., Indian Trader, Original letters in possession of the author.

MORGAN, George H., (U.S.A.) Original letters, in possession of the author.

MORRIS, Robert C., see *Wyoming*.

NEIHARDT, John G., Song of the Indian Wars. New York, 1925.

NICKERSON, Hiram G., Shoshone Indian Agent, Early History of Fremont county, Wyoming, in Wyoming Historical Department *Bulletin*, vol. 2, no. 1, 1924.

———, Original letters, in possession of the author.

OGDEN, Peter Skeene, Journals in Oregon Historical Society *Quarterly*, ed. T. C. Elliott. Portland, 1909-1910.

OLDEN, Sarah Emilia, Shoshone Folk Lore. Milwaukee, 1923.

"OPENING the Shoshone Reservation," in U. S. Land Office *Reports*, vol. 34, p. 640.

"PACIFIC Wagon Road," 35 Cong., 2 sess., doc. no. 108.

PARKMAN, Francis, Half Century of Conflict. Boston, 1903.

———, Oregon Trail. Boston, 1925.

PATTEN, James I., Shoshone Indian Agent, Original letters, in possession of the author.

PERKINS, J. R., Trails, Rails and War. Indianapolis, 1929.

PHILLIPPS, Paul C., see *Stuart*.

RAYNOLDS, W. F., Exploration of the Yellowstone. 40 Cong., 1 sess., doc. no. 77.

REES, John E., Idaho Chronology, Nomenclature, Bibliography. Chicago, 1918.

RICHARDSON, Alfred T., see *DeSmet*

ROBERTS, Reverend John, Missionary to the Shoshone indians, 1883-1929, Original letters, in possession of the author.

Ross, Alexander, Fur Hunters of the Far West. 2 vols. London, 1855.

RUSSELL, Isaac K. and H. R. Driggs, Hidden Heroes of the Rockies. New York, 1923.

RUSSELL, Osborne, Journal of a Trapper. Boise, 1921.

SAINT Louis (Missouri) *Republican*. October and November, 1851, articles, "Letters from the editor."

SCHUYLER, Walter A., (U.S.A.) Original letters, in possession of the author.

SIMPSON, J. H., Explorations across the Great Basin of the Territory of Utah in 1859. Washington, 1876.

SMITH, Jedidah Strong, see *Dale*.

SPARRENBERGER, Frederick H., (U.S.A.) Original letters, in possession of the author.

STANSBURY, Howard, Exploration of the Great Salt Lake. Washington, 1853.

STONE, Elizabeth Arnold. History of Uinta County (Wyo.). Evanston, 1924.

STUART, Granville, Forty Years on the Frontier, 2 vols., ed. Paul C. Phillips. Cleveland, The Arthur H. Clark Co., 1925.

———, Montana As It Is, 1865. Original manuscript, in the library of the University of Wyoming, Laramie.

TALBOT, Ethelbert, My People of the Plains. New York, 1906.

TYNDALL, Marion Roberts, Original letters in possession of the author.

U. S. Commissioners of Indian Affairs, *Reports*. Washington, 1852-1929.

———, Original letters, in possession of author.

U. S. Geographical Surveys, vol. 7, *Archaeology*. Washington, 1879.

U. S. Senate Exec. Doc., 36 Cong., 1 sess., doc. no. 42, 1860. Paragraphs in by F. W. Lander.

U. S. Superintendents of Indian Affairs, *Reports*. Washington, 1852-1929; Bulletin, 1922.

———, Original letters, in possession of the author.

U. S. War Department, Adjutant-general's Office, *Report* no. 37. Washington, 1887.

————, Original letters, in possession of the author.

VANDIVEER, Clarence A., The Fur-Trade and Early Western Exploration. Cleveland, The Arthur H. Clark Co., 1929.

WADSWORTH, H. E., Shoshone Indian Agent, Original letters, in possession of the author.

WASHAKIE, Chief Dick, Original manuscript signed by the chief, in possession of the author.

WELTY, Raymond L., Western American Frontier, in *Cavalry Journal*. Washington, 1927.

WHAM, J. W., Shoshone Indian Agent, *Report*, 1870.

WHEELER, Homer W., Original letters, in possession of the author.

————, Reminiscences of Old Fort Washakie in Wyoming Historical Department *Bulletin*. Cheyenne, 1924.

WIDTSOE, John A., see *Young*.

WILSON, E. N., White Indian Boy, ed. H. R. Driggs. New York, 1919.

WISSLER, Clark, Relation of Nature to Man in Aboriginal America. New York, 1926.

WISTER, Owen, Jimmyjohn Boss. New York, 1900.

WYOMING Historical Society *Collections*, vol. 1. Robert C. Morris. Cheyenne, 1897.

YOUNG, Brigham, Discourses, ed. John A. Widtsoe. Salt Lake City. 1925.

————, Report as Superintendent of Indian Affairs. Washington, 1852.

Index

Index